Dedication

To Ricky, who pestered me to write this book until I finally acquiesced.

The Critical Reader

The Complete Guide to SAT® Reading

Fifth Edition

Erica L. Meltzer

THE CRITICAL READER
New York

For information regarding bulk purchases, reprints, and foreign rights, please send correspondence to thecriticalreader1@gmail.com.

ISBN-13: 979-8-9873835-1-3

ALSO BY ERICA MELTZER

The Ultimate Guide to SAT® Grammar

SAT® Vocabulary: A New Approach (with Larry Krieger)

Reading & Writing Test Book for the Digital SAT®

The Critical Reader: AP® English Language and Composition Edition

The Critical Reader: AP® English Literature and Composition Edition

The Complete Guide to ACT® English

The Complete Guide to ACT® Reading

GRE® Vocabulary in Practice

How to Write for Class: A Student's Guide to Grammar, Punctuation, and Style

IELTS® Writing: Grammar and Vocabulary

Table of Contents

Preface

Eight years elapsed between my last SAT®, which I took as a senior in high school, and the first time I was asked to tutor reading for the SAT. I distinctly remember sitting in Barnes & Noble at 82nd Street on the Upper West Side of Manhattan, hunched over the *Official Guide*, staring at the questions in horror and wondering how on earth I had ever gotten an 800 at the age of 17. Mind you, I felt completely flummoxed by the SAT after I had spent four years studying literature in *college*.

Somehow or other, I managed to muddle through my first reading tutoring sessions. I tried to pretend that I knew what I was doing, but to be perfectly honest, I was pretty lost. I had to look up answers in the back of the book. A lot. I lost count of the number of times I had to utter the words, "I think you're right, but give me one second and let me just double-check that answer..." It was mortifying. No tutor wants to come off as clueless in front of a sixteen-year-old, but I was looking like I had no idea what I was doing. Grammar I could handle, but when it came to teaching reading, I was in way over my head. I simply had no idea how to put into words what had always come naturally to me. Besides, half the time I wasn't sure of the right answer myself.

Luckily for me, fate intervened in the form of Laura Wilson, the founder of WilsonPrep in Chappaqua, New York, whose company I spent several years writing tests for. Laura taught me about the major passage themes, answer choices patterns, and structures. I learned the importance of identifying the main point, tone and major transitions, as well as the ways in which that information can allow a test-taker to spot correct answers quickly, efficiently, and without second-guessing. I discovered that the skills that the SAT tested were in fact the exact same skills that I had spent four years honing.

As a matter of fact, I came to realize that, paradoxically, my degree in French was probably more of an aid in teaching reading than a degree in English would have been. The basic French literary analysis exercise, known as a linear textual explication, consists of close reading of a short excerpt of text, during which the reader explains how the text functions rhetorically from beginning to end—that is, just how structure, diction, and syntax work together to produce meaning and convey a particular idea or point of view. In other words, the same skills as those tested on the SAT. I had considered textual explications a pointless exercise (Rhetoric? Who studies *rhetoric* anymore? That's so nineteenth century!) and resented being forced to write them in college—especially during the year I spent at the Sorbonne, where I and my (French) classmates did little else—but suddenly I appreciated the skills they had taught me. Once I made the connection between what I had been studying all that time and the skills tested on the SAT, the test made sense. I found that I had something to fall back on when I was teaching and, for the first time, I found that I no longer had to constantly look up answers.

I still had a long way to go as a tutor, though. At first, I clung a bit too rigidly to some methods (e.g., insisting that students circle all the transitions) and often did not leave my students enough room to find their own strategies. As I worked with more students, however, I began to realize just how little I could take for granted in terms of pre-existing skills: Most of my students, it turned out, had significant difficulty even identifying the point of an argument, never mind summing it up in five or so words. A lot of them didn't even realize that passages contained arguments at all; they thought that the authors were simply "talking about stuff." As a result, it never even occurred to them to identify which ideas a given author did and did not agree with. When I instructed them to circle transitions like *however* and *therefore* as a way of identifying the key places in an argument, many of them found it overwhelming to do so at the same time they were trying to absorb the literal content of a passage. More than one student told me they could do one or the other, but not both at the same time. In one memorable gaffe, I told a student that while he often did not have to read every word of the more analytical passages, he did need to read all of the literary passages—only to have him respond that he couldn't tell the difference. He thought of all the passages as literary because the blurbs above them all said they came from books, and weren't all books "literary?" It had never occurred to me to tell him that he needed to look for the word *novel* in the blurb above the passage in order to identify works of *fiction*. When I pointed out to another student that he had answered a question incorrectly because he hadn't realized that the author of the passage disagreed with a particular idea, he responded without a trace of irony that the author had spent a lot of time talking about that idea. Apparently, no one had ever introduced him to the idea that writers often spend a good deal of time fleshing out ideas that they *don't* agree with. And this was a student scoring in the mid-600s!

Eventually, I got it. I realized that I would have to spend more time—sometimes a lot more time—explaining basic contextual pieces of information that most adult readers took for granted and, moreover, I would have to do so at the same time I covered actual test-taking strategies. Without the fundamentals, all the strategy in the world might not even raise a student's score by 10 points. My goal here is to supply some of those fundamentals while also covering some of the more advanced skills the exam requires. This book is therefore intended to help you work through and "decode" College Board material. To that end, I have done my best to select texts that reflect the content and themes of the SAT, with an approximately equal mix of fiction, humanities, social science, and natural science passages.

Unfortunately, though, there is no such thing as a "pure" reading test. To some extent, your ability to understand what you read is always bound up with your existing knowledge. Research shows that when students whose overall reading skills are weak are asked to read about subjects they are highly familiar with, their comprehension is *better* than that of students with stronger general reading skills.[1] The more familiar you are with a subject, the less time and energy you will need to spend trying to understand a passage about it. You'll also be familiar with any vocabulary associated with the topic, which means you won't have to worry about keeping track of new terminology.

Moreover, you will probably find it much easier to identify correct and incorrect answer choices. While it is true that answers that are true in the real world will not necessarily be right, it is also true that correct answers will not be false in the real world. If you see an answer that you know includes a false statement, you can start by eliminating it; and if you see one that you know is factually true, you can save yourself a lot of time by checking it first.

Finally, encountering a passage about a subject you already know something about can be very calming on a test like the SAT because you will no longer be dealing with a frightening unknown. Instead of trying to assimilate a mass of completely new information in the space of a few minutes, you can instead place what you are reading in the context of your existing knowledge.

Provided that you have solid comprehension skills and contextual knowledge, success in Reading is also largely a question of approach, or method. Because the test demands a certain degree of flexibility—no single strategy can be guaranteed to work 100% of the time—I have also tried to make this book a toolbox of sorts. My goal is to provide you with a variety of approaches and strategies that you can choose from and apply as necessary, depending on the question at hand. Whenever possible, I have provided multiple explanations for questions, showing how you might arrive at the answer by working in different ways and from different sets of starting assumptions. The ability to adapt is what will ultimately make you unshakeable—even at eight o'clock on a Saturday morning.

~Erica Meltzer

[1] Daniel Willingham, "How Knowledge Helps," *American Educator*, Spring 2006. https://www.aft.org/periodical/american-educator/spring-2006/how-knowledge-helps

How to Use This Book

As you may have noticed, this book contains a fair amount of material, and you might be wondering just how to go about using it. If that's the case, here's a quick guide:

Step 1: Take a full-length diagnostic test.

The College Board has released four full-length adaptive digital exams. Note that you will need to create an account and download the Bluebook app.

Step 2: Identify what you need to focus on.

Mark your right and wrong answers. Then, use the list of question stems on p. 131 to determine what type of material you need to work on. (**Note:** the question categories used in this book are slightly different from those used by the College Board.)

Step 3: Work through the relevant chapters.

If your errors are primarily concentrated in a few specific categories, you can start by focusing on the corresponding chapters.

If your errors are more random or encompass a wider range of question types, or if you have a significant amount of time before the exam, you will probably be best served by working through all of the chapters in order.

You may want to take practice tests periodically to gauge your progress, or you may prefer to work through the entire book before taking another complete test.

Step 4: Build a "bridge" to the test.

When you do the end-of-chapter exercises in this book, the strategy information will usually still be fresh, and you will also know in advance the concept that every question is testing. When you take full-length practice tests, however, all of the question types will be mixed together in unpredictable combinations. You will also need to recall a wide variety of strategies and, without any prompting, recognize when to apply them. That's a big strain on your working memory, and you may initially notice a gap between your performance on the individual exercises and your performance on practice tests.

If you find yourself in that situation, you must essentially create a "bridge" between the book and the test. Either set up a digital practice exam and ignore the timer; or, to remove the time constraint entirely, work through non-adaptive practice questions on Khan Academy.

Before you answer each question, stop and review the specific strategy it requires. For example, you can remind yourself to read before and after line references, consider answer choices in terms of whether they are positive or negative, or focus on the conclusion. If you find it helpful, you can even write yourself notes in the margins of your test. The goal is to practice identifying which strategies are most appropriate in a given situation, and to become accustomed to applying them when no one (me) is holding up a sign telling you where to start. (As I used to tell my students when they stared at me pleadingly, "Don't give me that look—I'm not going to be sitting there when you take the test. You tell *me* what you need to do to answer the question.")

To reiterate, it does not matter how much time you spend on this step. If you find it helpful, you can sit with this book next to your test and flip to the corresponding chapter for each question, reviewing the relevant sections as you work. At this point, it is much more important to work carefully than to work quickly, particularly if you have a tendency to lose points for careless errors. If necessary, you can even do a second test this way—however long it takes for the process to become automatic. When things seem to be coming together, take a timed test and see what holds.

Step 5: Review your mistakes.

I cannot stress how important this step is. Do not move on from a test until you have reviewed every mistake and understood where things went awry, as well as what you need to do to avoid similar errors in the future. Note that working this way also reduces the chance that you will use up all of the official College Board material early in your preparation process.

Step 6: Repeat as necessary until you are consistently scoring in your target range.

To be sure, there is no way to control for every possibility. Reading is inherently less predictable than Math, and there may indeed be times when a correct answer genuinely hinges on something you do not fully understand and could not have foreseen. In many other instances, however, getting the right answer is likely to be a matter of slowing down, making sure you know exactly what you're looking for, and going step by step. If you control for everything you can reasonably control for, you can usually get pretty far.

So yes, working this way is not always pleasant. Yes, it is more involved than simply crashing through practice test after practice test, hoping that somehow things will just work themselves out. But ultimately, it tends to be pretty effective. And when your scores come back, you're a lot more likely to be happy—and possibly even done with the SAT for good.

Question Stems by Category

Vocabulary

- Which choice completes the text with the most logical and precise word or phrase?
- As used in the text, what does the word x most nearly mean?

Big Picture/Main Idea

- Which choice best states the main idea of the text?
- Which choice best describes the overall structure of the text?

Literal Comprehension

- According to/Based on the text, what is true about…?
- According to/Based on the text, why does x occur?

Function

- Which choice best states the primary purpose of the passage?
- Which choice best states the function of the underlined sentence in the text as a whole?

Text Completion

- Which choice most logically completes the text?

Support/Undermine

- Which quotation from the text most effectively illustrates the claim?
- Which statement would most directly support the researchers' conclusion?
- Which statement would most directly undermine/weaken the researchers' conclusion?

Graphic

- Which choice best describes data from the graph/table that supports the researchers' claim?

Suggested Reading

The New York Times (particularly the Science section), www.nytimes.com or any other "serious" major newspaper.

Science Daily, www.sciencedaily.com

Smithsonian, www.smithsonianmag.com

Scientific American, www.scientificamerican.com

National Geographic, www.nationalgeographic.com

Newsweek, www.newsweek.com

Time, www.time.com

The Atlantic Monthly, www.theatlantic.com/magazine

Wired, www.wired.com

For links to many additional resources, Arts & Letters Daily: www.aldaily.com and Daily JSTOR: https://daily.jstor.org. University press releases and alumni magazines can also be an excellent source of SAT-level material.

Also see: Gerald Graff, Cathy Birkenstein, and Russel Durst: *They Say/I Say: The Moves that Matter in Academic Writing*, 2nd Edition. New York: W.W. Norton and Company, 2009.

Fiction, suggested authors: Julia Alvarez, Jane Austen, Charlotte/Anne Brontë, Michael Chabon, Amy Tan, Jhumpa Lahiri

Science and Social Science, suggested authors: Daniel Kahneman, Malcolm Gladwell, Adam Grant, Daniel Levitin, Brian Greene, Stephen Hawking, Lisa Randall

1 Overview of SAT Reading

The Reading and Writing portion of the digital SAT comprises two modules lasting 32 minutes with 27 questions each (54 questions total). Because the test is adaptable, performance during Module 1 determines the difficulty of the questions that appear in Module 2.

Questions can be answered in any order—the software permits skipping—so you should focus on answering everything you can answer easily upfront. If you do jump around, however, just make sure that you eventually answer every question. There is no additional penalty for incorrect answers, and thus there is no reason to leave questions blank.

Within the individual Reading/Writing modules, the first 15 questions or so are devoted to Reading, with the remainder testing Writing—the two types are not interspersed.

Nearly all passages consist of a one-paragraph text ranging from about 50 to 150 words, accompanied by a single question. The only exception is paired passages, which include two short texts accompanied by one question.

Each Reading section normally begins with fill-in-the-blank vocabulary questions and then progresses to more challenging items covering a variety of advanced reasoning skills. Passages cover a wide range of subjects but can be grouped into four major categories:

- **Fiction** (e.g., prose fiction, poetry, and very occasionally drama)
- **Humanities** (e.g., art, literature, music)
- **Social Science** (e.g., history, politics, sociology)
- **Natural Science** (e.g., biology, physics, astronomy)

Science passages, and less frequently Social Science passages, may also contain graphs or charts. In some instances, information from both the graphic and the passage will be needed to determine the answer; in others, the question can be answered based on the passage alone.

What Does SAT Reading Test?

The SAT reading test is a literal comprehension test in some regards, but it is also an *argument* comprehension test. **It tests not only the ability to find bits of factual information in a passage, but also the capacity to understand how arguments are constructed; what types of conclusions can logically be inferred from them; and what types of information would logically illustrate, support, or weaken them.** In other words, comprehension is necessary but not sufficient.

The skill that the SAT requires is therefore something called **"rhetorical reading."** Rhetoric is the art of persuasion, and reading rhetorically simply means reading to understand an author's argument as well as the rhetorical role or **function** that various pieces of information play in creating that argument.

Reading this way is an acquirable skill, not an innate aptitude. It just takes practice.

It is tested in various ways across a variety of different question types:

- **Vocabulary** questions test your ability to use context clues to complete texts in a logical manner, and to recognize alternate meanings of common words.

- **Literal Comprehension** questions test your understanding of straightforward meaning, although they may target portions of the passage that are written in potentially confusing ways or that contain vocabulary that many students find challenging.

- **Big-Picture/Main Idea** questions test your understanding of passages as a whole. They may ask you to identify the central point or overall structure of a passage.

- **Function** or **Purpose** questions ask you to identify the **rhetorical role** (e.g., support, refute, criticize) of a passage as a whole, or of information within it.

- **Text Completion** questions ask you to infer logical conclusions based on the information you have been given.

- **Support/Undermine** questions ask you to move beyond the passage and apply ideas in it to new situations.

- **Paired Passage** questions test your ability to compare texts with different, often conflicting, points of view, and to infer how each author—or figures discussed in one or both of the passages—would likely react to the other's point of view.

- **Graphic** questions test your ability to interpret information presented in graph or table form, and to determine how it relates to information in a passage.

Each chapter in this book is devoted to a specific type of question and is followed by exercises that allow you to practice that particular skill.

Managing the Reading Test as a Whole

The 64 minutes you are given to complete 54 questions are both a blessing and a curse. On one hand, passages are short and accompanied by only a single question, making the digital test feel less tedious than the paper-based version of the exam. On the other hand, some questions can be fairly taxing, and after you've read passage after passage for close to an hour without interruption, things can start to blend together. As a result, you should try to use your time as efficiently as possible to avoid becoming unnecessarily fatigued.

Regardless of whether you are aiming for a 600 or an 800, your goal is simple: to correctly answer as many questions as possible within the allotted time. You are under no obligation to read the passages and/or answer the questions in the order in which they appear. In each module, you can divvy up the 32 minutes and 27 questions—both Reading and Writing—any way you wish.

If you are a strong reader across the board, or if you have a very strong aversion to jumping around, you may find it easiest to simply read the passages and answer the questions in the order they appear—no need for fancy strategies.

However, if you have very pronounced strengths and weaknesses or consistently run out of time, you should try to answer questions in an order that allows you to leverage your skills to maximum effect. If you can generally answer certain question types very quickly, completing them first will allow you to save energy, helping you to remain focused on more difficult questions. Keep in mind also that the Reading/Writing portion is followed by an hour of Math, and you do not want to already feel fatigued when you begin.

While "easy" and "hard" are of course somewhat subjective, certain question types—for example, text completions, support/undermine, and graphics—tend to involve more steps of logic than others. Alternately, if you have trouble deciphering more literary language, you may find prose fiction and poetry passages difficult.

You should therefore practice recognizing which questions you are normally able to answer easily and which ones give you trouble so that you already have a clear sense of where to focus your attention when you walk into the test.

If time is consistently a serious issue, you may even be better off planning from the start to guess on a small number of questions in order to give yourself a bit of extra time on ones that you are more likely to get right. If you are not aiming for a perfect score, trying to answer every question may actually make it *more* difficult for you to achieve your goal.

Keep in mind that unless you are absolutely set on trying to score 1600, you probably have more wiggle room than you think. You do not need to answer every question correctly to obtain a score that will make you a serious candidate at any number of selective colleges to which you intend to submit test scores.

The Answer Isn't Always *in* the Passage

One of the great truisms of SAT prep is that "the answer is always in the passage," but in reality this statement is only half true: **the information necessary to answer the questions is always provided in the passage, but not necessarily the answer itself.** It's a subtle but important distinction.

The SAT tests the ability to draw relationships between specific wordings and general ideas, so while the correct answer will always be *supported by* specific wording in the passage, the whole point is that you must make the connection. That, in essence, is the test.

As a rule, therefore, the correct answers to most questions will usually not be stated word-for-word in the text. In fact, **if an answer repeats the exact phrasing from the passage, you should approach that option very cautiously.** The correct answer will usually refer to an idea that has been discussed in the passage and that has simply been **rephrased**. Your job is to determine that idea and identify the answer that restates it using **synonyms. Same idea, different words.**

Understanding Answer Choices

Although one or more incorrect answers may sound convincing, there is always a specific reason—supported by the passage—that wrong answers are wrong. Often, they describe a situation that *could* be true but that the passage does not explicitly indicate *is* true. They may also employ relatively abstract language that many test-takers find confusing or difficult to comprehend. That said, incorrect answers typically fall into the following categories:

- Off-topic
- Too broad (e.g., the passage discusses *one* scientist while the answer refers to *scientists*)
- Too extreme (e.g., they include words such as *never, always,* or *completely*)
- Half-right, half-wrong (e.g., right words, false statement)
- Could be true but not enough information; unsupported by the passage
- True for the passage as a whole, but not for the specific lines in question
- Factually true but not stated in the passage

On most questions, many test-takers find it relatively easy to eliminate a couple of answers but routinely remain stuck between two plausible-sounding options. Typically, the incorrect answer will fall into either the "could be true but not enough information" or the "half-right, half-wrong" category. In such cases, you must be willing to read very carefully in order to determine which answer the passage truly supports.

Strategies for Reading Passages

As a rule, you should always start by reading the question because it will tell you what aspect of the passage to focus on as you read. No less importantly, it will also tell you what information you do **not** need to worry so much about—knowledge that can prevent you from getting caught up in confusing language or irrelevant details, and from repeatedly reading sections of the passage that do not directly address the question.

Although passages on the digital SAT are very short, that **should not be confused with "easy."** Science passages may be fairly dense and technical; fiction/poetry passages may include challenging old-fashioned language; and passages of all types may involve topics you have had limited exposure to in high school. Your essential goal when you read, therefore, is to focus on getting the gist of the information necessary to answer the question. If there are sections of the passage you find confusing, try to avoid spending time puzzling over the details (which may or may not ultimately be relevant) and repeatedly rereading sections you do not immediately grasp.

For example, if you are looking for answer to a main-idea or primary-purpose question, you should pay particular attention to the beginning of the passage since that's where big-picture information is typically introduced; the middle of the passage is normally less important. (In a hundred-word passage, writers need to get to the point fast.)

On the other hand, if you are asked about the function of a sentence in the middle of a text, you probably want to skim through the beginning (for context) and then focus on the underlined sentence. If you cannot identify the answer from that portion alone, you can consider the information that comes immediately before and after.

Regardless of which portion of the text is most relevant, you should always be on the lookout for **words or phrases that indicate points, goals, and conclusions** (e.g., *point, intention, finding*); **the word *important* and any of its synonyms** (e.g., *significant, crucial, key*); and **italicized words**. If the author says something is important, it's important. There's no trick. You cannot determine what sort of information would illustrate, support, or weaken a point unless you know what the point is.

Second, you must be able to recognize when an argument changes, or when new and important information is introduced: transitions such as *however, therefore, in fact;* "unusual" punctuation such as dashes, italics, and colons; strong language such as *only* and *never;* and "explanation" words such as *reason* are "clues" that tell you to pay attention. If one of these elements appears in or near the aspect of the passage indicated by the question, **the answer will typically be located close by.**

What I would not recommend is reading the answer choices before you have looked at the passage. Unless you are a truly exceptional reader and test-taker with an intuitive sense of what correct answers sound like, this approach will almost certainly confuse you. Your goal should be to do some basic legwork before you look at the answers so that you have a sense of what you are looking for and are less likely to be distracted by plausible-sounding but incorrect options.

How to Work Through Reading Questions

While your approach will vary depending on the specific question, in general I recommend the following strategy:

1) Read the question <u>slowly</u>.

When you're done, take a second or two to make sure you know exactly what the question is asking.

This is not a minor step. If, for example, a question asks you the purpose of a sentence, you must reread it with the goal of understanding what role the sentence plays within the argument. If you reread it with a different goal, such as understanding what the sentence is literally saying, you can't work toward answering the question that's actually being asked.

2) Go back to the passage and find the relevant section. If the question seems to call for it, read from a sentence or two above to a sentence or two below.

Purpose/function questions often require more context and, as a result, you should be prepared to read both before and after the section reference. If the underlined portion begins close to the beginning of the passage, you should automatically read from the first sentence of the paragraph because it will usually give you the main point.

On the flip side, **only a very small section of a passage may sometimes be relevant, even—and perhaps especially—when a question asks about the text as a whole.** There is no sense in rereading fifteen lines when only a few key words at the beginning will suffice. Start by focusing on the first sentence or two, paying close attention to strong language, key transitions, and "interesting" punctuation such as colons or dashes, and you'll almost certainly have enough to go on.

3) Answer the question in your own words, and jot that answer down.

This step is unnecessary on very straightforward questions; however, it can be a big help on questions that require multiple steps of logic, particularly text completions, support/undermine questions, and Passage 1/Passage 2 relationship questions. Writing things down keeps you focused, reminds you what you're looking for, and prevents you from getting distracted by plausible-sounding or confusing answer choices.

The goal is not to write a dissertation or come up with the exact answer. You can be very general and should spend no more than a few seconds on this step; a couple of words scribbled down in semi-legible handwriting will suffice. The goal is to identify the general information or idea that the correct answer must include. Again, make sure you're answering the question that's actually being asked, not just restating what the passage says.

If you do this step, you should spend **no more than a few seconds** on it. If you can't come up with anything, skip to step #4.

4) Read the answers carefully, (A) through (D), in order.

If there's an option that contains the same essential idea you put down, choose it because it's almost certainly right. If it makes you feel better, though, you can read through the rest of the answers in order to be certain. Just make sure you don't get distracted by options that sound good and start second-guessing yourself. If you can't identify the correct answer…

5) Start by eliminating options that are clearly wrong.

Try not to spend more than a couple of seconds on each choice, and leave anything that's even a remote possibility. If answers are long, you may find it helpful to use your scratch paper and jot down the answers you are eliminating so that you do not accidentally click the wrong one. **Remember, though: your understanding of an answer has no effect on whether that answer is right or wrong.** You should never eliminate an option because you find it confusing or haven't really considered what it's saying.

If you get down to two answers, go back to the passage again and start checking them out. Whatever you do, do not just sit and stare at the screen (or the wall). The information you need to answer the question is in the passage, not in your head or on the other side of the room.

First, see if there are any major transitions or strong language you missed the first time; you may have been focusing on the wrong sentence, or you may not have read far enough before or after the line reference. If that is the case, the answer may become clear once you focus on the necessary information. The correct answer will usually contain a synonym for a key word in the passage, so if a remaining choice includes one, there's a good chance it's correct.

You can also pick one specific word or phrase in an answer to check out when you go back to the passage. For example, if the lines in question focus on a single scientist and the answer choice mentions "scientists," then the answer is probably beyond the scope of what can be inferred from the passage. Likewise, if an answer focuses on a specific person, thing, or idea not mentioned in the lines referenced, there's also a reasonable chance that it's off-topic. Keep in mind that **the more information an answer contains, the greater the chance that some of that information will be wrong.**

Finally, you can reiterate the main point of the passage, and think about which answer is most consistent with it. That answer will most likely be correct.

6) If you're still stuck, see whether there's a choice that looks like a right answer.

Does one of the answers you're left with use extremely strong or limiting language (*no one*, *always*, *ever*)? There's a pretty good chance it's wrong. Does one of them refer to the topic in the plural, whereas the passage has a narrow focus? It's probably too broad.

In addition, ask yourself whether all of the answers you're left with actually make sense in context of both the test and the real world. For example, an answer stating that no scientific progress has been made in recent years is almost certain to be wrong. Yes, you should be very careful about relying on your outside knowledge of a subject, but it's okay to use common sense too.

7) If you're still stuck, skip it or guess.

You can always come back to it later if you have time. And if you're still stuck later on, fill in your favorite letter and move on.

A Few Notes About Computer-Based Testing

While the computer-based SAT is shorter and more streamlined than the traditional paper version, you should not let the new format lull you into working too quickly or feeling overly confident. Essentially, you will have to separate the way you work on your laptop in everyday life—scrolling quickly through web pages, flipping between multiple tabs, pausing to check your phone—and the highly focused state that the test requires. Clicking through screens on a digital test on your personal device may *feel* easier than wrangling a number two pencil and a bubble sheet, but it does not mean that the exam is *actually* easier.

Furthermore, many people find that they are more likely to miss information when they read on a screen as opposed to paper. And a substantial body of research suggests that people tend to approach electronic devices "with a state of mind less conducive to learning than the one they bring to paper." (For a good SAT-style article on this topic, see "The Reading Brain in the Digital Age: The Science of Paper versus Screens," https://www.scientificamerican.com/article/reading-paper-screens/.) To be clear, it is perfectly fine to skim sometimes; however, you should do so deliberately, based on where important information is likely to be located—not because you associate reading on a screen with being in a semi-distracted state. When you study, you should practice reading more slowly and deliberately than you are accustomed to in order to counteract that tendency.

The adaptive nature of the test also means that you need to be extra careful to avoid careless errors during the first Reading/Writing module. While a strong performance on the first section will not automatically get you a high score, missing many questions there will prevent you from earning one. As a result, it is a good idea to get yourself into test mode before the exam begins. Try to do a few easy practice questions before you arrive at the testing center so that your brain is already warmed up when you begin.

General Tips for Reading Prep

And now, before we get started for real, some tidbits of test-prep wisdom:

If you're not in the habit of reading things written for educated adults, start. Now.

If you're unsure of where to begin, some good sources to start with are *Smithsonian* (www.smithsonianmag.com, covers humanities, natural and social sciences) and *Science Daily* (www.sciencedaily.com, a compilation of press releases from major research institutions around the world; includes natural and some social sciences). In addition, most university homepages have a link to a "News" section. These articles, particularly ones involving scientific research, can also be a very good source of SAT-style writing—and they're usually not too long either.

You cannot, however, read passively and expect your score to magically rise. Rather, you must **actively** and **consistently** practice the skills introduced in this book. Circle/underline the point, major transitions, and words that reveal tone; pay close attention to the introduction and conclusion for the topic and the author's opinion (see how quickly you can get the gist); notice when words are used in non-literal ways; and practice summarizing arguments briefly. The more you develop these skills independently, the easier it will become to apply them to the test. (And as a bonus, if you regularly read news from schools you plan to apply to, you can also obtain excellent material for "Why this college?" questions.)

Outside knowledge does matter.

One of the most frequently repeated pieces of SAT advice is that you have to forget all of your outside knowledge and just worry about what's in the passage. That's mostly true… but not completely. First, just to be clear, an answer can be both factually correct and wrong if is not supported by the passage. That's what most people mean when they say to forget about outside knowledge. The reality, however, is that reading does not exist in a vacuum. It is always dependent upon ideas and debates that exist outside of the SAT. The more you know about the world, the more easily you'll be able to understand what you're reading. And if you see an answer you know is factually correct, it can't hurt to check it first.

Read exactly what's on the screen, in order, from left to right.

This piece of advice may seem overwhelmingly obvious, but I cannot stress how important it is. When students feel pressured, they often start glomming onto random bits of information without fully considering the context. Although it is not necessary to read every word of a passage to get the gist of it, skipping around randomly is unlikely to help you either! Pay attention to what the author is telling you to pay attention to: when you see italics or words/phrases like *important* or *the point is*, you need to slow down and go word by word.

Be as literal as you possibly can.

While your English teacher might praise you for your imaginative interpretations, the College Board will not. Before you can understand the function of a piece of information or draw a conclusion about it, you have to understand exactly what it's saying—otherwise, you'll have a faulty basis for your reasoning. When you sum things up, stick as closely as possible to the language of the passage. People often get themselves into trouble because they think that there's a particular way they're supposed to interpret passages that they just don't "get," when in reality they're not supposed to interpret anything. **In short, worry about what the author is actually saying, not what she or he might be trying to say.**

Answering SAT Reading questions is a process.

Working through Reading questions is sometimes a process of trial-and-error. You make an assumption based on how texts are usually put together and how the test is typically constructed, and much of the time it'll turn out to be right (it is a *standardized* test, after all). If you work from the understanding that main ideas are often stated in the last sentence, for example, you may sometimes be best served by looking at a set of lines at the end of the passage first. In other instances, it may make more sense to focus on a key word and start halfway through the passage.

When your initial assumption doesn't pan out, then your job is to reexamine your original assumption and work through the answers one-by-one, trying to figure out what you overlooked the first time around. If you're a strong reader willing to approach the exam with the attitude that you can reason your way systematically through each question, you'll eventually hit on the answer. Yes, this does take some time, but if you can get through most of the questions quickly, having to slow down occasionally won't make much of an impact. No, working this way is not easy to do when you're under pressure, but it does get results.

Flexibility is key.

To obtain a very high score, you need to be able to adapt your approach to the question at hand. People who insist on approaching every question the same way tend to fall short of their goals, while those who start out scoring in the stratosphere tend to adjust automatically (even if they think they're just reading the passage and answering the question every time).

Sometimes you'll be able to answer a question based on your general understanding of the passage and won't need to reread anything. Sometimes you'll be able to go back to the passage, answer the question on your own, and then easily identify the correct answer when you look at the choices. Other times the answer will be far less straightforward, and you'll have to go back and forth between the passage and the question multiple times, eliminating answers as you go.

It's up to you to stay flexible and find the strategy that will get you to the answer most easily. For that reason, I have done my best, whenever possible, to offer multiple ways of approaching a given question.

The path to a perfect score is not linear.

Whereas math and writing scores can often be improved if you spend time internalizing just a few more key rules, the same cannot be said for reading. If you want a 750+ score, you *cannot skip steps* and start guessing or skimming through answers—you'll keep making just enough mistakes to hurt yourself. The SAT is a <u>standardized</u> test: if you keep approaching it the same way, you'll keep getting the same score. If you want your score to change radically, you have to approach the test in a radically different way. Raising your score is also not just about how much practice you do: it does not matter how well you know the test if you do not fully understand what you are reading. Getting into the right mindset can take five minutes or five months, but until you've absorbed it, your score will probably stay more or less the same.

Don't rush.

I took the SAT twice in high school: the first time, I raced through the reading section, answering questions mostly on instinct, not thinking anything through, and finishing every section early. I was an incredibly strong reader and even recognized one of the passages from a book I'd read for pleasure, but I got a 710.

The second time I understood what I was up against: I broke down every single question, worked through it step-by-step, wrote out my reasoning process, and worked every question out as meticulously as if it were a math problem. It was one of the most exhausting things I'd ever done, and when I stumbled out of the exam room, I had absolutely no idea how I'd scored. I'd literally been focusing so hard I hadn't left myself the mental space to worry about how I was doing. Working that way was *hard*, but it got me an 800.

Summoning that level of focus is not easy. It's also terrifying because you don't have the "well, I maybe didn't try as hard as I could have" excuse. If you bomb, you have nowhere to put the blame. If you have excellent comprehension and can stand to do it, though, working that precisely is almost foolproof. It might take longer than you're used to in the beginning, but the more you go through the process, the more accurate you'll become and the less time you'll take. Skipping steps might save you time, but your score will suffer as a result.

Understand what the College Board wants.

Every SAT passage has two authors: the author of the individual passage, and the writers of the test. The highest scorers are often able to use a combination of close reading skills and knowledge about the test itself (themes, biases, types of answers likely to be correct), and they are able to employ both of those skills as needed in order to quickly identify the answer choices most likely to be correct and then check them out for real.

When I was in high school and uncertain about an answer, I trained myself to always ask, "What would the test writers consider correct?" It didn't matter that I couldn't put the patterns into words then. The point was that I was able to convince myself that what *I* personally thought was irrelevant. To score well, you have to think of the test in terms of what the College Board wants—not what you want. You have to abandon your ego completely and approach the test with the mindset that *the College Board is always right, and what you think doesn't matter*. Then, once you've reached your goal, you can put the test out of your mind and never have to worry about it again.

Be willing to consider that the test might break its own "rules."

For example, you can usually assume that answers containing extreme language such as *always, never, awe, incomprehensible, impossible*, etc. are incorrect and cross them off as soon as you see them. But you can't *always* assume that a particular pattern holds without carefully considering what the passage is actually saying. Correct answers will very occasionally contain this type of phrasing. If you're trying to score 800 or close to it, you need to stay open to the possibility that an answer containing one of those words could on occasion be correct.

General patterns are just that: general. That means you will sometimes encounter exceptions.

Fit the answer to the passage, not the passage to the answer.

If an answer could only *sort of kind of maybe possibly be true if you read the passage in a very specific way*, it's not right. Don't try to justify anything that isn't directly supported by specific wording in the passage.

Every word in the answer choice counts.

One incorrect word in an answer choice is enough to make the entire answer wrong. It doesn't matter how well the rest of the answer works; it doesn't matter how much you like the answer or think it should be right. If the author of the passage is clearly happy about a new scientific finding and an answer says "express skepticism about a recent finding," that answer is wrong. The fact that the phrase *a recent finding* might have appeared in the passage is irrelevant. On the other hand…

Just because information is in a passage doesn't mean it's important.

One of the things the SAT tests is the ability to recognize important information and ignore irrelevant details. Reading SAT passages is not about absorbing every last detail but rather about understanding what you need to focus on and what you can let go. **If something confuses you, ignore it and work with what you do understand.**

Having a lot of time is different from needing a lot of time.

While you are given time to work carefully and methodically through the questions, you should not let the process become slower than necessary. Some questions are very straightforward and can be answered quickly, and you should avoid overthinking them. Save your energy for when you really need it.

Keep moving.

Students often become tired because they either 1) get hung up on a section of the passage that they find confusing—a part that sometimes turns out to be irrelevant—and fall into a loop of rereading it; or 2) get stuck between two answer choices and sit there staring at them. To avoid that trap, go back to the passage and check out a specific aspect of one of the answers, write down what you know, or highlight a key word in the text. Just do something to work towards the answer.

SAT Reading is not a guessing game.

Yes, you might be able to jack up your score a bit by guessing strategically on a relatively small number of questions, but there is still no substitute for carefully thinking your way through each question. The chances of your reaching your score goal simply by being a lucky guesser on more than a few questions are very small indeed.

If you consistently get down to two choices and always pick the wrong one, that's a sign that you either don't really know how to answer the questions or that you're not reading carefully enough. Many students told me they always got down to two options and then guessed wrong when in fact they were missing the entire point of the passage. That's not a test-taking problem; that's a comprehension problem.

If you are just not reading carefully enough, slow down, even try putting your finger on the screen (yes, seriously!), make sure you're getting every single word, and make a concerted effort to think things through before you pick an answer.

On the other hand, if you really aren't sure how to choose between answers, you need to figure out what particular skills you're missing and work on them. If you're misunderstanding the passage and/or answer choices because you don't know vocabulary, you need to keep a running list of unfamiliar words. Anything you see once is something you're likely to encounter again.

If you're getting thrown by complicated syntax, you need to spend more time reading SAT-level material. If you can't figure out what the author thinks, you need to focus on key phrases and places (e.g., the first sentence, places with strong language or unusual punctuation).

Finally, **remember: just because an answer is there doesn't mean it deserves serious consideration.** If you look for reasons to keep answers, you'll never get down to one.

But on the other hand...

Don't assume you'll always recognize the right answer when you see it.

Answers are written to make incorrect options sound right and correct ones sound wrong. You might get away with jumping to the answers on easy and medium questions, but you'll almost certainly fall down on at least some of the hard ones unless you do some work upfront. The fact that there are answer choices already there does not excuse you from having to think.

Moreover, **confusing does not equal wrong**. If there's any chance an answer could work, you have to leave it until you see something better. Sometimes the right answer just won't say what you're expecting it to say; in those cases, you need to keep an open enough mind to consider that you've been thinking in the wrong direction and be willing to go back and revise your original assumption.

There are no trick questions.

Reading questions may require you to apply very careful reasoning or make fine distinctions between ideas—but they're also set up so that you can figure them out. If you think your way carefully through a question and put the answer in your own words, then see an option choice that truly says the same thing, it's almost certainly correct.

Go back to the passage and read.

Even if you think you remember what the passage said, you probably need to go back and read it anyway (unless you can reason out the answer based on the main point). Stress makes memory unreliable, so don't assume you can trust yours. Don't play games or be cocky. Just take the extra few seconds and check.

Don't ever read just half a sentence.

Context counts. If you read only the first or last half of a sentence, you might miss the fact that the author thinks the *opposite* of what that half of the sentence says. You might also overlook the exact information you need to answer a question.

If the answer isn't in the section you're given, it must be somewhere else.

If you read the underlined portion referenced in the question and can't figure out the answer, chances are the information you need is located either before or after. Don't just assume you're missing something and read the same set of lines over and over again or, worse, guess. Again: be willing to revise your original assumption and start over. Yes, this will take time (although probably not as much as you think), but you have enough of it overall that you probably won't run out.

When in doubt, reread the first and last sentences.

The point of the passage is more likely to be located in those two places than it is anywhere else. If you get lost and start to panic, stop and reread it to focus yourself. It won't work all the time, but it will work often enough.

Scratch paper is your friend.

Most people don't have a huge problem writing down their work for math problems; the same, alas, cannot be said for reading. Unfortunately, one of the biggest differences between students scoring pretty well vs. exceptionally well is often their degree of willingness to write down each step of a problem. The very highest scorers tend to view writing each step down as a crucial part of the process necessary to get the right answer, whereas lower scorers often view writing as a drag on their time or a sign of weakness that they should be above. It's not either of those things. You can jot things down quickly, and the only person who has to read your handwriting is you.

Writing also keeps you focused and takes pressure off of your working memory. If you're really certain what you're looking for, you probably don't need to spend the time. If you have any hesitation, though, it's worth your while. When you're under a lot of pressure, having even one less thing to worry about is a big deal. Besides, you probably wouldn't try to figure the hardest math problems out in your head, so why on earth would you work that way for reading?

Don't fight the test.

It doesn't matter how much you want the answer to be (C) instead of (B). It never will be, and unless you want to file a complaint with the College Board, you're stuck. Instead of arguing about why your answer should have been right, try to understand why it was wrong. Chances are you misunderstood something or extrapolated a bit too far along the way. If you're serious about improving, your job is to adapt yourself to the mindset of the test because it certainly won't adapt itself to yours. Who knows, you might even learn something.

2 Vocabulary in Context

We're going to start by looking at vocabulary-in-context questions, which are among the most frequently appearing questions on the SAT: **you can expect about 10 of these questions per test, the vast majority of which will be sentence completions**. Compared to other question types, they are quite straightforward; however, you do need to work carefully so as not to overlook key information.

The prefix CON- means "with," so *context* literally means "with the text." Vocabulary-in-context questions thus require you to use clues in the passage to determine the meanings of particular words. In some cases, you may also need to rely on your knowledge of literal definitions, or your ability to use information such as prefixes and roots to make reasonable assumptions about those definitions; other times, however, the standard dictionary definition will be beside the point and may even appear as a wrong answer.

On the digital SAT, there are two main types of vocabulary questions:

1) Sentence Completions

These are a version of traditional (pre-2016) SAT vocabulary questions, which have been revived for the digital exam. You will be given a short passage with one word omitted and will be asked to select the most fitting option. While you will need to use the information in the passage to determine the logical definition of the missing word, you will also generally need to know—or be able to make educated guesses about—the standard meanings of the various answer choices, which may include some challenging academic words such as *epitomize* and *succinct*.

2) Meaning in Context

These questions are primarily designed to test your ability to recognize when common words (e.g., *poor, want*) are being used in alternate definitions. So as a general rule, if you see the usual definition of a word among the answer choices (e.g., "knock over" for *spill*), you should assume that it is incorrect and only reconsider it if no other option fits. As long as you are able to 1) use information from the passage to determine the intended meaning; and 2) match one of the choices to that meaning, you should be able to find your way to the answer.

Do you Really Need to Study Vocabulary?

The answer: it depends. While the vocabulary tested on the digital exam will not be outrageously difficult, you will be expected to be familiar with terms commonly found in advanced high school-level academic texts.

If you attend a rigorous school and have taken very challenging classes that require a substantial amount of reading and writing, you may already know most of the vocabulary that appears on the exam. If you have not been required to read and write extensively throughout high school, however, you may need to spend some time filling in the gaps. The only way to accurately gauge your level of preparation is to take a practice test or two: if you find yourself consistently missing questions because you do not know what various words mean, that's a sign you need to devote some time to learning new vocabulary.

That said, even if you are already a strong reader, it is still a good idea to spend 15 or so minutes a day reading a moderately serious publication such as the *New York Times* or *Scientific American*, keeping a running list of the vocabulary you do not know. As a general rule, any word whose meaning you are not 100% certain of, or that you cannot define out of context, should be looked up and written down. Encountering new words in relation to specific topics—ideally, ones that you find interesting—will make you more likely to remember them.

Keep in mind that a strong vocabulary will help you on the Reading and Writing test as a whole. Some of the same words that appear as answer choices to sentence completions will likely appear in passages accompanying other question types. Furthermore, **some Reading questions that appear to ask about other concepts may indirectly test vocabulary as well**. In certain cases, you may even be unable to determine an answer because you do not know the meaning of a word <u>not</u> specifically mentioned in the question. And finally, you do not want to get stuck on unfamiliar vocabulary in a passage and panic, overlooking the fact that you can get the gist of the passage and answer the question without knowing precisely what those words mean.

How to Work Through Sentence Completions

As is true for everything on the SAT, working carefully and systematically through sentence completions is the key to answering every question correctly that you are capable of answering correctly. It does not matter how strong your vocabulary is if you make careless errors. The scoring software will not care whether you actually knew the answer—it will just assign a score based on the buttons you clicked.

1) Read the entire passage, and identify the key words or phrases.

It is crucial that you consider the missing word in context of the full passage. If you focus exclusively on the line with the blank, you are likely to miss important information and may even end up looking for a word that means the opposite of the correct answer. As you read, look for clues to the definition of the missing word, which will always be built into sentences or passages.

2) Plug your own words into the blank.

If you do this and one of the words is contained in an answer choice, check it first. There's no guarantee that it'll be right, but when it is, you can save yourself a lot of time.

You should spend no more than a couple of seconds attempting to fill in your own word. It also doesn't matter if you just scribble down an approximate definition. The point is to reduce your margin of error by getting an idea, even a general one, of what belongs in the blank. You do not need to come up with the actual word (although if you can do that, great).

Important: If you can't define with certainty the word that belongs in a blank, do NOT try to plug in something that might only sort of work. Plugging in a word when you're not really sure what belongs is a great way to set yourself up to overlook the right answer. If you're not sure exactly what belongs in a blank, skip this step and go to step #3.

3) Play positive/negative.

Determine whether the word in question is positive or negative—it won't always be clear, but when it is, this is an incredibly effective strategy. If the blank is positive, draw a (+) on your scratch paper; if it's negative, draw a (-) on your scratch paper. Writing this down will reduce the strain on your memory and help keep you focused.

If you know that the word in the blank is clearly negative, for example, go through each answer from (A) to (D) and eliminate any **positive or neutral** word.

Do not skip around. Going in order keeps you thinking logically and systematically and reduces the chances that you'll make a careless error. This is especially important during the first Reading and Writing section, where incorrect answers can prevent you from receiving the more difficult second section and thus limit your score early on.

If you're unsure of whether an answer fits, keep it.

In many if not most cases, this approach should allow you to get rid of at least two answers, and if you're really lucky, three. Plug in the remaining options, if any, and see which works better.

Remember: worry about what a word means, not how it sounds.

While some words can clearly be eliminated immediately because they sound thoroughly incorrect in context, you need to consider things much more closely if you get stuck between two answers. At that point, you need to ignore the fact that a particular word, one whose meaning is consistent with what the sentence requires, may sound odd or unusual to you (especially if a second meaning is involved). Whether you yourself would think to use a given word is irrelevant—you are simply responsible for identifying the word with the most appropriate meaning.

Using Context Clues to Predict Meanings

Whenever you read a sentence, one of the first things you should look for is the presence of transition words: words that indicate logical relationships between parts of the sentence. Transitions fall into three basic categories:

1) Continuers

Continuers are words that indicate an idea is continuing in the direction it began.

• Also • And • As well as • Furthermore • In addition	• Just as • Likewise • Moreover • Not only … but also • Similarly

When continuers appear, you need to look for words with a similar meaning, or the same meaning, as the word in the blank.

For example:

> One of the hardiest types of grain, sorghum is frequently used to make flour as well as to replace a variety of wheat-based products. It can be cultivated in unusually dry conditions and is especially important in regions where soil is poor and resources are ______.

The fact that the continuer *and* links the blank to the phrase *soil is poor* tells us that the word we're looking for goes along with the idea of poor soil and must be negative.

2) Cause-and-Effect Words

Continuers also include cause, effect, and explanation words, which indicate that something is causing a particular result or explain why something is occurring.

Note that both words and punctuation marks can signal a cause-and-effect relationship.

• As a result • Because • Consequently • In that • Therefore • Thus	• Colons • Dashes

For example:

> Before the launch of the first space shuttle in 1961, the astronauts were required to undergo mental evaluation **because** the _____ danger inherent in space travel was judged to be as important as the physiological one.

The transition *because* indicates that the word in the blank must go along with the idea of mental evaluation—it must mean something like "psychological."

3) Contradictors

Contradictors are words that indicate that a sentence is shifting directions, or that contrasting information is being introduced.

• Although/Though	• Meanwhile
• But	• Nevertheless
• In contrast	• On the other hand
• Despite/In spite of	• Unlike
• For all (= despite)	• Whereas
• However	• While

When these types of words appear, you need to look for an answer that means the opposite of, or that is inconsistent with, key words in the sentence. For example:

> From the outside, the Afar Triangle, one of the most geologically active regions in the world, seems quite _____. **However**, its external appearance is deceptive, obscuring the presence of the fiery pools of lava lying just beneath its surface.

The word *however* tells us that the two parts of the sentence contain opposite ideas, and the phrase *fiery pools of lava* tells us that the word in the blank must indicate the opposite of this description—it must mean something like "calm" or "peaceful."

Important: Two key phrases that test-takers often find confusing are *for all*, which means "despite," and *all but*, which means "essentially" or "more or less," not "everything except." If you do not know what these phrases mean, you can very easily misinterpret an entire sentence.

Even if the words in the answer choices are quite straightforward, fill-in-the blank questions have the potential to be quite challenging. The difficulty lies in determining what the correct word must mean. To answer these types of questions, you must be able to navigate lengthy, complex sentences, and to understand the relationships between different parts of them.

Parallel Structure

Parallel structure simply refers to the fact that the constructions on either side of a transition (e.g., *and*, *but*) or word pair (e.g., *not only...but also*) must match. In such cases, the structure of the sentence itself tells you what sorts of words belong in the blanks. For example:

> Emily Wilson's translation of *The Odyssey* has been praised for being both accessible and _____: while it captures the clarity of the original, it does so without sacrificing any of the work's <u>subtlety</u> or <u>complexity</u>.

Alternately, the sentence could be phrased in this way:

> Because it captures the (1) <u>clarity</u> of the original without sacrificing any of its (2) <u>subtlety or complexity</u>, Emily Wilson's translation of *The Odyssey* has been praised for its (1) accessibility as well as its (2) _____.

In both cases, the description in the first half of the sentence is intended to run parallel to the two ideas expressed after the comma. Part 1: clarity = accessibility; Part 2: subtlety and complexity = _____.

The colon in the first version and the word *because* in the second indicate that the missing word must explain or elaborate on the idea that the translation is both subtle and complex.

Two Negatives Equal a Positive

One construction that many students find particularly challenging involves the negation of negative words to indicate a positive idea. In such cases, it is necessary to distinguish between the "charge" of the individual words and the opposite meaning they create when put together.

For example, consider the question below.

> Despite their physical attractiveness, some butterfly species are regarded as **pests** because in their larval stages they are capable of causing damage to crops or trees. Other species play a **less** _____ role in the ecosystem, however, because their caterpillars consume harmful insects.

The first sentence indicates that certain butterfly species are viewed negatively (*regarded as pests*) because they can damage crops.

In the second sentence, the contradictor *however* indicates an opposing relationship to the first sentence. That plus the statement *caterpillars consume harmful insects* indicate that the second sentence must convey a positive idea.

When we look at the blank, however, we can notice that it is modified by the word *less*. *Less* + something good = negative, which is the opposite of what we want. Logically, the sentence must be talking about something that is less *bad*. So even though the idea is positive, the word itself must be negative.

That is extremely important to work out upfront, because otherwise you might get confused when you look at the answer choices.

Despite their physical attractiveness, some butterfly species are regarded as **pests** because in their larval stages they are capable of causing damage to crops or trees. Other species play a less ______ role in the ecosystem, however, because their caterpillars consume harmful insects.

1 Mark for Review

Which choice completes the text with the most logical or precise word or phrase?

Ⓐ exceptional

Ⓑ beneficial

Ⓒ significant

Ⓓ detrimental

If you mistook "positive idea" for "positive word," you would probably seize on (B). In reality, however, "beneficial" (root *bene-*, good) is positive, as are "exceptional" and "significant." "Detrimental," meaning "harmful" (prefix *de-*, not), is the only negative option and thus the only possible answer.

Roots Can Help You (to a Point)

As we've just seen, a familiarity with roots will allow you to make educated guesses about the meanings of words and to quickly identify answers likely to be correct and/or incorrect. In fact, learning how to take words apart in order to make reasonable assumptions about their meanings is just as important as knowing lots of words.

In some ways, it is actually *more* important: if you've simply memorized definitions, you'll have no way of figuring out whether an unfamiliar word works or not. Knowing how the components of a word can reveal its meaning, however, gives you much more flexibility as well as more control, which in turn can give you more confidence. The bottom line is that if you have a little background knowledge and think calmly and logically about what's being asked, you can usually come to a reasonable conclusion. You don't need to be 100% sure to get questions right.

So if you haven't been paying attention in Spanish or French class, you might want to start. For example, consider the word *facility*. In its first definition, *facility* is a noun referring to a building. On the SAT, however, this word is much more likely to be used in its second definition, "ease" (e.g., a *facility with numbers*). Even if you're not familiar with that usage, if you know that *fácil* means "easy" in Spanish, or that *facile* means "easy" in both French and Italian (albeit with different pronunciations), you can make a pretty good assumption about its meaning on the test.

To illustrate, let's look at the following question.

An award-winning reporter as well as the author of several books, Maria Elena Fernandez is considered an ______ in her field because unlike the vast majority of present-day journalists, her work is characterized by a prose style that readers find highly distinctive, even unique.

1 Mark for Review

Which choice completes the text with the most logical or precise word or phrase?

Ⓐ anomaly

Ⓑ innovator

Ⓒ explorer

Ⓓ activist

The passage tells us that Fernandez's work is *highly distinctive, even unique*, so the correct answer must reflect that idea.

"Explorer" and "activist" both clearly do not make sense, but let's say that you get stuck between "innovator" (which you know) and "anomaly" (which you don't). How do you decide?

It might seem like "innovator"—someone who does things in new ways—could fit because someone who does new things could be considered unique, right? The problem is that this word does not **by definition** mean "unique." If that were the correct option, the passage would contain words or phrases that pointed directly to it, e.g., *groundbreaking* or *novel* (new) *approach*. But that is not the case here.

To confirm that "anomaly" is correct, consider that Fernandez is *unlike the majority of present-day journalists*—that is, she is not something. The prefix *a-* means "not," which is consistent with that requirement. (And if you wanted to go deeper, the root *nom-* means "name," so *anom* = without a name, which is also consistent with the idea of being completely unlike others.)

That said, roots and especially prefixes can on occasion mislead you: some positive words may have prefixes that normally indicate a negative, e.g., *discerning*, a positive word meaning "able to make fine distinctions"; or *provoke*, which can mean "deliberately attempt to anger." But those are exceptions. In general, any solid logical process you use will stand a good chance of getting you to the correct answer.

Watch Out for Second Meanings

Although second definitions are the focus of meanings-in-context questions, it is entirely possible that fill-in-the-blank questions will test alternate usages as well. As a result, if you see what appears to be an extremely simple, common, and obviously wrong word among the answer choices, you should think twice before eliminating it.

To take a straightforward example:

In the two-dimensional world of maps, sharp lines are used to demarcate where one country ends and another begins. In reality, however, boundaries between nations are typically much more ______, with border regions that are characterized by multiple languages and cultures.

1 Mark for Review

Which choice completes the text with the most logical or precise word or phrase?

Ⓐ fluid

Ⓑ precise

Ⓒ rigid

Ⓓ identifiable

If you looked at (A) and immediately eliminated it because not only does "stuff you can pour" have nothing to do with maps and countries and borders, but it's also the wrong part of speech, guess again.

First, all four answer choices will always be given in the same, correct part of speech. So if you see a word normally used as a noun appear along with three adjectives (as is true above), that word is being used as an adjective as well—a sure sign that a second meaning is involved.

That is exactly the case here. A common second meaning of *fluid* is "able to change shape" or "not rigid." And that is exactly the definition required here: the word *however* sets up a contrast between the *sharp lines* on maps and the word in the blank, so (A) must be correct.

Important: When second meanings appear in answers to non-vocabulary Reading questions, you should pay extra attention to those choices. While these options are by no means guaranteed to be correct, they probably stand a higher chance of being right simply because so many test-takers will either misunderstand or jump to eliminate them.

Exercise: Sentence Completions

1 Mark for Review

In Ancient Egyptian art, human figures are presented in a rigid and ______ manner. In contrast, animals are often very well-observed and lifelike.

Circle or underline key words

Definition or (+/ –): ____________________

Ⓐ dazzling

Ⓑ artificial

Ⓒ impressive

Ⓓ realistic

2 Mark for Review

Female hyenas remain within their clan and inherit their mother's rank. As a result, sisters must compete with one another to obtain a ______ position in the hierarchy.

Circle or underline key words

Definition or (+/ –): ____________________

Ⓐ relative

Ⓑ dominant

Ⓒ regular

Ⓓ secure

3 Mark for Review

Because music plays an essential role in facilitating social functions and is more effective than speech at improving people's moods, researchers are beginning to question whether it truly is as ______ as they once believed. In fact, they believe it may have evolved to promote societal cohesion.

Circle or underline key words

Definition or (+/ –): ____________________

Ⓐ demanding

Ⓑ prevalent

Ⓒ frivolous

Ⓓ important

4 Mark for Review

The camera obscura—a darkened room with a small hole or lens through which an image is projected—was perhaps the earliest known imaging device. First referred to in a fourth-century Chinese text known as *Mozi*, it was ______ of the modern-day photographic camera.

Circle or underline key words

Definition or (+/ –): ____________________

Ⓐ a forerunner

Ⓑ a relic

Ⓒ an heir

Ⓓ a proponent

5	Mark for Review

For centuries, ______ have questioned the authorship of Shakespeare's plays. In total, no fewer than 50 alternative candidates, including Francis Bacon, Queen Elizabeth I, and Christopher Marlowe, have been proposed as the true writer.

Circle or underline key words

Definition or (+/ –): ____________________

Ⓐ partisans

Ⓑ zealots

Ⓒ advocates

Ⓓ skeptics

Now, try some questions without the intermediate step.

All of the factors that allowed the Great Barrier Reef to ______ are changing at unprecedented rates. Over the next several decades, marine biologists believe, it is likely to decline below a crucial threshold from which it is impossible to recover.

6	Mark for Review

Which choice completes the text with the most logical or precise word or phrase?

Ⓐ flourish

Ⓑ diminish

Ⓒ extend

Ⓓ succumb

Although traditional historians and historical filmmakers differ in their choice of medium, the most respected ones share a scrupulous regard for facts and the rules of evidence that ______ their acceptability.

7 Mark for Review

Which choice completes the text with the most logical or precise word or phrase?

Ⓐ deny

Ⓑ complete

Ⓒ dictate

Ⓓ rely on

In the past, psychologists dismissed fiction as a way of understanding human emotions. In more recent times, however, they have developed a new ______ for the insights that stories can provide into human behavior.

8 Mark for Review

Which choice completes the text with the most logical or precise word or phrase?

Ⓐ disregard

Ⓑ explanation

Ⓒ responsibility

Ⓓ appreciation

Okakura Kakuzo is credited with the revival of Nihonga, painting done with traditional Japanese techniques, at a time when Western-style painting was threatening to ______ it. When, in 1897, it became clear that European methods were to be given prominence at the Tokyo Academy of Fine Arts, he resigned his directorship and shortly after helped found the Japanese National Arts Academy.

9 Mark for Review

Which choice completes the text with the most logical or precise word or phrase?

Ⓐ supplant

Ⓑ deny

Ⓒ salvage

Ⓓ challenge

Like many of the surgeons general before her, Joycelyn Elders became an outspoken advocate for a variety of controversial health issues. As a result, she quickly established a reputation for being ______.

10 Mark for Review

Which choice completes the text with the most logical or precise word or phrase?

Ⓐ a pragmatist

Ⓑ a polemicist

Ⓒ a curiosity

Ⓓ an amateur

Chicago epitomized the remarkable ______ of urbanization during the nineteenth century. In 1830, the city was home to only a few hundred residents. Just eight decades years later, it had expanded to a population of two million.

11 Mark for Review

Which choice completes the text with the most logical or precise word or phrase?

Ⓐ velocity

Ⓑ significance

Ⓒ mastery

Ⓓ influence

Lynn Margulis's revolutionary theory of eukaryotic cell development was initially met with almost unanimous ______ because it built upon ideas that had largely been discredited. In fact, her groundbreaking 1967 paper, "On the Origin of Mitosing Cells," was published only after being rejected by fifteen journals.

12 Mark for Review

Which choice completes the text with the most logical or precise word or phrase?

Ⓐ scorn

Ⓑ jubilation

Ⓒ consideration

Ⓓ impatience

Proponents of the Arts and Crafts movement claimed that its simple but refined aesthetics would ______ the new experience of industrial consumerism. Individuals would become more rational and society more harmonious.

13 Mark for Review

Which choice completes the text with the most logical or precise word or phrase?

Ⓐ contain

Ⓑ elevate

Ⓒ compromise

Ⓓ enjoy

The whale is a remarkably ______ navigator, migrating thousands of miles each year without a compass and always arriving in precisely the same spot.

14 Mark for Review

Which choice completes the text with the most logical or precise word or phrase?

Ⓐ docile

Ⓑ advantageous

Ⓒ adept

Ⓓ precocious

At its peak, roughly corresponding to the Middle Ages, Constantinople was one of the largest and most influential cities in the world. It ______ a powerful cultural pull and dominated economic life throughout the Mediterranean basin.

15 Mark for Review

Which choice completes the text with the most logical or precise word or phrase?

Ⓐ defended

Ⓑ exerted

Ⓒ restrained

Ⓓ thwarted

The International Space Station is intended to accelerate scientific progress, speeding the development of new technologies and ______ their integration into industry and medicine.

16 Mark for Review

Which choice completes the text with the most logical or precise word or phrase?

Ⓐ hindering

Ⓑ containing

Ⓒ facilitating

Ⓓ relating

Until well into the nineteenth century, most people in Europe obtained the majority of their nutrients from bread. Workers commonly devoted half of their earnings to it and lived in constant dread of ______.

17 Mark for Review

Which choice completes the text with the most logical or precise word or phrase?

Ⓐ scarcity

Ⓑ distress

Ⓒ abundance

Ⓓ rejection

Smallpox, believed to have emerged in human populations around 10,000 BCE, is one of only two infectious diseases to have been fully ______: the first effective vaccine, made from a modified cowpox virus, was developed at the end of the eighteenth century by the British physician Edward Jenner, and the last natural case was reported in 1977.

18 Mark for Review

Which choice completes the text with the most logical or precise word or phrase?

Ⓐ investigated

Ⓑ described

Ⓒ sequenced

Ⓓ eradicated

Contemporary readers of Mark Twain's autobiography may occasionally become bored with some of the more obscure references to nineteenth-century scandals. Nevertheless, the work as a whole is seldom less than ______.

19 Mark for Review

Which choice completes the text with the most logical or precise word or phrase?

Ⓐ tedious

Ⓑ engaging

Ⓒ relevant

Ⓓ descriptive

Historians often hold conflicting views about when the Harlem Renaissance began and ended. While some scholars believe that it was largely over by the early 1930s—the beginning of the Great Depression—others argue that in fact many of the movements associated with the period ______, influencing artists and thinkers decades later.

20 Mark for Review

Which choice completes the text with the most logical or precise word or phrase?

Ⓐ prevailed

Ⓑ persisted

Ⓒ emerged

Ⓓ declined

Researchers in Japan have discovered two brain signals in the prefrontal cortex that play a role in humans' ability to predict what types of decisions other people will make. Their results suggest that these signals strike a balance between expected and observed outcomes, enabling people to ______ others' choices, even when those individuals hold different values.

21 Mark for Review

Which choice completes the text with the most logical or precise word or phrase?

Ⓐ anticipate

Ⓑ mimic

Ⓒ dispute

Ⓓ assess

Because genetic factors play a role in influencing personality, early life experiences are not solely responsible for determining an individual's character. However, significant events in childhood have been shown to establish neural pathways that can either be changed or ______ by later events.

22 Mark for Review

Which choice completes the text with the most logical or precise word or phrase?

Ⓐ affected

Ⓑ restored

Ⓒ reinforced

Ⓓ undermined

The lack of centralization among the Igbo-speaking peoples of southeastern Nigeria has been ______ the development of a great variety of artistic styles and cultural practices. Objects range from pottery to carved decorative instruments to masks made of wood and fabric, and some art forms such as elaborate clay statues of families are produced by only a single group.

23 Mark for Review

Which choice completes the text with the most logical or precise word or phrase?

Ⓐ detrimental to

Ⓑ conducive to

Ⓒ adopted by

Ⓓ attributed to

Social psychologists David Dunning, Chip Heath, and Jerry Suls have shown that the correlation between self-ratings of skill and actual performance in many domains can be ______. The researchers found that on average, people claim to be "above average" in a series of common skills—a conclusion that defies statistical possibility.

24 Mark for Review

Which choice completes the text with the most logical or precise word or phrase?

Ⓐ tenuous

Ⓑ clear

Ⓒ narrow

Ⓓ predictable

Found in the Ukaguru mountains, for which it is named, *Hyperolius ukaguruensis* is among the few frogs around the world that do not croak or sing. Because these amphibians are unable to ______ auditory information to identify other members of their species, scientists speculate that they might use tiny spines on their throats to compensate, employing touch instead.

25 Mark for Review

Which choice completes the text with the most logical or precise word or phrase?

Ⓐ interfere with

Ⓑ ignore

Ⓒ rely on

Ⓓ relate to

The early twentieth-century pianist and composer Helen Hagan made use of ______ influences in her work. Although much of the music she wrote was grounded primarily in the nineteenth-century European tradition, it also incorporated a diverse set of genres including ragtime and African American spirituals.

26 Mark for Review

Which choice completes the text with the most logical or precise word or phrase?

Ⓐ unexpected

Ⓑ complex

Ⓒ contemporary

Ⓓ eclectic

Native to southern Mexico, the shortfin mollie is unique among aquatic animals in that it can survive in water with high concentrations of hydrogen sulfide. Genetic biologist Joanna Kelley led a 2016 study to investigate the mechanism by which the fish are able to thrive in what is normally a toxic environment, finding that about 170 of the fish's 35,000 genes are activated not to ______ the absorption of hydrogen sulfide but rather to detoxify and remove it once it is present.

27 Mark for Review

Which choice completes the text with the most logical or precise word or phrase?

Ⓐ intensify

Ⓑ streamline

Ⓒ regulate

Ⓓ impede

Beginning in the mid-1600s, the gradual transformation of the English economy was accompanied by improvements in general welfare. As economists Sara Horrell, Jane Humphries, and Jacob Weisdorf found from their research on historical family living standards, from that period on, men's salaries alone could rarely ______ a family comfortably; women's participation in the labor force was also necessary.

28 Mark for Review

Which choice completes the text with the most logical or precise word or phrase?

Ⓐ sustain

Ⓑ uphold

Ⓒ entertain

Ⓓ defend

Joy Harjo's memoir *Poet Warrior* is ______ work. As the title suggests, the book includes many poems, including ones by Federico García Lorca and Meridel LeSueur, whom Harjo cites as major influences on her writing; however, the narrative also interweaves prose and songs, creating a work that defies easy classification.

29 Mark for Review

Which choice completes the text with the most logical or precise word or phrase?

Ⓐ a hybrid

Ⓑ an innovative

Ⓒ a controversial

Ⓓ a significant

Unlike other bat species, nectar-feeding bats evolved extra-long whiskers that allow them to ______ as they drink from flowers. Biologist Eran Amichai and colleagues used high-speed cameras to capture how the forward-facing whiskers provide enhanced spatial information, permitting the bats to remain briefly suspended in mid-air as they feed.

30 Mark for Review

Which choice completes the text with the most logical or precise word or phrase?

Ⓐ recline

Ⓑ hover

Ⓒ balance

Ⓓ glide

How to Work Through Meaning-in-Context Questions

Meaning-in-context questions are less common than sentence completions, but you may encounter them occasionally. The principle on which they are based can be summarized as follows:

Context determines meaning.

Essentially, words can be used to mean whatever an author happens to want them to mean, regardless of their dictionary definitions.

As a result, when you see a question that says, *As used in the text, what does the word "fine" most nearly mean?* You can think of the question as saying, *As used in the text, what does the word ________ most nearly mean?* The fact that *fine* rather than some other word happens to be used is essentially irrelevant.

That said, in some cases a familiarity with common second meanings may be helpful. For example, *a want of* is often used to mean "a lack of," especially in old-fashioned writing. In other cases, though, words will be used in ways unlikely to appear on any vocabulary list. A common alternate meaning may even appear as an *incorrect* answer. So while you may find the list of second meanings on p. 62 helpful, you should also be aware that it does not cover the full range of potential definitions.

Strategies

Although the process for working through meaning-in-context questions is not radically different from the process for working through sentence completions, it often involves a slightly different approach.

1) Read the entire passage, and identify the key words.

As is true for Sentence Completions, focusing only on the text immediately surrounding the blank can cause you to miss key information; however, you must also be careful to focus on what is truly important and ignore what is not.

2) Plug in your own word and find the answer choice that matches.

If you are able to use this strategy effectively, it is the simplest and fastest way to answer these questions. The only potential difficulty is that sometimes, even if you provide a perfectly adequate synonym for the word in question, the correct answer will be a word that you find odd, or that you do not recognize as having the same meaning as the term you supplied. If you are a strong reader with a solid vocabulary, however, those issues should not pose a serious problem.

3) Plug each answer choice into the sentence.

Frequently, you'll be able to hear that a particular choice does not sound correct or have the right meaning in context. The only potential downside is that sometimes, as is true for #1, the correct word is not a word you would think to use, causing you to avoid it. As always, be careful with answer choices that are themselves second meanings.

4) Play positive/negative, then plug in.

Additional Points:

While some students feel most comfortable using a single approach for all vocabulary-in-context questions, it is also true that certain questions lend themselves better to certain approaches. On some straightforward questions you may find it easiest to plug in your own word, while on other, less clear-cut questions, a combination of positive/negative and process of elimination might provide the most effective strategy.

Second, you should pay particular attention to clues indicating that a word in question has a similar or opposite meaning to another word. For example, in the phrase *quiet and reserved*, the word *and* tells you that *reserved* must mean something similar to *quiet*; and in the phrase *delicate but sound*, the word *but* tells you that *sound* must mean roughly the opposite of *delicate*. On the other hand, if you cannot determine the meaning of a word from the sentence in which it appears, you must establish a slightly larger context. Read from the sentence above to the sentence below—one of those sentences will very likely include the information you need to answer the question.

Finally, don't get distracted by unfamiliar words in the answer choices. **It doesn't matter whether you know the definition of the wrong answers as long as you can identify the right answer.** The test writers are fond of using distractors whose definitions students are unlikely to know, while making correct answers relatively simple. As a result, you should never choose an answer because it looks sophisticated. If anything, it's more likely to be wrong. **As a rule, always work from what you do know to what you don't know**. If you're not sure about a word, ignore it and deal with everything you know for sure first.

Let's look at some examples.

Meaning in Context #1

Every time a car drives through a major intersection, it becomes a data point. Magnetic coils of wire lie just beneath the pavement, registering each passing car. This starts a cascade of information: Computers tally the number and speed of cars, shoot the data through underground cables to a command center and finally translate it into the colors red, yellow and green.

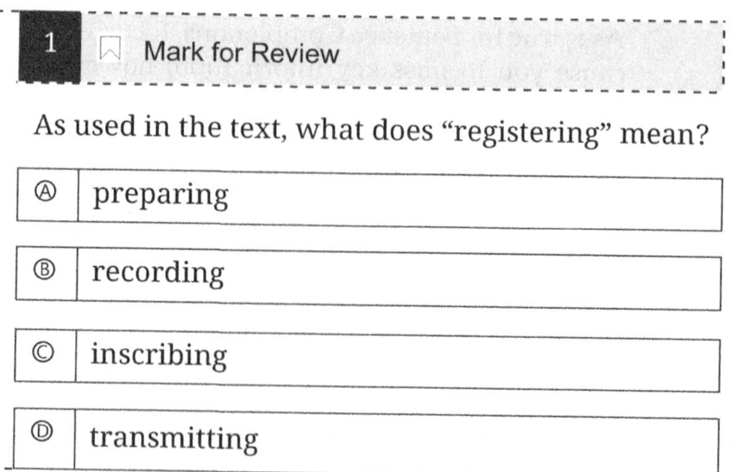
1 Mark for Review

As used in the text, what does "registering" mean?

Ⓐ preparing

Ⓑ recording

Ⓒ inscribing

Ⓓ transmitting

The passage is talking about *magnetic coils of wire* that notify computers of the cars' presence, beginning *a cascade of information*. Logically, the coils of wire must be "recording" each car.

Otherwise, you can play process of elimination. "Preparing" doesn't fit, so (A) can be crossed out. If you don't know what "inscribing" (engraving) means, ignore (C) for the moment and deal with the words you do know first.

Now, be very careful with (D): the passage implies that the coils of wire transmit information about the cars to computers, but it is illogical to say that coils of wire "transmit" each passing car.

If you're stuck between (B) and (C), don't fall into the trap of assuming that the harder-looking word must be right. Instead, plug (B) into the sentence: *Magnetic coils of wire lie just beneath the pavement, recording each passing car.* Yes, that makes sense. So the answer is (B).

Meaning in Context #2

Until the past few years, physicists agreed that the entire universe is generated from a few mathematical truths and principles of symmetry, perhaps throwing in a handful of parameters like the mass of an electron. It seemed that we were closing in on a vision of our universe in which everything could be calculated, predicted, and understood.

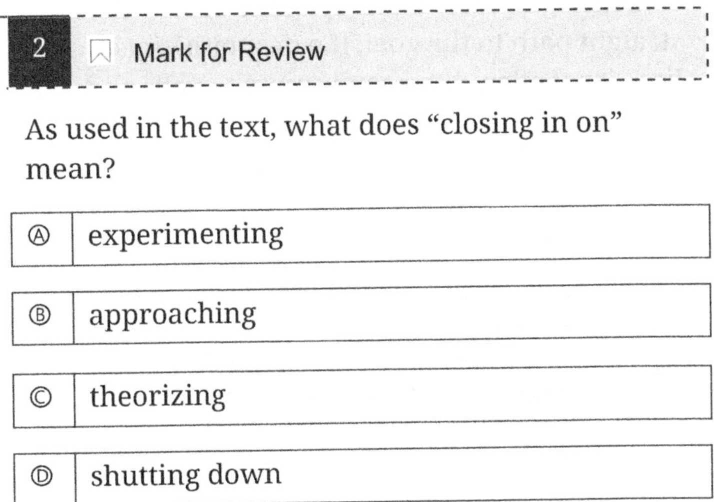

2 Mark for Review

As used in the text, what does "closing in on" mean?

Ⓐ experimenting

Ⓑ approaching

Ⓒ theorizing

Ⓓ shutting down

The beginning of the passage discusses the fact that physicists believed they were beginning to understand how to describe the universe mathematically. Given that context, *closing in on* must mean something like "getting close to." That is the definition of "approaching," so (B) is correct.

Playing process of elimination, (A) can be crossed out because it does not make sense to say *It seemed that we were experimenting a vision of our universe...* Scientists could conduct experiments to gain a greater understanding of the universe, but it is not grammatically or logically possible to "experiment" a vision.

Be careful with (C). It is true that a synonym for this word, *predicted*, does appear in the passage, but that meaning does not make sense in this context. The two sentences make it clear that physicists believed they were on the verge of possessing a thorough understanding of how the universe works. They were not predicting *a vision of [the] universe in which everything could be calculated*, etc. because that vision was already firmly in place.

To eliminate (D), you can play positive/negative. The fact that scientists agreed that a major problem in physics was about to be solved tells you that all of the information before the word *however* has a positive focus. As a result, you can assume that the correct answer will be positive as well. Shutting down is negative and thus can be eliminated.

That again leaves us with (B) as the only possibility.

Meaning in Context #3

When Saburo joined the track and field team at Bukkyo High School, the sport was enjoying a popularity it had not known before the war. At the time, few schools could afford baseball bats or gymnastic equipment. And there was something in the simplicity of the sport—the straight path to the goal, the dramatic finish line—that <u>stirred</u> the community to yells and often tears.

3 Mark for Review

As used in the text, what does "stirred" mean?

Ⓐ forced

Ⓑ transformed

Ⓒ disturbed

Ⓓ inspired

This is an excellent example of a question that lends itself well to playing positive/negative. The passage is clearly positive – track and field is enjoying a new popularity, and families came outside to cheer – so you can assume that the correct answer will be positive as well. Don't get thrown off by the reference to yells and tears. "Forced" and "disturbed" are negative, so (A) and (C) can be eliminated. "Transformed" is positive, but it does not make any sense when it is plugged back into the sentence. That leaves (D), which fits: logically, the spectators were "inspired" by the athletes.

Exercise: Meaning in Context

Neuroscientists and humanists are tackling similar questions—by joining forces, they might vastly refine our understanding of the role that narrative plays in human cognition, for example, or explore with empirical precision the power of literature to represent consciousness.

1 Mark for Review

As used in the text, what does “refine” mean?

Ⓐ purify

Ⓑ filter

Ⓒ improve

Ⓓ explain

In recent years, scientists have used powerful genome-sequence tools to investigate the associations between genes and disease risk, with the goal of preventing illnesses before symptoms occur. However, some researchers have cautioned against relying too heavily on genetic factors, arguing that estimates of an individual’s chances of developing a particular malady are more confounded by environmental factors than is usually recognized.

2 Mark for Review

As used in the text, what does “confounded” mean?

Ⓐ confused

Ⓑ influenced

Ⓒ deceived

Ⓓ puzzled

Among humans, even thinking about yawning can trigger the reflex, leading some to suspect that catching a yawn is linked to our ability to empathize with other humans. For instance, contagious yawning activates the same part of the brain that governs empathy and social know-how. And some studies have shown that humans with more fine-tuned social skills are more likely to catch a yawn.

3 Mark for Review

As used in the text, what does “governs” mean?

Ⓐ elects

Ⓑ requires

Ⓒ controls

Ⓓ suppresses

The following text is from Emily Brontë's 1847 novel *Wuthering Heights*. The narrator is bringing a boy named Linton to his father.

The boy was fully occupied with his own cogitations for the remainder of the ride, till we halted before the farmhouse garden-gate. I watched to catch his impressions in his countenance. He surveyed the carved front and low-browed lattices, the straggling gooseberry-bushes and crooked firs, with solemn intentness, and then shook his head: his private feelings entirely disapproved of the exterior of his new abode.

4 Mark for Review

As used in the text, what does "catch" mean?

Ⓐ acquire

Ⓑ gather

Ⓒ attain

Ⓓ observe

The following text is from James Weldon Johnson's 1922 poem "Mother Night."

Eternities before the first-born day,
Or ere the first sun fledged his wings of flame,
Calm Night, the everlasting and the same,
A brooding mother over chaos lay.
And whirling suns shall blaze and then decay,
Shall run their fiery courses and then claim
The haven of the darkness whence they came;
Back to Nirvanic peace shall grope their way.

5 Mark for Review

As used in the text, what does "claim" mean?

Ⓐ return to

Ⓑ pick up

Ⓒ plea for

Ⓓ assert

As a painter, Georgia O'Keeffe is so closely tied to the American Southwest that it is hard to imagine her anywhere but the desert. In 1939, however, she accepted a commission to travel to Hawaii and paint scenes for a campaign promoting pineapple juice. Although serious artists did not normally take on commercial work, O'Keeffe was won over by images of palm trees and sandy white beaches.

6 Mark for Review

As used in the text, what does "tied to" mean?

Ⓐ held down

Ⓑ engaged with

Ⓒ fastened to

Ⓓ associated with

One reason piracy was often an act or a phase rather than a way of life was that humans are not designed to live at sea for long stretches. The open water is a hostile place, offering few of the pleasures of life on land. Pirates needed to clean and repair their ships, collect wood and water, gather crews, obtain paperwork, and fence their goods. Gold and silver have no value in the middle of the ocean.

7 Mark for Review

As used in the text, what does "stretches" mean?

Ⓐ expansions

Ⓑ periods

Ⓒ areas

Ⓓ distortions

Mangroves, which have extensive root networks, are essential to some coastal ecosystems because they help check erosion and capture carbon dioxide that would otherwise be released into the atmosphere. However, while these tropical trees and shrubs grow relatively quickly, they can take years to achieve full maturity.

8 Mark for Review

As used in the text, what does "check" mean?

Ⓐ determine

Ⓑ reveal

Ⓒ impede

Ⓓ seize

Around 12,000 years ago, the Neolithic revolution radically changed the economy, diet, and structure of the first human societies in the Fertile Crescent. With the beginning of the cultivation of grains such as wheat and barley and the domestication of animals, the first cities emerged in a new social context marked by a productive exchange of goods.

9 Mark for Review

As used in the text, what does "marked" mean?

Ⓐ imprinted

Ⓑ labeled

Ⓒ represented

Ⓓ distinguished

The following text is from Willa Cather's 1918 novel *My Antonia*. The narrator is teaching Antonia English.

We were so deep in the grass that we could see nothing but the blue sky over us and the gold tree in front of us. It was wonderfully pleasant. After Antonia had said the new words over and over, she wanted to give me a little chased silver ring she wore on her middle finger. When she coaxed and insisted, I repulsed her quite sternly. I didn't want her ring, and I felt there was something reckless and extravagant about her wishing to give it away.

10 Mark for Review

As used in the text, what does "repulsed" mean?

Ⓐ refused

Ⓑ frustrated

Ⓒ defeated

Ⓓ obstructed

Essential Academic Vocabulary

Make a Claim

Advance

Assert

Conjecture (also a noun)

Posit

Proffer

Speculate

Hypothesize

Support a Claim

Bolster

Buttress

Substantiate

Acknowledge a Claim

Concede

Question a Claim

Ambivalence

Skepticism

Rebut

Refute

Think about

Grapple with

Mull over

Ruminate about

Coming Together

Converge

Integrate

Intersect

Moving Apart

Diverge

Draw a Conclusion

Infer

Surmise

Provide Sources

Attribute

Cite

Large Amount

Copious

Multitude

Plethora

Profusion

Small Amount

Dearth

Paucity

Different, Diverse

Disparate

Heterogeneous

Eclectic

Noticeable, Striking

Conspicuous

Distinctive

Salient

Harmless

Benign

Innocuous

Inborn

Inherent

Innate

Intrinsic

Key Science-Related Terms	Branches of Science
Advantageous – providing an advantage Empirical – relying on hard data Fauna – animal life Flora – plant life Hierarchy (adj., hierarchical) – system of rank; opposite of *egalitarian* Isotope – alternate form of an element Indigenous – native Inhibit – prevent, impede (e.g., a response) Metabolism – the process of converting food to energy Methodology – system of methods or procedures Microbial – relating to microscopic organisms Pigment – color Predisposed – having a tendency toward Regenerate – regrow Replicate – repeat with the same result Saturate – to become completely soaked with Simulation – realistic (computer) model Stimulus (pl., Stimuli) – something that provokes a specific response Symbiosis (adj., Symbiotic) – interaction between two organisms living close together, benefits both Taxonomy – classification system Trait – characteristic Vegetation – plants (not vegetables) Velocity – speed	Astronomy – study of stars and planets Botany – study of plants Cognitive Science, Neuroscience – science of the brain Ecology – study of the natural world Entomology – study of insects Epidemiology – study of diseases and public health Genetics – study of genes Geology – study of rocks Ornithology – study of birds Paleontology – study of fossils Zoology – study of animals **Branches of Social Science and Humanities** Anthropology – study of human behavior and social organization, usually on a large scale; can include linguistics, biology, and archaeology Archaeology – study of historical human activity through the recovery or **excavation** (digging up) of physical objects Economics – study of monetary systems Ethnography – study of individual cultures Folklore – study of traditional stories and myths Sociology – study of everyday human social behaviors and interactions at a specific time

Additional Words to Know	
Positive	**Negative**
Adept – skilled	Adversary – opponent
Align (oneself with) – support or adopt the position of	Bureaucracy (adj. Bureaucratic) – Administrative portion of a government or organization; usually has a connotation of unnecessary hassle or complication
Authentic – genuine	Conventional – traditional, what has always been done; usually has a negative connotation on the SAT. Most of the researchers described in science and social science passages are arguing **against** conventional approaches or understandings.
Centrality – state of being central or essential	Displace – to force someone or something from its home or habitat
Complement – to complete or perfect	Disparity (adj., Disparate) – difference, gap
Comprehensive – thorough, complete (NOT to be confused with *comprehensible*, which means "understandable")	Feign (v.) – to fake or pretend
Contingent – dependent upon	Fruitful/Fruitless – productive/unproductive
Confer – give, grant	Haphazard – careless
Cultivate – grow, raise, e.g., crops	Impede, Inhibit – prevent; get in the way of
Elucidate – make clear	Indecipherable – incomprehensible
Esteemed- held in high regard	Impenetrable – impossible to understand or access
Invigorating – Intensely energizing, exciting	Marginal – unimportant
Extant – still in existence; be careful not to confuse this word with *extinct*	Rudimentary – very basic
Fervor (adj., Fervid) – excitement, intensity	Trivial – unimportant
Innovative – new and revolutionary	
Mirth – happiness	
Mitigate – make less severe	
Precocious – done at an earlier age than usual	
Prevail – win; adj. Prevalent, Prevailing – widespread; generally accepted	
Sovereignty – political independence, self-rule	

Neutral (Positive/Negative Depending on Context)	
Acquisition – something received or purchased Constitute – make up, compose; often used as a more sophisticated synonym for *is*, e.g., *the new theory* ***constitutes*** *a challenge to the traditional view* Corollary – a statement or condition that logically results from a proven argument Contemporary – current Contrive – think up Disposition – personality Ethics – moral principles Epistemology – branch of philosophy dealing with theory of knowledge Ideology – belief system Fluctuate – go back and forth, be unstable Inherent, Innate, Intrinsic – inborn, existing in something by definition Intuitive – without thought, done instinctively Lineage – a family sequence Judicial – related to the law Magnitude – large size Mutable – changeable; Immutable, not changeable Preliminary – occurring before the main event Premeditated – planned beforehand (often negative, but not always) Reciprocate – respond to an action or behavior with the same action/behavior Successor – person who inherits another's position	

Common Roots and Prefixes

Positive

Co, Con – With
Converse = speak with

Multi – Many
Multitude = many, numerous

Poly – Many
Polymath = person accomplished in many fields

Pro – In favor of
Proponent = one who is in favor of something

Ver – True
Verity = truth

Vit – Life
Revitalize = bring back to life

Negative

An(a) - Not, without
Anaerobic = without oxygen

Anti – Against
Antipathy = dislike

Contra – Against
Contrarian = one who is constantly against things

De – Off, From
Desalinate = Remove salt from

Dis – Lack of
Disinterested = objective; not having an interest in

Fict – False
Fictitious = Not real

In, Un – Not
Insignificant = not significant

Ob, Op – Against
Opponent = someone a person is against

Neutral

Ante – Before
Antecedent = one who came before

Chron – Time
Chronic = ongoing (all the time)

Cog – Think
Cognition = thinking

E, Ex – From
Exude = discharge (something that is exuded comes from something else)

Hetero – Different
Heterogeneous = consisting of different things

Homo – Same
Homogeneous = consisting of the same things

Peri – Around
Periphery = around the edges

Re – Again
Replicate = do again in the same way

Sent – Feel
Sentient = capable of feeling

Spec – See
Spectacle = something that is highly visible

Seq – Follow
Sequential = one following the other

Temp – Time
Temporary = lasting a short time

Terr – Earth
Terrestrial = earth-dwelling

Trans – through
Transport = move through

Common Second Meanings

Afford – grant (e.g., an opportunity)

Appreciate – to take into account, recognize the merits of, OR to increase in value

Arrest – to stop (not just put handcuffs on a criminal)

Assume – to take on responsibility for, acquire (e.g., to assume a new position)

Austerity – financial policy to reduce excess spending on luxury or non-essential items

Badger – to pester or annoy (e.g., reporters repeatedly badgered the candidate after the scandal broke)

Bent – liking for

Capacity – ability

Chance – to attempt

Channel – to direct something (e.g., energy, money) toward a specific purpose

Check – to restrain, control, or reduce (e.g., the vaccine checked the spread of the disease)

Coin – to invent (e.g., coin a phrase)

Compromise – to endanger or make vulnerable (e.g., to compromise one's beliefs)

Constitution – build (e.g., a football player has a solid constitution)

Conviction – certainty, determination. Noun form of *convinced*.

Couch – to hide

Discriminating – able to make fine distinctions (e.g., a discriminating palate)

Doctor – to tamper with

Economy – thrift (e.g., a writer who has an economical style is one who uses few words)

Embroider – to falsify, make up stories about

Execute – to carry out

Exploit – make use of (does not have a negative connotation)

Facility – ability to do something easily (e.g., a facility for learning languages)

Foil – to put a stop to (e.g., to foil a robbery)

Grave/Gravity – serious(ness)

Grill – to question intensely and repeatedly (e.g., the police officers grilled the suspect thoroughly)

Hamper – to get in the way of, hinder

Harbor – to possess, hold (e.g., to harbor a belief)

Hobble – prevent, impede

Plastic – able to be changed, malleable (e.g., brain plasticity)

Provoke – elicit (e.g., a reaction)

Realize – to achieve (a goal)

Reconcile – to bring together opposing or contradictory ideas

Relay – to pass on to someone else (e.g., to relay information)

Relate – to tell, give an account of (a story)

Reservations – misgivings

Reserve – to hold off on (e.g., to reserve judgment)

Ruffled – flustered, nonplussed

Sap – to drain (e.g., of energy)

Scrap – to eliminate, get rid of

Shelve/Table – to reject or discard (e.g., an idea or proposal)

Solvent – able to pay all debts (usually used in a business context)

Sound – firm, stable, reliable, valid (e.g., a sound argument)

Spare, Severe – unadorned, very plain

Static – unchanging (i.e., in a state of stasis)

Sustain – to withstand

Uniform – constant, unvarying

Unqualified – absolute

Upset – to interfere with an expected outcome

Words that Look Negative but Aren't

Critic/Criticism – a critic is a person who writes commentary—either positive or negative—about a subject, e.g., art, music, or sports.

Discern – to recognize or distinguish; adj., Discerning – highly perceptive

Imminent – about to happen

Immune, Invulnerable – not affected by something, e.g., a disease

Improvise – spontaneously invent

Incentivize – provide someone with a reward for doing something

Incisive – sharply focused and accurate

Induce – persuade, Bring about a desired action

Infallible – unable to be wrong

Infuse – fill with

Ingenious – clever, brilliant

Inimitable – unique, one-of-a-kind

Innate, Intrinsic – inborn, natural

Innocuous – harmless

Invaluable – having immense value, priceless

Unassuming – modest

Unqualified – absolute

Answers: Sentence Completions

1. B

Negative; key words: *rigid, in contrast, lifelike.* "Artificial" is the only negative answer and is the opposite of *lifelike.*

2. B

Positive; key words: *inherit their mother's rank, compete with one another.* The correct word must mean something like "high." A "dominant" animal is the one that has high status, so (B) is correct. Don't get distracted by "secure": the focus is on achieving a <u>high</u> rank within the pack, not a <u>stable</u> rank as "secure" would imply.

3. C

Negative; key words: *essential role, more effective than speech, questioning.* The correct word must mean something like "unimportant." "Demanding" and "prevalent" (dominant, widely accepted) do not make sense, and "important" means the opposite of the required word. "Frivolous" means "unserious," so (C) is correct.

4. A

Neutral/positive; key words: *earliest known imaging device;* the correct word must mean something like "ancestor." A "forerunner" is something that comes <u>before</u>, so (A) is correct. A "relic" (something surviving from an earlier time) and an "heir" are both things that come <u>after</u>, eliminating (B) and (C). A "proponent" is a person who is in favor of something, a definition that does not fit at all. (D) can thus be eliminated as well.

5. D

Negative; key words: *questioned;* the correct word must describe people who question whether something is true. That is the definition of "skeptics," so (D) is correct. "Partisans" (people who take sides) and "zealots" (people who are fanatical about a cause) do not fit, eliminating (A) and (B). In (C), "advocates" are people who are in favor of something, the opposite of the required word.

6. A

The passage indicates that the Great Barrier Reef is *changing* in a way that will eventually result in its destruction, so the blank must be a positive word that indicates the <u>opposite</u> of *decline.* "Diminish" (become smaller) and "succumb" (give into, e.g., a disease) are both negative and can be eliminated. "Extend" (get longer) is positive but does not make any sense in context. Only "flourish" is a positive word that fits as the opposite of *decline.*

7. C

The sentence indicates that the *most respected [filmmakers]* hold facts in *scrupulous regard* (i.e., very high regard) along with the rules that ______ whether they (those facts) are acceptable. Logically, the word in the blank must be neutral/positive and mean something like "determine." "Deny" is negative, so (A) can be eliminated immediately. "Complete" does not make sense in context, so (B) can be eliminated as well. Be careful with (D): this answer states things backwards. Historians and historical filmmakers "rely on" the rules of evidence to decide which facts are sufficiently well-documented—the rules of evidence do not rely on the acceptability of facts. Only (C) creates a logical meaning. "Dictate" can be used to mean "determine" in the sense of "set the rules for," so this choice is correct.

8. D

The contradictor *however* indicates that the passage is contrasting the situation *in the past* with the situation in the present. If psychologists formerly *dismissed fiction*, then logically they must now have a much higher opinion of it. The blank must therefore be filled with a positive word meaning something along the lines of "liking for." "Disregard" is negative, so (A) can be eliminated immediately. "Explanation" and "responsibility" do not make sense, eliminating (B) and (C) as well. That leaves (D): if psychologists have revised their formerly negative opinion of fiction, they have developed a new "appreciation" for it.

9. A

Although the passage includes two sentences, this question can be answered with information from the first sentence only. There, we learn that Kakuzo is considered responsible for *the revival of Nihonga*—the implication is that this art form was dying out. Why? Because *Western-style painting was threatening to* ______ it. Logically, the blank must be filled with a word meaning something like "replace." That is the definition of "supplant," so (A) is correct. "Deny," "salvage" (save), and "challenge" all do not make sense in context.

10. B

Elders is described in the passage as *an outspoken advocate for a variety of controversial issues*, and the word in the blank must indicate how she was perceived *as a result*. Logically, the correct word must be somewhat negative and describe a person who is involved in controversy, or who is perceived as difficult. (A) does not fit because a "pragmatist" is someone who is concerned with practical solutions. (C) does not work either because someone who is "a curiosity" is viewed as odd or puzzling, which has nothing to do with controversy. The same is true for "amateur" (non-professional) in (D). A "polemicist," on the other hand, is someone who takes sides very strongly, which is consistent with being an outspoken advocate for controversial issues.

11. A

The second sentence indicates that Chicago grew from almost nothing to a city of two million in the space of just 80 years, so the blank must be filled with a word meaning "speed." That is the definition of "velocity," so (A) is correct. "Significance," "mastery," and "influence" do not fit the required definition.

12. A

The first sentence indicates that Margulis's theory *built upon ideas that had largely been discredited* (become considered inaccurate), and the second sentence illustrates that idea by emphasizing the many journals that rejected her groundbreaking paper. Given that context, the blank must be filled with an extremely negative word meaning "dislike." (A) is correct because something that is "scorned" is viewed as worthless. (B) is incorrect because "jubilation" is an extremely positive word meaning "joy"; in (C), "consideration" is positive as well. Although "impatience" is negative, this word is not a good match because it does not have a connotation of strong dislike.

13. B

The key phrases *simple but refined* and *rational and more harmonious society* indicate that the word in the blank must be very positive and mean something like "improve." "Compromise" (weaken the quality of) has a negative connotation in this context, and "contain" is neutral/negative so (A) and (C) can be eliminated. "Enjoy" is positive but does not make sense when plugged in. *Simple but refined aesthetics* (concepts of beauty) cannot "enjoy" anything—only people can do that. (B) is correct because "elevate" (raise to a more sophisticated level) logically describes how proponents (people in favor of; prefix *pro-*) of an artistic movement with *simple but refined aesthetics* would view its effect.

14. C

The sentence indicates that the whale *migrat[es] thousands of miles each year without a compass*, so logically the whale is an "excellent" or "exceptional" navigator. "Docile" (tame) and "advantageous" (bringing advantages) do not make sense. Someone who is "precocious" (pre-CO-cious, not pre-cious!) acquires or demonstrates an ability earlier than usual, but there is no information in the sentence consistent with that specific definition. Only "adept" (highly skilled) is both positive and makes sense in context, so (C) is correct.

15. B

If Constantinople was *one of the...most influential cities in the world*, then it "had" or "possessed" *a powerful cultural pull and dominated economic life throughout the Mediterranean*. "Defended" does not have the required connotation because the sentence says nothing about Constantinople being attacked. "Restrained" (held back) and "thwarted" (prevented) are both negative and do not make sense. Only "exerted" fits: something that "exerts a pull" brings force or power. (B) is thus correct.

16. C

The key words in the passage are *accelerate* and *speeding*; they indicate that the word in the blank must be positive and have a similar meaning. "Facilitating" (making easier) is the only positive option directly consistent with the required definition, so (C) is correct. "Hindering" (preventing, getting in the way of) is strongly negative, and "containing" is slightly negative, so (A) and (B) do not fit. "Relating" is neutral/positive but does not make sense in context.

17. A

If workers *commonly obtained the majority of their nutrients from bread,* then logically they would experience *dread* at not being able to obtain any. The correct word must therefore be negative and convey the idea of lack or absence. The only word that is a direct match for this definition is "scarcity." Something that is scarce is present in very small amounts, and "scarcity" is the state of being scarce. "Abundance" (large amount) means the opposite, so (C) does not fit. "Distress" (emotional upset) and "rejection" are negative, but neither matches the required meaning.

18. D

If *the last natural case* of smallpox was reported in 1977, then the disease must have been eliminated completely, i.e., "eradicated." "Investigated," "described," and "sequenced" are all things that can be done to diseases, but none of these options fits the logical definition of the word in the blank.

19. B

The first sentence indicates that readers may become *bored* by Twain's references to nineteenth-century scandals, and the second sentence begins with *Nevertheless,* indicating that it will convey an opposing, positive idea. Be careful with the double negative at the end of the sentence: we are told that Twain's overall work is *seldom* (rarely) *less than* ______. In other words, it is usually ______, with the blank meaning the opposite of "boring." The only logical fit is "engaging," so (B) is correct. (A) does not fit because "tedious" is a synonym for "boring." Remember, however, that it does not matter whether you know what this word means as long as you can recognize that "engaging" fits. "Relevant" and "descriptive" are both positive, but neither fits the required definition. Although a book that was one of those things *could* be interesting, it would not necessarily be interesting by definition.

20. B

The key phrase *influencing artists and thinkers decades later* indicates that the blank must be filled with a word conveying the idea that *many of the movements associated with [the Harlem Renaissance]* lasted beyond the early 1930s. The correct word must therefore be positive and mean "lasted" or "endured." That is the meaning of "persisted," so (B) is correct. "Prevailed" (won) does not fit because the passage makes no mention of a struggle or conflict between movements. "Emerged" does not make sense either because this word is inconsistent with the idèa of long-term influence, and because the passage focuses on the end of the Harlem Renaissance rather than the beginning. "Declined" has the opposite of the required meaning.

21. A

The key information appears in the first sentence, which indicates that the brain signals are involved in *humans' ability to predict* others' decisions. The last sentence reiterates this idea, with the word in the blank serving as a synonym for *predict.* "Anticipate" is a direct match, making (A) correct. "Mimic" does not fit because the passage is not talking about imitation, and "assess" does not work because the passage is not talking about judgment. Even though *individuals [who] hold different values* might be inclined to "dispute" each other's choices, that is not the focus of the passage—the word in the blank concerns the ability to imagine what another person would choose regardless of whether they hold the same values.

22. C

The word *or* before the blank signals that the correct word must be the opposite of *changed*. The only direct match for this meaning is "reinforced" (made even stronger). "Affected" is a synonym for *changed*, so (A) does not fit. "Restored" (changed back) is also very similar in meaning, so (B) can also be eliminated. In addition, something cannot be restored unless it has been changed, and the passage is discussing pathways that have been *established*. "Undermined" (weakened) does not fit the required definition, eliminating (D).

23. B

Although the passage contains two sentences, you can answer the question based on the information in the first sentence only—the second sentence merely expands on it. Logically, the *great variety of artistic style and cultural practices* resulted from the *lack of centralization among the Igbo* (pronounced Ee-bo), so the correct word must be positive and mean something like "good for" or "helpful to." "Detrimental (harmful) to" is negative, so (A) can be eliminated immediately. "Adopted" is positive but makes absolutely no sense in context: a lack of centralization cannot "adopt" the development of artistic styles. "Attributed" is positive as well but gets the relationship backwards: the development of diverse artistic styles could be "attributed" to a lack of centralization, but a lack of centralization could not logically have been caused by a variety of artistic styles. (B) is correct because something "conducive" is something that leads to a particular result (*con* = with; *duc* = lead), which is what the sentence is describing here.

24. A

The word *actual* in the first sentence provides a clue that there is a gap between how people rate themselves and how skilled they truly are. In addition, the fact that the frequency with which people claim to be above average *defies statistical probability* indicates that their self-assessments are not very accurate. The word in the blank is used to describe the correlation between belief and reality, so it must be negative and mean something like "not very good." If you don't know what "tenuous" means, play process of elimination with the other answers. "Clear," "narrow" (implying a strong correlation), and "predictable" all do not fit the required definition, leaving (A) as the only option. Indeed, "tenuous" means "weak," so (A) is correct.

25. C

The passage indicates that the frogs in question do not *croak or sing* and that they may use touch rather than sound to identify other members of their species. Given that context, the blank must mean something like "use"—if these animals do not vocalize, they would be unable to use sound to identify one another. "Interfere with," "ignore," and "relate to" all do not make sense: the frogs cannot get in the way of, deliberately not pay attention to, or feel a connection with sounds that do not exist. That eliminates (A), (B), and (D). Only "rely on" makes sense: because the auditory information does not exist, there is no way for the frogs to depend on it. (C) is thus correct.

26. D

The key phrase used to describe Hagan's musical influences is *diverse set of genres*, so the correct word must be a synonym for *diverse*. "Eclectic" (varied) is a direct match, making (D) the answer. "Unexpected," "complex," and "contemporary" are all words that could potentially be used to describe musical influences; however, none of these matches the definition indicated by the passage.

27. D

The construction *not to* ______ *but rather to* indicates a contrast between the word in the blank and the fact that the hydrogen sulfide is detoxified and removed *once it is present*. If the hydrogen sulfide is present, that means it is absorbed, i.e., it is not blocked. The correct word must therefore mean something like "block" or "prevent." That is the definition of "impede," so (D) is correct. "Intensify" and "streamline" (facilitate, make less complex) mean the opposite of the required word, eliminating (A) and (B). Be careful with (C): the point is that the genes do not serve to prevent hydrogen sulfide from entering, not that they do not "regulate" (control) its entrance. This word is not a direct fit in the same way that "impede" is.

28. A

If *women's participation in the labor force was also necessary*, then the implication is that *men's salaries alone* were not enough for a family to live on comfortably. The word in the blank must therefore be positive and mean something like "support." "Sustain" is a direct match for that meaning, making (A) correct. "Uphold" is similar in meaning, but this is something that can only be done to an idea, decision, or position—it cannot refer to financially supporting people, so (B) is incorrect. "Entertain" is positive but does not otherwise fit: the issue is that men's earnings alone were insufficient to live comfortably, not whether they could provide entertainment. That eliminates (C). "Defend" does not make sense because the passage makes no mention of an attack or threat, eliminating (D).

29. A

The passage indicates that Harjo's memoir includes different types of writing: poems, prose, and songs. A "hybrid" is something made up of different elements (e.g., a hybrid vehicle uses two or more sources of power), so (A) is correct. Be careful with (B): Harjo's use of different genres could be perceived as "innovative" (groundbreaking), but the passage does not directly provide information indicating that this is the case; rather, the focus is on the fact that it *defies classification*, making (A) the stronger answer. Likewise, the book could be "controversial" or "significant," but the passage does not actually indicate that either of these things is true. There is nothing to suggest that the book provokes strong and opposing opinions, eliminating (C), or that it is exceptionally important, eliminating (D).

30. B

The key phrase appears in the last sentence, which tells us that the bats can *remain briefly suspended in mid-air*—the correct word must convey the idea of suspension. Note that without this piece of information, there is no way to determine the answer. "Hover" is the only option that matches the required definition. "Recline" (lean back) and "glide" both do not fit, eliminating (A) and (D). Be careful with "balance," though. One balances *on* an object, whereas here the point is that the bats are not resting on anything. As a result, (C) can also be eliminated.

Answers: Meaning in Context

1. C

If *[n]euroscientists and humans are…joining forces,* then logically they might "improve" our understanding of narrative's role in human cognition. (C) is a direct match. "Purify" and "filter" are words commonly associated with "refine," but they do not fit the definition indicated by the passage, so (A) and (B) can be eliminated. Be careful with (D): neuroscientists and humanists want to "explain" the role of narrative in cognition, not *our understanding* of that role. (D) can thus be eliminated as well.

2. B

To determine the meaning of the underlined word, back up and read the sentence from the beginning. If *some researchers have cautioned against relying too heavily on genetic factors*, that is logically because *estimates of an individual's chance of developing a particular malady* (illness) *are "affected" by environmental factors*. "Confused" is the literal definition of *confounded*, but this word does not make sense at all in context. (A) can thus be eliminated. "Deceived" and "puzzled" are similarly illogical, eliminating (C) and (D). Only "influenced" means something like "affected" and fits in context: if people's chances of developing a particular disease are influenced by their environment, then genetic factors should not be given too much weight. (B) is thus correct.

3. C

The passage is discussing the part of the brain that ______ contagious yawning along with empathy and social-know how. The body's abilities are controlled by the brain, so in this context, *governs* must mean "controls." (C) is thus correct. "Elect" is a word that is often associated with governing, but in the context of the brain, it does not make sense. That eliminates (A). "Requires" does not mean "controls," so (B) can be eliminated as well. "Suppresses" (prevents) is exactly the opposite of the required meaning. The passage states that *catching a yawn is <u>linked</u> to our ability to empathize*, so all those skills must be activated together. That eliminates (D).

4. D

The beginning of the passage indicates that the boy was *fully occupied with his own cogitations* (that is, lost in his thoughts) during the ride, and the last sentence indicates that the narrator carefully watched the boy as he inspected his new surroundings. Given that context, *catch* must logically mean something like "see" (*countenance* means "face"). The best fit for this definition is "observe"—the sentence is essentially saying that the narrator wanted to see how the boy would react. (A) does not fit because it does not make sense to say that someone "acquired" another person's impressions. (B) does not fit because it is illogical to say that a person "gathered" (collected) impressions <u>in</u> someone's face. (C) likewise does not make any sense because a person must "attain" (achieve) their own facial reaction. (D) is thus correct.

5. A

Although you are given a fairly lengthy excerpt from this poem, the key phrase appears in the same sentence as the underlined word. Johnson indicates that the *whirling suns [s]hall...claim the haven of the fiery darkness whence they came* (from which they came). In other words, he is saying that the suns will "return to" the darkness that they emerged from. (A) is thus correct. Neither "pick up" nor "plea for" is consistent with this meaning, so (B) and (C) can be eliminated. Although "assert" is a common meaning of *claim*, it is being used in a very different sense here, so (D) does not fit either.

6. D

The passage indicates that *it is hard to imagine [O'Keeffe] anywhere but the desert*, so logically, she must be strongly "identified with" or "associated with" the American Southwest. (D) is a direct match for this meaning, so it is correct. "Held down" and "fastened to" do not make any sense in context, so (A) and (C) can be eliminated. O'Keeffe may have been "engaged with" the American Southwest in her paintings; however, this phrase does not fit the definition indicated by the passage.

7. B

The passage indicates that pirates had many practical tasks that they needed to accomplish on land (*clean and repair ships, collect wood and water*, etc.). Given that context, *stretches* must logically mean something like "amounts of time," i.e., "periods of time." That corresponds to (B). "Expansions" (taking up larger amounts of space), areas, and "distortions" (deformations) all do not fit the required meaning.

8. C

The first sentence indicates that mangroves are beneficial to some coastal ecosystems, so logically they must help stop or prevent, i.e., "impede," erosion. (C) is the only option that fits. "Determine" and "seize" do not make sense at all, eliminating (A) and (D), and (B) does not quite fit either because "revealing" erosion would not directly help coastal ecosystems in the same way that preventing it would.

9. D

The sentence in question is talking about the first cities with a new feature—*the productive exchange of goods*—so the correct word must logically mean something like "characterized." Although "imprinted" and "labeled" both have literal meanings similar to "marked," neither word is even close to the required definition, so (A) and (B) can be eliminated right away. "Represented" in (C) is not as straightforwardly incorrect, but don't get distracted by it. The sentence is talking about an internal characteristic of the first cities, not something that symbolized them publicly. (D) is correct because in this context, "distinguished" is a synonym for "characterized." This word also captures the idea that the exchange of goods was something that made it distinct from other, earlier cities.

10. A

The key phrase *I didn't want [Antonia's] ring* indicates that the narrator "refused" her offer, which corresponds directly to (A). "Frustrated" and "defeated" do not make sense at all, eliminating (B) and (C). "Obstructed" (blocked) does not have the right connotation: the narrator turned Antonia down—he did not physically get in her way, as "obstructed" implies.

3 Making the Leap

Before we look more closely at the various question types, we're going to examine a key element of SAT reading—namely, the ability to move between specific wording and more abstract or general ideas. While you probably won't see questions that directly test this skill, it is nevertheless crucial for navigating challenging passages, no matter how short.

Let's start with the fact that one of the most common ways that both the authors of SAT passages and the test-writers themselves move between specific phrasings and more general language is by using **pronouns** (e.g., *it*, *this*) and **abstract nouns**, which refer to ideas (*observation*, *claim*, *conclusion*) rather than to physical objects. As a result, you must be able to connect pronouns back to their referents because without the ability to "track" an idea through a passage, you can easily lose the thread of the text's focus and argument.

For example, compare the following two versions of this passage. The first version uses only nouns, no pronouns. Notice how incredibly awkward and repetitive it is.

> ...Crowdsourcing is a wonderful tool, but **crowdsourcing** still fails in a very particular way, which is that any evaluation is swayed by the evaluations that have come before **that evaluation**. A barbershop with a one-star rating on Yelp as **that barbershop's** first review is subsequently more likely to accrue more negative reviews—and **that same barbershop**, were **that barbershop** to receive a four-star rating on Yelp as **that barbershop's** first review, would be more likely to accrue more subsequent positive reviews.

Now look at this version, which replaces the repeated nouns with pronouns:

> ...Crowdsourcing is a wonderful tool, but **it** still fails in a very particular way, which is that any evaluation is swayed by the evaluations that have come before **it**. A barbershop with a one-star rating on Yelp as **its** first review is subsequently more likely to accrue more negative reviews—and that same barbershop, were **it** to receive a four-star rating on Yelp as **its** first review, would be more likely to accrue more subsequent positive reviews.

Notice how much smoother this version is. You don't get tangled up in the constant repetition of the same phrase, so the meaning is much easier to process.

Pronouns won't always appear by themselves, though. Typically, a pronoun such as *this, that,* or *these* will appear in front of a noun, e.g., *this notion, these movements, such developments.* More straightforward, right? Well...maybe yes, maybe no.

Sometime around third grade, you probably learned that a noun was a person, place, or thing. Pretty self-explanatory. When you learned that a noun was a "thing," however, you probably understood "thing" to mean an object like a bicycle or an apple or a house. That's certainly true. But words like *idea* or *assertion* or *concept*—words that don't refer to actual physical objects—are also nouns. These nouns are sometimes referred to as **abstract nouns** or **"compression" nouns** because they compress lots of information into a single word.

The ability to recognize the relationship between abstract nouns and the ideas that they refer to is central to making sense out of many passages. If you can't draw the relationship between the noun, say, *phenomenon*, and the specific occurrence that it refers to, you probably can't answer a question that asks you to do exactly that. And you certainly can't answer a question that asks you to draw a conclusion from it or determine what sort of information would be most likely to support it.

What's more, these nouns, like pronouns, may appear **either before or after** the particular idea (argument, assertion, description, etc.) has been discussed. If you encounter a question that requires you to identify what such a noun refers to, you must generally **back up and read from <u>before</u> the place where the noun appears**, although in rare instances that information may be found afterward.

Very often, when students are confused about this type of phrase, they either reread the phrase in isolation and try to figure out what it's talking about (impossible) or start reading at the phrase and continue on for several lines, then become confused as to why they have no clearer an understanding of the phrase than they did when they started. As a result, they get caught in a loop of reading and rereading the wrong spot and consequently have no reliable means of determining the correct answer.

Starting on the next page, we're going to look at some examples in order to help you avoid getting stuck in this pattern.

Pronoun: Example #1

Let's start with something simple.

> In a step toward creating robots capable of spontaneous learning, **a new approach** has expanded training data sets for robots that work in cluttered environments. Developed by Dmitry Berenson and Peter Lozano, doctoral students at the University of Michigan, **it** could cut learning time for new materials and environments down to a few hours rather than a week or two.

As Reading passages go, this one is fairly straightforward; however, it is useful to work with for illustrative purposes.

In the third line from the bottom, the pronoun *it* appears not only three lines down from its referent, *a new approach*, but in a different sentence altogether. If you read the full passage, the meaning of the pronoun would probably be so obvious you would not even think about. If you began reading at the pronoun and never backed up, however, you would have no way of figuring out what *it* referred to.

Next, we're going to look at something slightly trickier.

Pronoun: Example #2

> The distance between the Earth and the sun varies gradually over the course of the year because of the elliptical nature of Earth's orbit. At **its** closest approach, known as perihelion, **the Earth** is about 3 million miles closer to the sun than at **its** farthest point, called aphelion. As a result, sunlight on Earth is about 7% more intense at perihelion than **it** is at aphelion.

When you look at this passage, you can notice that *it* and *its* appear in both the second and third sentences. Although these words are both part of the same description, they do not all refer to the same singular noun.

In the second sentence, *it* and *its* both refer to *the Earth*. Note, however, that the first appearance of *its*, at the beginning of the second sentence, actually comes before the noun (although you may be able to assume that the referent is *Earth* based on the information in the first sentence).

In the third sentence, *it* refers to not to Earth but to *sunlight*. Although the pronoun is the same, the referent is different.

Next, we're going to look at some examples with compression nouns.

Pronoun: Example #3

To track pronoun-referent relationships, you must know whether nouns are singular or plural. **Singular pronouns must have singular referents, and plural pronouns must have plural referents.**

So far, we've looked at examples that require only singular pronouns. Now we're going to consider an example that involves a plural one.

> Many Artificial Intelligence (AI) systems involving speech recognition, computer vision, and medical imaging make use of neural networks—computing systems inspired by the architecture of the human brain. In neuroscience, **they** are often used to model the same kinds of tasks that the brain performs, in hopes that the models could lead to new insights in understanding how the brain itself performs those tasks.

In this case, the pronoun *they* indicates that the referent must be plural—that is, the noun that it corresponds to most likely ends in -s.

If we back up to the previous sentence, we can figure out that the referent of the pronoun *they* is the noun *neural networks*—logically, these would be used to *model the same kinds of tasks that the brain performs* (neural = referring to the brain).

Next, we're going to look at some examples of compression nouns. These nouns often end in ***-ment***, ***-ion***, ***-ness***, and ***-ude***, and they are generally built from verbs or, less commonly, adjectives. Sometimes the ending is simply added onto the noun (e.g., *object* → *objection*), and sometimes there is a slight modification before the ending, as in the nouns below.

Verb or Adjective	Noun
Comply	Compliance
Contemplate	Contemplation
Justify	Justification
Modify	Modification
Obey	Obedience
Propel	Propulsion
Relative	Relativity
Rely	Reliance
Wide	Width

Exercise: Forming Compression Nouns

Using the model provided, write the noun form of each word. Notice when the stem changes.

	Example	Noun
1.	Admit → Admission	Commit → ______________________
2.	Resolve → Resolution	Dissolve → ______________________
3.	Receive → Reception	Deceive → ______________________
4.	Depend → Dependency	Tend → ______________________
5.	Relate → Relation	Mutate → ______________________
6.	Advance → Advancement	Enhance → ______________________
7.	Converge → Convergence	Emerge → ______________________
8.	Realize → Realization	Revitalize → ______________________
9.	Produce → Production	Deduce → ______________________
10.	Responsible → Responsibility	Susceptible → ______________________

Compression Noun: Example #1:

> [T]he evolution of our communications system from a broadcast model to a networked one has added a new dimension to the mix. The Internet has made us all less dependent on professional journalists and editors for information about the wider world, allowing us to seek out information directly via online search or to receive it from friends through social media. But **this enhanced convenience** comes with a considerable risk: that we will be exposed to what we want to know at the expense of what we need to know.

The phrase *this enhanced convenience* (bold) is a classic example of a compression noun. It refers not to a single thing but rather to an entire idea presented in the sentence before it:

> The Internet has made us all less dependent on professional journalists and editors for information about the wider world, allowing us to seek out information directly via online search or to receive it from friends through social media.

The phrase *this enhanced* (improved) *convenience* thus refers to the fact that the Internet has made people's lives much easier because it allows them to obtain information on their own.

If the author did not "compress" the information into the phrase *this enhanced convenience,* the second sentence would include a long and exceedingly awkward construction restating a large portion of the previous sentence, and the sentence would read like this:

> The Internet has made us all less dependent on professional journalists and editors for information about the wider world, allowing us to seek out information directly via online search or to receive it from friends through social media. But **the fact that the Internet has made us less dependent on professional journalists and editors for information about the wider world**, allowing us to seek out information directly via online search or to receive it from friends through social media, comes with a considerable risk...

Compression Noun: Example #2

While humpback dolphins look quite similar to other dolphins, their genetics tells a different story. Researchers collected 235 tissue samples and 180 skulls throughout the animals' distribution, representing the biggest dataset assembled to date for the animals. The team analyzed mitochondrial and nuclear DNA from the tissue, which revealed significant variations. Although the line between species, sub-species and populations is a blurry one, in this case, the researchers are confident that <u>the humpback dolphin is distinct enough to warrant the "species" title</u>. The mitochondrial DNA turned up genetic signatures distinct enough to signal a separate species, and likewise, differences in the dolphins' skulls supported **this divergence**. Although the nuclear DNA provided a slightly more confounding picture, it still clearly showed differences between the species.

The bolded phrase *this divergence* (i.e., *this difference*, fourth- and third-to-last lines) is another typical example of the type of language that frequently causes trouble.

A test-taker who looked to the following sentence for clarification would be mostly out of luck: although there is a mention of the *differences between the species*, humpback dolphins are not mentioned there. The student might grasp that different types of dolphins are involved somehow but could easily miss the main idea: humpback dolphins are sufficiently different genetically from other dolphins to be considered a separate species. That is something a question could easily ask about.

Furthermore, it is necessary to back up five lines to find the beginning of the sentence that mentions humpback dolphins. (Remember: never start reading in the middle of a sentence.) That's a long way back; however, there is no other way to determine exactly what *this divergence* refers to.

The Former and the Latter

One set of compression nouns that has a tendency to cause confusion is "the former" and "the latter." These words are used when two referents are involved: *the former* refers back to the noun or phrase mentioned first, and *the latter* refers back to the noun or phrase mentioned second. Let's start with a straightforward example:

> In the nineteenth century, both Thomas Edison and Nikola Tesla were well-known scientists, but <u>the former</u> quickly came to be regarded as one of the greatest American inventors, while <u>the latter</u> fell into obscurity.

The beginning of the sentence refers to two individuals: Thomas Edison and Nikola Tesla. In the second half, *the former* refers to Edison because his name occurs first, while *the latter* refers to Tesla because his name occurs second (*latter* is like *later*). That's easy enough to follow, but some passages may use these words in ways that you may have to work somewhat harder to follow. For example:

> All bodies in the solar system are heated by sunlight. They rid themselves of this heat in two ways: (1) <u>by emitting infrared radiation</u> and (2) <u>by shedding matter</u>. In long-lived bodies such as Earth, **the former process** prevails; for others, such as comets, **the latter** dominates.

Let's look closely at what's going on in these sentences. First, the author states that bodies in the solar system eliminate heat from the sun in two ways. Next, he lists those two ways. The first way is by emitting infrared radiation, and the second is by shedding matter. When he refers to those ways again in the following sentence, *the former* = emitting infrared radiation, and *the latter* = shedding matter.

Therefore, the final sentence means that old planets like Earth eliminate heat by emitting infrared radiation, but other objects like comets eliminate heat by shedding matter.

Note that occasionally, *the latter* may appear **before** *the former*. For example, the paragraph above could be written the way it is below. Although the order of *the former* and *the latter* is switched, the last sentence has exactly the same meaning as the previous version.

> *All bodies in the solar system are heated by sunlight. They rid themselves of this heat in two ways: (1) <u>by emitting infrared radiation</u> and (2) <u>by shedding matter</u>. For some objects such as comets, **the latter** dominates; in long-lived bodies such as Earth, **the former process** prevails.*

Exercise: Pronouns and Compression Nouns

In the passages below, underline the word, phrase, or sentence(s) within the passage that each indicated pronoun or noun refers to.

Artificial neural networks leverage the architecture of the human brain in order to improve systems ranging from medical diagnostics to credit card fraud to translation. In some areas, such as computational speed, **(A) they** demonstrate superhuman performance; however, when they learn sequentially, old information is often overwritten by new information. **(B) This loss**, which occurs when new pathways are formed, is known as catastrophic forgetting.

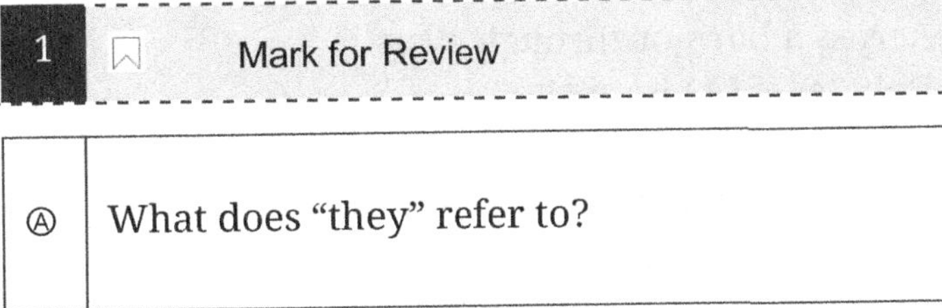

Ⓐ What does "they" refer to?

Ⓑ What does "this loss" refer to?

In the past, efforts to identify cacao in ancient Mayan pottery centered on highly decorated ceramic vessels used in elite ceremonial contexts, an approach that resulted in the assumption that **(A) it** was only available to members of the elite. A study by Anabel Ford and Mattanjah de Vries casts doubt on **(B) this claim**, however, suggesting that cacao was widely accessible and used in celebrations by all members of Mayan society.

2 Mark for Review

Ⓐ What does "it" refer to?

Ⓑ What does "this claim" refer to?

Soon after the Big Bang, there were tiny ripples: quantum fluctuations in the density of the seething ball of hot plasma. Billions of years later, **(A) those seeds** have grown into galaxy clusters — sprawling groups of hundreds or thousands of galaxies bound together by gravity. But there seems to be **(B) a mismatch**. Research suggests that as much as 40% of galaxy-cluster mass is missing when compared with the amount of clustering predicted by the ripples. **(C) The findings** have led theorists to propose physics beyond the standard model of cosmology to make up the difference.

3 Mark for Review

Ⓐ What does "those seeds" refer to?

Ⓑ What does "a mismatch" refer to?

Ⓒ What does "the findings" refer to?

The following text is adapted from Emily Dickinson's 1890 poem "Beclouded."

The sky is low, the clouds are mean,
A travelling flake of snow
Across a barn or through a rut
Debates if **(A)** **it** will go.

A narrow wind complains all day
How some one treated him;
Nature, like us, is sometimes caught
Without **(B)** **her** diadem.

4 Mark for Review

Ⓐ What does "it" refer to?

Ⓑ What does "her" refer to?

Flash organizations are teams that assemble temporarily to tackle specific, complex problems. Drawn from online labor markets, **(A)** **they** combine the flexibility of crowdsourcing with the managerial complexity of traditional companies. The workforce in a flash organization is fluid, called together quickly and often on short notice. In most cases, **(B)** **it** is organized into a clear hierarchy but can adapt by adding new teams or allowing workers to shift roles as the work evolves.

5 Mark for Review

Ⓐ What does "they" refer to?

Ⓑ What does "it" refer to?

The following text is adapted from Jane Austen's 1814 novel *Mansfield Park*.

To the education of her daughters Lady Bertram paid not the smallest attention. She had not time for **(A)** **such cares**. She was a woman who spent her days in sitting, nicely dressed, on a sofa, doing some long piece of needlework, of little use and no beauty, thinking more of her pug than her children, but very indulgent to **(B)** **the latter** when it did not put herself to inconvenience, guided in everything important by Sir Thomas, and in smaller concerns by her sister.

6 Mark for Review

Ⓐ What does "such cares" (line 3) refer to?

Ⓑ What does "the latter" refer to?

Carolyn Bertozzi's development of bioorthogonal chemistry stemmed from her interest in complex carbohydrate molecules known as glycans. Along with proteins and nucleic acids such as DNA, **these compounds** are one of the key building blocks of life. However, they are not well understood: because **(B) they** are challenging to synthesize in the laboratory, they have traditionally been among the most difficult molecules for scientists to analyze.

7 Mark for Review

Ⓐ What does "these compounds" refer to?

Ⓑ What does "they" refer to?

The following text is adapted from Nikolai Gogol's 1842 short story "The Overcoat."

It would be difficult to find another man who lived so entirely for his duties. It is not enough to say that Akakiy laboured with zeal: no, he laboured with love. In his copying, he found a varied and agreeable employment. Enjoyment was written on his face: some letters were even favourites with him; and when he encountered **(A) these**, he smiled, winked, and worked with his lips, till it seemed as though each letter might be read in his face, as his pen traced **(B) it**.

8 Mark for Review

Ⓐ What does "these" refer to?

Ⓑ What does "it" refer to?

An ancient New Mexican lakebed is home to the preserved footprints of life that roamed the American southwest thousands of years ago. In addition to giant sloths and mammoths, ancestors of modern humans also left **(A) their mark**. Research published in *Science* in 2021 claimed that these footprints were "definitive evidence" of human presence in North America during the last ice age, which ended around 25,000 years ago; however, a study by geologists and paleontologists in Kansas, Oregon, and Nevada disputes **(B) that conclusion**. The researchers argue that it is more likely humans entered the Americas sometime between 14,000 and 16,000 years ago.

9 Mark for Review

Ⓐ What does "their mark" refer to?

Ⓑ What does "that conclusion" refer to?

The following text is adapted from Emily Pauline Johnson's 1917 poem "Rainfall."

From out the west, o'erhung with fringes grey,
The wind preludes with sighs its roundelay,

Then blowing, singing, piping, laughing loud,
(A) **__It__** scurries on before the grey storm-cloud;

Across the hollow and along the hill
It whips and whirls among the maples, till

With boughs upbent, and green leaves blown wide,
The silver shines upon **(B)** **__their__** underside.

10 Mark for Review

Ⓐ What does "it" refer to?

Ⓑ What does "their" refer to?

Most of the planets orbiting stars like the Earth's sun fall into one of two categories: the first group is around one-and-a-half times the size of the Earth, whereas the other faction is twice as large. Astronomers theorize that while members of **(A)** **__the former__** have retained their atmospheres, the atmospheres of **(B)** **__the latter__** may have dissipated over time, leaving nothing but rocky cores behind. Researchers studying **(C)** **__this phenomenon__**, known as planetary escape, developed models of it in order to more fully understand how heat and radiation could affect planets' atmospheres. Then, they created 70,000 simulated planets of different sizes, varying their atmospheric compositions and types of suns, and modeled what would happen to **(D)** **__them__**.

11 Mark for Review

Ⓐ What does "the former" refer to?

Ⓑ What does "the latter" refer to?

Ⓒ What does "this phenomenon" refer to?

Ⓓ What does "them" refer to?

Answers: Forming Compression Nouns

1. Commission (act of committing)

2. Dissolution (act of dissolving or breaking up)

3. Deception (act of deceiving)

4. Tendency (inclination toward a particular type of behavior)

5. Mutation (change; typically used in the context of genes)

6. Enhancement (improvement)

7. Emergence (coming into view or existence)

8. Revitalization (process of bringing new life into something; typically used in the context of cities)

9. Deduction (process of inferring a particular case from a general rule or principle)

10. Susceptibility (state of being susceptible, i.e., likely to be affected or harmed by something)

Answers: Pronouns and Compression Nouns

1. (A): they = artificial neural networks; (B) this loss = old information is overwritten by new information

2. (A): it = cacao; (B): this claim = [cacao] was only available to members of the elite

3. (A): those seeds = tiny ripples; (B) and (C): the mismatch, the findings = 40% of galaxy-cluster mass is missing when compared with the amount of clustering predicted by the ripples

4. (A): it = a travelling flake of snow; (B): her = Nature

5. (A): they = flash organizations; (B): it = the workforce

6. (A): such cares = the education of her daughters; (B): the latter = her children

7. (A), (B): these compounds = (complex carbohydrate molecules known as) glycans

8. (A): these = some letters; (B): it = each letter

9. (A): their mark = footprints; (B): that conclusion = these footprints were "definitive evidence" of human presence in North America during the last ice age

10. (A): It = The wind; (B): their = the maples

11. (A): the former = the first group [that] is one-and-a-half times the size of the Earth; (B): the latter = the other faction [that] is twice as large; (C): this phenomenon = the atmospheres may have dissipated over time, leaving nothing but rocky cores behind; (D) them = 70,000 planets of different sizes

4 The Big Picture

Every SAT is virtually guaranteed to contain questions that test your ability to identify main ideas, claims, and purposes, as well as statements that would support or illustrate them. These questions can ask about the passage as a whole, or an idea that is presented in just one specific section.

While these questions are worded in a straightforward manner, they can also be challenging because they require a leap from seeing passages as masses of details to understanding them as coherent texts with larger ideas and purposes. This jump is obviously easier when texts are short, for the simple reason that there is less information that could potentially distract or confuse you. But even in the space of 10-15 lines, you will need to navigate complex sentence structure as well unfamiliar topics, names, references, and vocabulary in order to move beyond the individual words and recognize what they are actually saying.

Very often, smart, detail-oriented students have a tendency to worry about every single thing that sounds even remotely odd while missing something major staring them in the face. Frequently, they blame this on the fact that they've been taught in English class to read closely and pay attention to all the details. But this type of reading simply does not work on the SAT. It is much closer to the type of skimming you will need to do in college, where you may be assigned hundreds of pages of reading to be completed in a relatively short time.

Your professors will not expect you to read every last word, however. Rather, you will be expected to skim through it, identifying key points and then focusing more closely on a few key areas. As a result, the ability to quickly identify major points of interest in a text is one of the most important skills you can bring with you to college. (Unlike the books that are generally assigned in high school, most of what you read in college will not have easily digestible summaries available courtesy of www.sparknotes.com!) If you get the gist, you can figure a lot of other things out, whereas if you focus on one little detail, you'll get . . . one little detail.

All that said, to make the leap from specific information to larger ideas, you must start by identifying the most basic feature of the passage: the topic.

Identifying Topics

The topic is **the person, thing, or idea that is the primary subject or focus** of the passage. In most cases, **it is the word or phrase that appears most frequently throughout the passage**, either by name or in rephrased form (pronoun or compression noun). For example, a computer could also be referred to as *the machine, the invention*, or *the technology.*

Generally speaking, the topic will be presented in either **the first sentence of the passage or shortly afterward**. On the digital exam, passages are simply too short for topics to be introduced any later.

For example, look at the following sample first sentences. Each clearly indicates to readers what the text that follows will focus on.

- Make no mistake—**Dolley Madison** was as fiercely partisan as any male politician.
- Hidden inside the Earth—within the first several hundred kilometers below the crust—there is **another ocean**.
- Some scientists conclude that **music's influence** may be a chance event, arising from its ability to hijack brain systems built for other purposes such as language, emotion and movement.

The ability to identify topics is crucial because **correct answer choices to main idea questions will refer to the topic**. In fact, the correct answer will sometimes be the *only* answer to mention it. Moreover, many incorrect answers are wrong because they are off-topic, and **you cannot recognize when a statement is off-topic unless you are clear about what the topic *is***.

Let's look at an example of how that could play out in a passage.

> Admired primarily for her exquisite calligraphy, **Otagaki Rengetsu (1791-1875) was among Japan's most celebrated artists**. She was also a writer and ceramicist, often inscribing her poems in her own calligraphy onto clay vessels—a distinctive blending of art forms not replicated by any other artist in Japanese history. Her work was in such great demand during the nineteenth century that every household in Kyoto was said to own her pottery, and today scrolls and ceramics bearing her calligraphy are sought after by collectors.

Here, the topic—Otagaki Rengetsu's art—is introduced in the very first sentence and then referred to in other words (*her work, her pottery, scrolls and ceramics*) in the following lines.

In this case, the connection between the various terms is evident; however, if you have difficulty drawing the connection between an original term and its variations, your comprehension may suffer. You may also misunderstand the **scope** of the passage—that is, whether it's **general** or **specific**.

When asked for the topic of a passage such as this, students sometimes say things like, "Ummm... it talks about Japan," or "it mentions calligraphy," or, a bit closer to the mark, "Japanese artists." (Incidentally, I've witnessed this type of uncertainty even in high-scoring students.)

As a matter of fact, the focus is not on "artists." It is actually on one specific artist, namely **Otagaki Rengetsu**. That fact would become very important if you saw a question like the one below.

Admired primarily for her exquisite calligraphy, Otagaki Rengetsu (1791-1875) was among Japan's most celebrated artists. She was also a writer and ceramicist, often inscribing her poems in her own calligraphy onto clay vessels—a distinctive blending of art forms not replicated by any other artist in Japanese history. Her work was in such great demand during the nineteenth century that every household in Kyoto was said to own her pottery, and today scrolls and ceramics bearing her calligraphy are sought after by collectors.

1 Mark for Review

Which choice best states the main idea of the passage?

Ⓐ Otagaki Rengetsu's artistic creations are prized for their unique qualities.

Ⓑ Inscribed clay vessels have traditionally played an important role in Japanese art.

Ⓒ The collaboration between writers and ceramic workers produced highly distinctive works of art in Japan.

Ⓓ Many households in Kyoto once featured scrolls produced by Otagaki Rengetsu.

Answering this question requires you to take information from multiple parts of the passage and recognize how they combine into a single overarching idea. This process is made considerably easier, however, if you start by focusing on the topic: Otagaki Rengetsu – one artist, singular – and her work. Only (A) directly refers to that information, and it is in fact the answer. (In the second sentence, *distinctive blending of art forms not replicated by any other artist in Japanese history* corresponds directly to "unique qualities.")

(C), on the other hand, mentions *writers and ceramics workers*, plural, but as we've established, the passage focuses on only one person.

(B) is directly contradicted by the passage – the second sentence states that Rengetsu's calligraphy inscriptions of her poems on clay vessels were *not replicated by any other artist in Japanese history.*

(D) takes information from the passage and misstates it slightly. The last sentence states that *every household in Kyoto was said to own [Rengetsu's] pottery;* however, the answer refers to Rengetsu's scrolls. In addition, this answer focuses on a detail from the passage rather than its overall meaning.

What's the Point?

The point, aka the main idea, of a passage is the **primary idea** that the author wants to convey. After the topic, the point should be the first thing you look for. Once you have clearly identified it, you can often skim through the rest of the passage.

I cannot state this strongly enough: If you keep the main point in mind, you can often eliminate answers simply because they do not make sense in context of it or, better yet, identify the correct answer because it is the only option that is consistent with it.

What's more, **focusing on finding the point means you don't have a chance to get distracted.** It gives you a clear goal and reduces the chance that you'll spend unnecessary minutes trying to absorb a single confusing line while losing sight of the bigger picture.

That said, let me begin by saying what a main point (sometimes referred to as a **central claim**) is **not**.

- It is not a **topic** such as "social media" or "the disappearance of bees."
- It is not a **theme** such as "oppression" or "overcoming."

A main point is an **argument** that answers the question "so what?" It tells us *why* the author thinks the topic is important, or what primary information about it he or she wants to convey.

You can use this "formula" to determine the point:

Topic + So What? = Main Point

Sometimes the author will directly state the point, **most often in the first sentence or two, and then state or refer to it again for emphasis in the last sentence.** For example:

> Although **dark matter cannot be seen, its effects are visible in the world, and so scientists know that it must exist**. Over the course of the twentieth century, particle physics and astronomy developed in tandem. As physicists were piecing together the standard model, which explains three out of four known fundamental forces (electromagnetic, weak and strong interactions, although not gravity), astronomers were beginning to discover that stars moved away from the Earth—proof of the universe's expansion. That movement was occurring too quickly to be explained by the stars' gravity, however. **This finding ultimately led researchers to conclude that it was only possible because of the presence of matter that could not be perceived visually.**

Here, the author presents the topic (dark matter) along with the "so what" (it is invisible but must exist) right at the beginning of the first sentence; devotes the following sentences to explaining how scientists arrived at that conclusion; and then reiterates the main takeaway at the end. When the point is presented this clearly, you may find it helpful to highlight it on the screen.

In other passages, however, the main point may not be presented quite so directly or quickly, or it may involve integrating information from the middle of the text.

In such cases, you should pay particular attention to any words or phrases that indicate the author is making a point: ***the point is*** (or: the *point is not*), ***key, goal***, etc., along with words such as ***important, significant, central***, and any **italicized words**. You should also be on the lookout for **dashes** and **colons** which signal explanations.

If the author does not state the point—or if you want to reduce your margin of error—you should jot it down, by hand, on your scratch paper yourself. The physical act of writing will reinforce the idea in a way that hitting letters on a keyboard cannot.

Even though the passages will be short, **do not underestimate the importance of this step**. Remember that the incorrect answers are explicitly designed to distract and confuse you. Your job is to not allow that to happen—and having key information written down in front of you makes it much easier to keep your head clear and stay laser-focused on the information that the correct answer must contain. This is particularly true for text completions, support/undermine questions, and graph-based questions, which may require multiple steps of logic.

In order to write a strong main point, you must understand just what it is and how it differs from simply summarizing the text.

> **Describing Content** - Recounting the information presented in the text without necessarily distinguishing between main points and supporting evidence and/or counterarguments. The goal is simply to relate a condensed version of what is being conveyed, often in sequential *first x, then y, and finally z* form.
>
> **Summarizing an Argument** - Identifying the essential point that the author, or a person discussed in the passage, wants to convey and eliminating any unnecessary detail. This requires you to move beyond simply recounting information (concrete) to recognizing which parts of the passage are most important and relating them to more general ideas (abstract).

To illustrate, we're going to work with the following passage.

> Sometime near the end of the Pleistocene, a band of people left northeastern Asia, crossed the Bering land bridge when the sea level was low, entered Alaska and became the first Americans. **Since the 1930s, archaeologists have thought these people were members of the Clovis culture.** First discovered in New Mexico in the 1930s, the Clovis culture is known for its distinct stone tools, primarily fluted projectile points. For decades, Clovis artifacts were the oldest known in the New World, dating to 13,000 years ago. **But in recent years, researchers have found more and more evidence that people were living in North and South America before the Clovis.**

When many students are asked to summarize the main point of a passage like the one on the previous page, they generally respond in one of two ways:

1) They state the topic

The Clovis People

2) They summarize the content

Uh... so the guy basically talks about how these people, I think they were called the Clovis people, right? They were like the first people who came across the Bering Strait to America... Oh no, wait, they weren't actually the first people to come across, it's just that they thought that those people were first. But so anyway those people settled in New Mexico, I think it said like 13,000 years ago? Only now he's saying that there were other people who were actually there before the Clovis.

Notice how long, not to mention how vague, this version is. It doesn't really distinguish between primary and secondary information; everything gets mushed in together, and frankly it doesn't make a lot of sense. That summary gives us exactly zero help in terms of figuring out the main point. It also wastes *colossal* amounts of time.

This is not what you want to do.

Argument Summary:

New evidence shows the first inhabitants of the Americas were NOT Clovis people.

Notice how this version just hits the big idea and omits the details. All the details.

Argument Summary in super-condensed SAT terms:

New: CP ≠ 1st/ Am.

Now notice how this version cuts out absolutely everything in order to focus on the absolute total utter bare essentials. It doesn't even attempt to incorporate any sort of detail beyond the subject of the passage (the first inhabitants of the Americas) and its result, the "so what?"- the part that tells us why the main focus of the passage is important (it's new evidence, which means that an old theory has been overturned).

So in four words and a number, we've managed to capture the essential information *without wasting any time*. It doesn't matter if anyone else would understand it as long as we know what it's saying.

Same Idea, Different Words

As mentioned earlier in this chapter, correct answers to main idea questions may refer to the topic or a key figure verbatim, or they may reword it using close synonyms.

For example, consider the following question.

Kente, the traditional fabric of Ghana's Asante people, **has evolved into a symbol of many meanings**—political and cultural, African and American, honorary and everyday. "What is called kente is many things," says Doran H. Ross, director of the Fowler Museum of Cultural History, though he notes its origin is Ghana's strip-woven cloth. But Ross says kente appears just as widely today in Western-style tailored clothing, and in other ways that make it the most recognizably African textile.

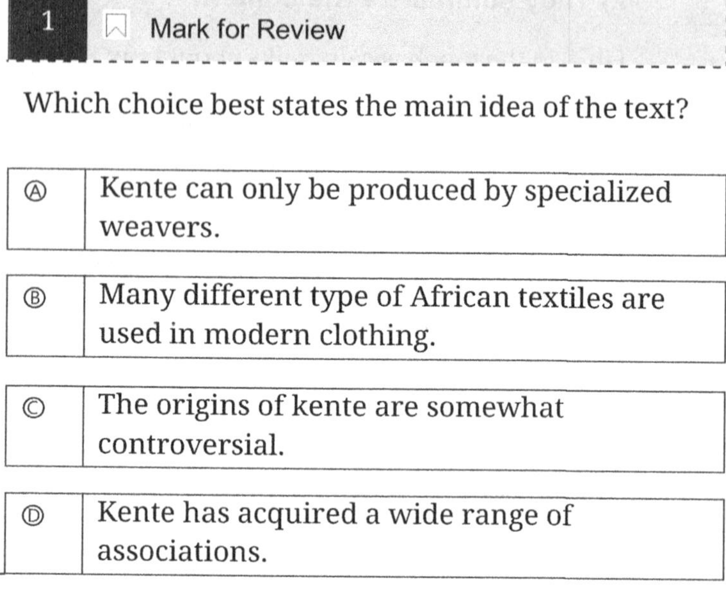

1 Mark for Review

Which choice best states the main idea of the text?

Ⓐ Kente can only be produced by specialized weavers.

Ⓑ Many different type of African textiles are used in modern clothing.

Ⓒ The origins of kente are somewhat controversial.

Ⓓ Kente has acquired a wide range of associations.

In this case, the correct answer essentially rephrases the first sentence. The fact that kente *has evolved into a symbol of many meanings*, which are then listed, directly corresponds to the statement in (D) that it "has become associated with a wide range of areas." The answer merely phrases the information from the text in different, slightly more general language.

Note that the information you need to answer the question is located right around the dash. This is a classic instance of a key statement being signaled by "interesting" punctuation.

Old Idea vs. New Idea

The "old idea" vs. "new idea" template is one of the most important concepts necessary for making sense out of social science and science passages. It can essentially be summed up as "people used to believe *x*, but now they believe *y*" or "many people believe *x*, but in fact *y* is true." Authors using this model typically devote the first paragraph or two to discussing a traditionally accepted idea or theory, then shift to explaining why that theory is wrong and why a new theory—the theory that scientists or other researchers now believe—is actually correct.

Although authors will sometimes state flat-out that a particular idea is wrong, in other cases they will be less direct. They'll imply skepticism by putting particular words or phrases in quotation marks, or ask rhetorical questions such as *but is this really the case?* When the shift to the "new idea" occurs, you must pay close attention to that place because **the result or theory discussed will almost certainly be the point of the passage**. In some cases, opposing arguments or potential objections to the theory (counterarguments) will be discussed later in the passage, but in general, authors tend to stick to discussing "new ideas" once they've transitioned to them.

Certain words and phrases commonly signal when authors are discussing old vs. new ideas:

Old Idea

- Some/Many/Most people (scientists, researchers) believe…
- It is commonly thought that…
- Accepted/conventional wisdom holds that…
- In the past/For decades, people thought that…
- Traditionally it was believed that…

New Idea

- However, But in fact…
- Actually, In reality…
- But is it really true/the case that…?
- It now seems (clear)/Researchers now think that…
- Recently, it has been found that…
- New research/evidence shows/suggests that…
- Another possibility is that…

As you read, it's up to you to keep track of what the old vs. new ideas are, and why they are false vs. true. **Don't rely on your memory: write each viewpoint on your scratch paper in very abbreviated terms.** Yes, this can be annoying; it can also be extremely effective.

If you are a strong reader, this is less about trying to get questions right than about ensuring you don't get them wrong. You may remember most things, but if you don't make the main positions clear for yourself, you might eventually choose an answer that says the opposite of the correct one.

Note: In earlier versions of *The Critical Reader*, this framework is presented in terms of the "They Say/I Say" model developed by Gerald Graff and Cathy Birkenstein in their book of the same name. Although I have eliminated that discussion because the passages used on the post-2016 SAT are less aligned with the type of reading they discuss, I do still strongly recommend their book as a superb aid for the transition to college-level reading and writing.

Using the "Old Idea" to Predict Main Point and Attitude

One of the reasons it is so crucial you be able to recognize the types of phrases that signal "old ideas" is that those phrases often allow you to identify the point of the passage *before the author even states it.*

Think of it this way: if a phrase such as *many people think...* appears near the beginning of a passage, that's an absolute giveaway that the idea that follows has been questioned or discredited, and that the researchers discussed in the passage will view it negatively. Moreover, you can infer that the "new idea" – the one that scientists now view positively – will be the opposite.

Likewise, the word *however* or *but* in the middle of a passage often signals the presence of this structure: the "new idea" will virtually always be introduced **after** that transition.

Knowing whether the author, or a particular figure discussed in the passage, agrees or disagrees with a given idea can also help you on Text Completions and Support/Undermine questions, as well as on Passage 1/Passage 2 relationship questions. If you know that a person's attitude toward the "old idea" is negative, and that their attitude toward the "new idea" is positive, you can easily make a solid assumption about whether they would agree or disagree with a particular statement. For example, consider the following opening lines:

Example #1

> Conservationists have **historically** been at odds with the people who inhabit wildernesses.

The word *historically* implies that conservationists are no longer in conflict with people who inhabit wildernesses. Their attitude toward them is now more positive.

Example #2

> **Some scientists** conclude that music's influence may be a chance event, arising from its ability to hijack brain systems built for other purposes such as language, emotion and movement.

The phrase *some scientists* suggests that the writer is presenting an "old idea," (disagree, negative opinion), and that the passage will go on to explain why music's influence is not in fact a chance event.

Example #3

> **Most people** believe that there is an objective reality out there and that our senses and our science directly convey information about the material world.

The phrase *most people* suggests that the writer is about to discuss a theory based on the idea that there is no such thing as objective reality.

Now let's come back to a passage we looked at earlier. This time, we're going to examine it from the perspective of old idea/new idea.

Sometime near the end of the Pleistocene, a band of people left northeastern Asia, crossed the Bering land bridge when the sea level was low, entered Alaska and became the first Americans. Since the 1930s, archaeologists have thought these people were members of the Clovis culture. First discovered in New Mexico in the 1930s, the Clovis culture is known for its distinct stone tools, primarily fluted projectile points. For decades, Clovis artifacts were the oldest known in the New World, dating to 13,000 years ago.	Old Idea
<u>But</u> in recent years, researchers have found more and more evidence that people were living in North and South America before the Clovis.	New Idea

In this case, the "new idea" is not introduced until the very last sentence, although the phrase *Since the 1930s, archaeologists have thought...* hints that it is coming. It is, however, the key piece of information.

In order to avoid confusion, jot down for yourself the "old idea" and the "new idea." And by "jot down," I mean scribble in shorthand. You don't get points for neatness, and it should take you a few seconds at most.

Old = CP 1st NA	(Clovis people first in North America)
New = Ppl in NA pre-CP	(People were in North America before Clovis)

As you answer the question, **you must remember to look back at your notes!** I've witnessed many students identify the exact sentence where an answer was located but still get the question wrong because they forgot to look back at what they'd written. And that was in paper format—the chances you will skip important steps or overlook essential information when working on the computer is considerably greater.

Main Point and Fiction Passages

In terms of writing main points, fiction passages pose a challenge because they are obviously not written to make arguments or discuss findings from studies. Nevertheless, these passages do generally focus on a particular trait or quality of a character or place.

Furthermore, in fiction passages key information is often located in the same places as in other passages, namely the beginning and the end. That's hardly a surprise because most writers, regardless of genre, tell their readers upfront why a topic or situation is important and then make sure to reemphasize that idea as they conclude. So **if you're not sure what's important**, focus on those two places and do your best not to get overly caught up in the details.

That said, fiction passages can be structured more unpredictably than non-fiction passages, and **if you are a strong reader accustomed to quickly getting the gist of social science and science passages**, you may need to slow down. Try to get a sense of who's involved and what they want (or don't want) while being careful not to waste too much time on unfamiliar or confusing language.

As is true for all other types of passages, you should also pay careful attention to major transitions, unusual punctuation (semicolons, colons, dashes, quotation marks, and italics), and strong language because they will virtually always appear in important places.

In addition, you should be careful to consider only the information provided by the author and not attempt to speculate about any larger meaning. What counts is your ability to understand the literal events of the passage and how they are conveyed by specific words and phrases. That's it. If you do go looking for some larger symbolism or start to make assumptions not explicitly supported by the passage, you can easily lose sight of the basics. In fact, most students have difficulty with passages like these not because there's a profound interpretation that can only be perceived through some mystical process, but rather because they aren't sufficiently *literal*.

Let's look at an example.

The following text is adapted from Virginia Woolf's 1919 novel *Night and Day*. Katherine is attending a party hosted by her mother.

Considering that the little party had been seated round the tea-table for less than twenty minutes, the animation observable on their faces, and the amount of sound they were producing collectively, were very creditable to the hostess. It suddenly came into Katherine's mind that if some one opened the door at this moment he would think that they were enjoying themselves; he would think, "What an extremely nice house to come into!" and instinctively she laughed, and said something to increase the noise, for the credit of the house presumably, since she herself had not been feeling exhilarated.

Although the passage contains a fair amount of information, it also follows the "key information at the end" pattern. Most of the paragraph provides a description of how an observer would view the party—that is, the person would believe the guests were enjoying themselves—but in the last sentence, the narrator states outright that Katherine is <u>not</u> particularly excited to be present.

For a main point, then, we could write something like:

- **Guests seem to enjoy, BUT K. no**

Or, from a slightly different angle:

- **K. pretends to enjoy party**

Note that these statements do not even try to cover all of the details, nor do they "interpret" anything—they merely condense the information directly stated by the narrator and summarize the **main idea** that she wants to convey.

Since we now have a good idea of the point, we're going to look at a question:

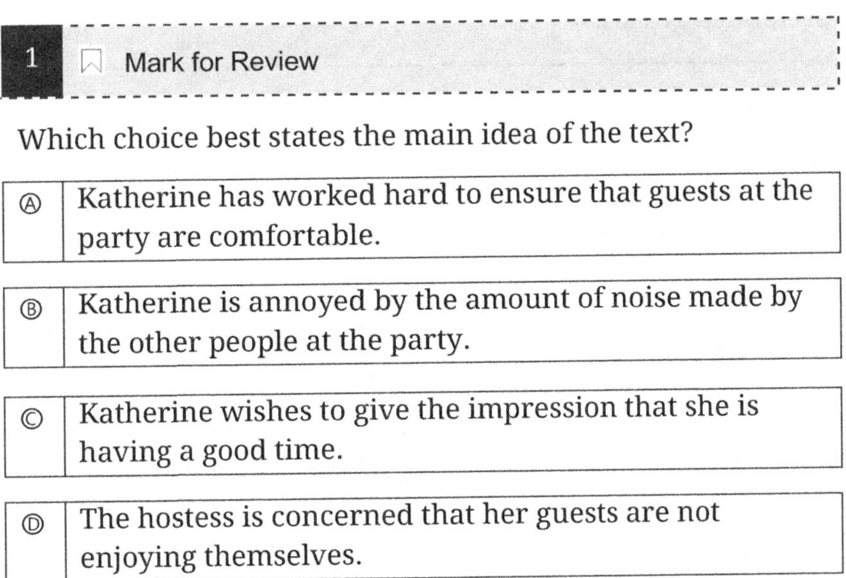

1 Mark for Review

Which choice best states the main idea of the text?

Ⓐ Katherine has worked hard to ensure that guests at the party are comfortable.

Ⓑ Katherine is annoyed by the amount of noise made by the other people at the party.

Ⓒ Katherine wishes to give the impression that she is having a good time.

Ⓓ The hostess is concerned that her guests are not enjoying themselves.

Knowing the main point allows you to jump pretty much directly to the answer here: (C) fits so well that there is no need to seriously consider the other options, allowing you to save both time and energy.

Not all big-picture questions will be this straightforward, but if you take those few extra seconds to scribble down the main point for yourself, you might be surprised at how quickly you're able to answer some of them.

Main Point and Poetry Passages

Finding the "point" of a poem can be tricky because the literal meaning may sometimes not be directly stated—a poet may convey the central idea indirectly, using images or metaphors. At the same time, though, you cannot make assumptions that are not clearly supported by the specific words in the text.

Let's start with a relatively straightforward example.

> I'd love to write of the beautiful,
> I'd love to write of the brave,
> And read the minds of others,
> And note their winning ways.
>
> I would not judge the beautiful
> By the beauty of their faces,
> By suppositions or the like,
> Or their pretended graces.

The text is divided into two equal parts, each consisting of four lines: in the first section, the speaker describes wanting to study and record the actions of admirable people; then, in the second section, indicates an intention to look beyond people's surface qualities or superficial actions (*the beauty of their faces/their pretended graces*) when assessing who is "beautiful."

As a result, we could say that the main idea is that the speaker is uninterested in superficial characteristics, or wishes to portray people who are internally beautiful. Knowing that information upfront would lead you directly to the answer for the question below.

The following text is adapted from Maggie Pogue Johnson's 1910 poem "Virginia Dream."

I'd love to write of the beautiful,
I'd love to write of the brave,
And read the minds of others,
And note their winning ways.

I would not judge the beautiful
By the beauty of their faces,
By suppositions or the like,
Or their pretended graces.

1 Mark for Review

Which choice best states the main idea of the text?

Ⓐ The speaker is drawn to people who are attractive and graceful.

Ⓑ The speaker does not feel suited to the task of judging others.

Ⓒ The speaker believes that external features are a reliable indicator of internal ones.

Ⓓ The speaker is unconcerned with superficial appearances.

(D) states the main point we determined beforehand, so it is correct.

Sequence of Events

A slightly more involved type of big-picture question involves identifying how passages are structured. This simply involves identifying the events that occur as well as a character's, or characters', reactions to them.

Although the answer choices accompanying these questions may seem very complex, you can simplify them by focusing on a straightforward section of each option. For example, if each choice refers to the end of the passage, identify what happens there, and eliminate any answer that says something else. For example:

The following text is adapted from George Orwell's 1936 novel *Keep the Aspidistra Flying.*

The gaslight shone yellow through the frosted transom above the door of Number 31. Gordon took out his key and fished about in the keyhole—in that kind of house the key never quite fits the lock. The darkish little hallway—in reality it was only a passage—smelt of dishwater and cabbage. Gordon glanced at the japanned tray on the hall-stand. No letters, of course. He had told himself not to hope for a letter, and nevertheless had continued to hope. A stale feeling, not quite a pain, settled upon his breast. Rosemary might have written! It was four days now since she had written [...] The one thing that made the evening bearable was to find a letter waiting for him when he got home. But he received very few letters—four or five in a week at the very most.

1 Mark for Review

Which choice best describes the overall structure of the text?

Ⓐ It presents a character who has repeatedly failed to receive an important letter and then explains why it has not been sent.

Ⓑ It depicts a character's inability to enter his home and retrieve a letter and then describes his reaction to that situation.

Ⓒ It describes the reaction of a character to an upsetting occurrence followed by his happiness at receiving a letter.

Ⓓ It portrays a character's desire to receive a letter and subsequent disappointment when none is found.

Try not to get too caught up in the details of each answer choice. If you read the passage straight through and take a moment to sum it up for yourself, you should be able to identify the correct answer without too much trouble.

What is the essential action? A character (Gordon) arrives home, enters his house, checks to see whether a letter has arrived, and does not find it (*No letter, of course*). How does he feel about this? Not happy (*A stale feeling, not quite a pain, settled upon his breast*). The correct answer must be consistent with those events.

(B) can quickly be eliminated because Gordon does enter his home—he merely has a bit of trouble with the lock. The same is true for (C) because he does not receive a letter and is unhappy.

(A) does not fit because the passage does not explain why the letter has not been sent.

(D) is correct because it is consistent with the idea that Gordon hopes for a letter and is then disappointed not to find one.

Exercise: The Big Picture

The following text is adapted from Henry James' 1880 novel *Washington Square*. Mrs. Penniman is a widow who lives with her brother.

Mrs. Penniman was a tall, thin, fair, rather faded woman, with a perfectly amiable disposition, a high standard of gentility, a taste for light literature, and a certain foolish indirectness and obliquity of character. She had a passion for little secrets and mysteries—a very innocent passion, for her secrets had hitherto always been as unpractical as addled eggs. She was not absolutely veracious; but this defect was of no great consequence, for she had never had anything to conceal.

Which choice best states the main idea of the text?

Ⓐ Mrs. Penniman is a puzzling and mysterious figure.

Ⓑ Mrs. Penniman is a passionate reader of novels.

Ⓒ Mrs. Penniman is frequently difficult to get along with.

Ⓓ Mrs. Penniman is romantic and sentimental.

Among the thousands of species that have made their way around the world since European exploration began in the fifteenth century, knotweed is widely regarded as one of the most intractable. Removing it completely requires extracting the land itself; if anything is left behind, the weed can return repeatedly, regenerating from minuscule fragments after as long as twenty years. One study found that knotweed could regrow from a root fragment weighing just 0.3g—about as much as a pinch of salt.

2 Mark for Review

Which choice best states the main idea of the text?

Ⓐ Knotweed was among the earliest plant species to be transported between continents.

Ⓑ Knotweed can regenerate even when the land it grows on has been removed.

Ⓒ Knotweed is exceptionally difficult to eradicate permanently.

Ⓓ In comparison to other plants, knotweed takes much longer to reach its full size.

The following text appeared in Josephine Heard's 1890 work, "On receiving Tennyson's Poems from Mrs. M. H. Dunton, of Brattleboro, Vt."

Dear Friend, since you have chosen to associate
My humble thoughts with England's poet laureate,
I trust that he will bear me pleasant company,
And soon we shall far more than mere
acquaintance be.
Since childhood's days his name I have revered,
And more and more it has become to me
endeared;
I blush not for the truth, I but confess,
I very wealthy feel since I his "works" possess.

3 Mark for Review

Which choice best states the main idea of the text?

Ⓐ She is impressed by her friend's personal acquaintance with Tennyson.

Ⓑ She views Tennyson with respect and wishes to understand his work deeply.

Ⓒ She is embarrassed by her poor understanding of Tennyson's work.

Ⓓ She believes that her own poetry is equal to Tennyson's.

Navajo pawn originated in the 1870s as a bartering system that was altogether different from traditional banking. Based on relationships of mutual trust, it evolved to be a fully integrated part of Navajo life. By the middle of the twentieth century, it had become a highly sophisticated and complex practice, with more than 150 active trading posts. Today it remains a pivotal aspect of Navajo society.

4 Mark for Review

Which choice best states the main idea of the text?

Ⓐ Pawn has played a significant role in modern Navajo culture.

Ⓑ During the twentieth century, pawn was gradually replaced by other banking options.

Ⓒ Pawn is more complex than traditional banking.

Ⓓ Pawn became popular in Navajo society because it was based on personal relationships.

Although publishers and critics classified Octavia Butler's novels as science fiction—a genre that Butler enjoyed deeply and referred to as "potentially the freest genre in existence"— her works attracted a diverse readership, and Butler resisted being associated exclusively with that form. Indeed, she was also the author of a number of essays, and her book *Parable of the Sower* was adapted into an opera by the mother-and-daughter team Bernice Johnson Reagon and Toshi Reagon. Combining African-American spirituals, soul, rock and roll, and folk music, it debuted at The Public Theater in New York City in 2015.

5 Mark for Review

Which choice best describes the overall structure of the text?

Ⓐ A work is presented, and its effects are considered.

Ⓑ An interpretation of a novel is described, and an opposing view is introduced.

Ⓒ Examples of an author's writing are given, and their significance is discussed.

Ⓓ A claim is made, and supporting examples are provided to illustrate it.

When the titanium sapphire laser was introduced in the 1980s, it represented a major advance in laser technology. Critical to its success was the material used as its gain medium, the material that amplifies the laser's energy. Sapphire and titanium ions proved to be a particularly potent combination, providing a much wider emission bandwidth than conventional lasers—an innovation that led to fundamental discoveries and countless applications in physics, biology, and chemistry.

6 Mark for Review

Which choice best states the main idea of the text?

Ⓐ Unlike conventional lasers, titanium sapphire lasers employ a gain medium to increase their power.

Ⓑ Titanium sapphire lasers have better heat conductivity than other types of lasers, making them more efficient.

Ⓒ Titanium sapphire lasers are exceptionally powerful because they combine ions in a way that increases emission bandwidth.

Ⓓ The adjustable emission bandwidth of titanium sapphire lasers has led to discoveries in a variety of scientific fields.

For centuries, griots have passed down the epics of North Africa's Sahel region through songs and stories, with each person adding details from their lives and the lives of their audiences. As a result, contemporary listeners can appreciate the tales much the way their ancestors did. One of the most famous epics tells the story of Sunjata, the legendary founder of the Mali Empire. There are numerous versions, however, and some historians believe that if all of the different versions were combined, the tale would take several days to recite.

7 Mark for Review

Which choice best states the main idea of the text?

Ⓐ Modern audiences would have difficulty appreciating the stories told by griots of previous generations.

Ⓑ Griots' flexible approach to storytelling allows their work to remain relevant.

Ⓒ The epic of Sunjata lacks a definitive version.

Ⓓ Many listeners learn about the Mali Empire through griots' stories.

The following text is adapted from the 1911 novel *The Crux* by Charlotte Perkins Gilman. Vivian is a woman who lives in a New England village.

When Vivian reached her own gate she leaned her arms upon it and looked first one way and then the other, down the long, still street. The country was in sight at both ends—the low, monotonous, wooded hills that shut them in. It was all familiar, wearingly familiar. She had known it continuously for such part of her lifetime as was sensitive to landscape effects, and had at times a mad wish for an earthquake to change the outlines a little.

8 Mark for Review

Which choice best describes the overall structure of the text?

Ⓐ It portrays a character arriving home, and then describes her dissatisfaction with her surroundings.

Ⓑ It presents a character who is unhappy with her environment, and then explains how she plans to change it.

Ⓒ It introduces a character who is eager to return home, and then describes her reaction when she arrives.

Ⓓ It depicts a character's love of nature, and then details how she is affected by it.

Wanting to give residents of flood-prone neighborhoods in New Orleans an easy and inexpensive way to protect their homes, architect Elizabeth English founded the Buoyant Foundation Project and began working with a group of architecture and engineering students to devise a method for adapting houses to high water levels. Unlike traditional buildings, the amphibious structures created by the group respond to floods by rising up and floating on the water's surface. English and her colleagues have now designed prototypes for regions in Jamaica and Nicaragua that are vulnerable to flooding, and amphibious buildings are becoming more common in countries from the United Kingdom to Bangladesh.

9 Mark for Review

Which choice best states the main idea of the text?

Ⓐ Amphibious structures will eventually replace traditional houses in some regions.

Ⓑ Although amphibious houses can help residents of flood-zones temporarily, they do not represent a long-term solution.

Ⓒ As an architect, Elizabeth English has had a longstanding interest in amphibious construction.

Ⓓ Amphibious structures provide a practical solution for allowing people to remain in homes located in flood zones.

Experiences that elicit powerful emotional responses such as awe or anger are more likely to be shared than neutral or technical pieces, and ones that include surprises also provoke this reaction. For example, when audiences see a movie with a big twist at the end, they often want to discuss it with friends immediately. Thus, in addition to drawing our attention to new information, surprising items also can rapidly spread through networks. The result is that surprise not only has individual effects on beliefs and attitudes, but also collective effects on a culture.

10 Mark for Review

Which choice best states the main idea of the text?

Ⓐ Surprises promote positive social interactions.

Ⓑ Surprises can have a significant social impact.

Ⓒ Surprises help individuals make sense of new information.

Ⓓ Surprises facilitate the creation of societal networks.

Answers: The Big Picture

1. D

Throughout the passage, Mrs. Penniman is described as someone unserious and unconcerned with everyday matters: she has *a taste for light literature* and *a passion for little secrets and mysteries*, and is *unpractical as addled eggs*. These phrases convey an image of someone who is "romantic and sentimental," making the answer (D). (A) and (C) are both entirely unsupported by the passage—there is nothing to suggest that Mrs. Penniman is either mysterious or difficult to get along with. (B) is incorrect because the passage states only that Mrs. Penniman has *a taste* (a liking) *for light literature*, which is much less extreme than a "passion."

2. C

The main focus of the passage is on the difficulty of eradicating (getting rid of) knotweed: the first sentence states that it is *intractable* (immovable), and the second indicates that the only way to remove it completely is to extract the land it sits on. That corresponds directly to (C). (A) is incorrect because the passage does not state that knotweed was one of the earliest plants to travel. (B) is directly contradicted by the passage, which states that knotweed can be removed when the land it sits on is extracted. (D) is entirely off-topic: the figure (0.3g) mentioned in the last sentence serves only to emphasize the minuscule amount of knotweed capable of regenerating a new plant.

3. B

The lines *Since childhood's days [Tennyson's] name I have revered/And more and more it has become to me endeared*, and *I very wealthy feel since I his "works" possess* indicate that Heard is extremely proud to have received Tennyson's poems and has an extremely positive attitude toward the poet. (C) is negative and can be eliminated. (A) misstates the essential situation: Heard's friend does not personally know Tennyson; as indicated in the title in the blurb before the passage, she has merely given a book of his poems as a gift. (D) is incorrect because Heard refers to her *humble thoughts*, indicating that she does not consider herself Tennyson's equal. Only (B) correctly characterizes Heard's attitude of "respect" and desire to "understand [Tennyson's] work deeply."

4. A

The key information appears in the second sentence and last sentence, where pawn is described as *a fully integrated part of Navajo life* and *a pivotal aspect of Navajo society*. In other words, it "plays a significant role in Navajo culture," making (A) correct. (B) is entirely unsupported by the passage. (C) and (D) are incorrect because the passage states only that pawn is *different from traditional banking* and is *based on relationships of mutual trust*—it cannot be inferred that pawn is "more complex than traditional banking" or that it "became popular...because it was based on personal relationships."

5. D

Don't get too caught up in the seeming complexity of the answer choices. In reality, the structure of the passage is fairly straightforward. The first sentence presents a claim—Octavia Butler resisted being identified exclusively with science fiction novels (i.e., *that form*)—and the rest of the passage serves to support it with specific examples (she also wrote essays and had one of her books turned into an opera). The only answer that corresponds to that organization is (D). The passage does not focus on one specific work or novel, eliminating (A) and (B). (C) does not fit either because the passage does not discuss the significance of either of the works mentioned.

6. C

The dash in the third sentence as well as the strong word *potent* (powerful) provides a clue about where important information is located. The statement that *sapphire and titanium ions proved to be a particularly potent combination, providing a much wider emission bandwidth than conventional lasers* is merely reworded in (C), making that answer correct. (A) does not work because the passage implies only that conventional lasers with other gain mediums are less effective, not that they do not contain gain mediums at all. (B) is entirely off-topic—the passage does not even mention heat conductivity. Be careful with (D): the last sentence does indicate that sapphire ion lasers are responsible for discoveries in many different scientific fields; however, that is because their emission bandwidth is wider than that of other lasers'—not because it is adjustable.

7. B

The focus of the passage is on how the griots' work has remained "relevant" because of a "flexible" approach that allows it to evolve. That makes (B) correct. (A) is phrased in negative terms, whereas the passage overall is positive. Although (C) is supported by the text, the discussion of the Sunjata epic is restricted to one section—it is not the overall focus. (D) is unsupported by the passage and, as is true for (C), stories about Sunjata/the Mali Empire are mentioned only to support the main idea.

8. A

The simplest way to answer this question is to use the main point. What is the primary thing we learn about Vivian from the passage? She's tired of what's around her. It's *monotonous* (all the same), *wearyingly familiar*, and she has a *mad wish* that an earthquake would come along and shake things up (literally and figuratively). If you condense that into something like "Vivian is bored," you can jump to (A). Both (C) and (D) are too positive, and (B) does not work because Vivian simply wishes for change—there is no indication that she herself wishes to make a change.

9. D

The first sentence indicates that English's work—amphibious architecture—provides people living in flood zones with *an easy and inexpensive way to protect their homes*. In other words, it offers "a practical solution." That corresponds to (D). (A) is incorrect because the passage states only that English and her colleagues are designing *prototypes for regions in Jamaica and Nicaragua*. It cannot be assumed that these new structures will replace traditional ones; moreover, this discussion is restricted to one section of the passage. (B) is negative, whereas the passage is quite positive towards amphibious architecture. (C) is incorrect because the passage focuses on the actual structures that English and her colleagues have produced/hope to produce, not on the history of her interest in amphibious architecture.

10. B

The key information appears in the first and last sentences: information including surprises is *more likely to be shared than neutral or technical pieces* and *surprise [has]...collective effects on a culture*. In other words, it can have "a significant social impact." That makes (B) correct. (A) does not work because the passage indicates only that surprises increase the likelihood that an experience will be shared—it says nothing about whether those interactions will be positive or not. (C) is unsupported by the passage. The focus is on how surprises cause people to spread new information; how surprises do or do not affect how new information is processed is not mentioned. (D) is also incorrect because the creation of societal networks themselves is not facilitated (made easier) by surprises. Rather, surprises travel throughout societal networks in order to spread widely.

5 Literal Comprehension: Same Idea, Different Words

Literal comprehension questions ask you to identify what a passage states or indicates. They can be phrased in the following ways:

- According to the text, what is true about character X?
- According to the text, why was the team's discovery significant?
- Based on the text, how does character X respond?

Although these types of questions are not a major focus of the digital SAT, you can expect to encounter one or two of them during a given Reading and Writing module.

As the most straightforward type of comprehension question, they essentially require you to understand ideas well enough to recognize accurate **summaries** of them. Because this is the SAT, however, those summaries will not use the exact same wording as that found in the passage—that would make things too easy! The test is whether you understand the ideas well enough to recognize when they're stated using **different, often more general, language**.

Correct answers thus require you to recognize **paraphrased** versions of ideas, ones that contain **synonyms for key words** in the passage. Essentially, you can treat these questions as a sort of matching game. If you understand the idea, you'll probably be fine; if you're too focused on the details, or do not read the correct lines—something that may require you to back up to the beginning of a sentence or passage—you might miss it completely.

Although these questions are asked in a straightforward way, they can also be challenging because you must sometimes navigate very challenging syntax and vocabulary. Furthermore, you must connect the specific words of the correct set of lines to the more abstract language of the answers.

Starting on the following page, we're going to look at some examples.

According to new research, viral DNA embedded in human genomes during ancient infections protects human cells against certain modern-day viruses. Earlier studies have shown that fragments of ancient viral DNA—known as endogenous retroviruses—in the genomes of mice, chickens, cats and sheep provide immunity against modern viruses that originate outside the body by preventing them from entering host cells. Though the new study, conducted by researchers at Cornell University, was performed with cultured human cells in a laboratory, it shows that the antiviral effect of endogenous retroviruses likely also exists for humans.

1 Mark for Review

Based on the text, what is true about the study conducted by Cornell researchers?

Ⓐ It tested for the presence of viral material in a range of species.

Ⓑ It suggests that endogenous retroviruses behave differently in humans than in animals.

Ⓒ It did not test for the presence of retroviruses in human bodies.

Ⓓ It demonstrated that fragments of ancient viral DNA can infect modern humans.

Although the question itself is asked in a straightforward way, it does have the potential to be quite tricky if you do not focus on the necessary section of the passage.

A very common approach would be to scan the passage for the information about the Cornell study, which is mentioned in the last sentence, and then focus on the information after the word *shows*. That is an entirely logical approach, but unfortunately it won't get you the answer. **To reiterate: never read just half a sentence.** If you back up to the beginning of the sentence, you'll find the key information: the Cornell study involved *cultured human cells in a laboratory*, i.e., not actual human bodies. And that is what (C) says. Same idea, different words—but maybe not in the place you were expecting. All of the other answers are either unsupported or directly contradicted by the passage.

Let's look at a fiction question.

The following text is adapted from the 1920 short story "Anything Once" by Isabel Ostrander. Lou is traveling from Buffalo to New York City with Jim.

Lou was trying her best to appear her old self with [Jim], but dissimulation was an art in which she was as yet unversed, and her whole nature rebelled against playing a part. Only her pride kept her from betraying her disappointment in him and running away. She told herself fiercely that he didn't care what she thought of him; they were only partners met by chance on the road, and perhaps never to see each other again after the city was reached.

5 Mark for Review

Based on the passage, what is true of Lou?

Ⓐ She is uncomfortable with being dishonest.

Ⓑ She is disappointed in her own behavior.

Ⓒ She is eager to gain Jim's respect.

Ⓓ She does not want to see Jim again after they arrive in the city.

The question and answers are quite straightforward here; the real challenge is unpacking the language of the passage. The key information appears in the first sentence, which tells us that *dissimulation* (pretending or lying) *was an art in which [Lou] was as yet unversed*, and that *her whole nature rebelled against [it]*. In other words, she doesn't have much experience pretending to be something she isn't, and having to behave that way makes her uncomfortable. That corresponds directly to (A).

(B) does not work because the passage indicates that Lou is disappointed in *Jim*, not in herself. (C) is unsupported by the passage, which states only that Lou believe Jim *didn't care what she thought of him*. Be careful with (D): the passage says only that Lou and Jim were *perhaps never to see each other again after the city was reached*. Even though Lou is clearly irritated with Jim, it is a step too far to infer that she does not wish to see him after they arrive. Notice that if you have difficulty with the language in the first sentence but are able to recognize that (B), (C), and (D) do not fit, you can still answer the question correctly.

One more question.

Much of what we know about the physical and mental toll of chronic stress stems from seminal work by Robert Sapolsky beginning in the late 1970s. Sapolsky, a neuroendocrinologist, was among the first to make the connection that the hormones released during the fight-or-flight response—the ones that helped our ancestors avoid becoming dinner—have deleterious effects when the stress is severe and sustained. Especially insidious, chronic exposure to one of these hormones, cortisol, causes brain changes that make it increasingly difficult to shut the stress response down.

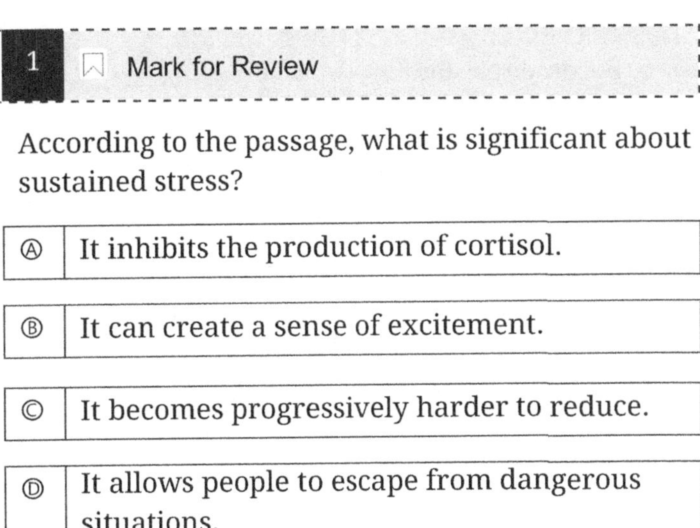

Don't get bogged down in the scientific language. Instead, focus on the last sentence, where the phrase *especially insidious* (dangerous in a sneaky way) and the word *cause* indicate the presence of key information. What do we learn there? That *chronic exposure to...cortisol causes brain changes that make it increasingly difficult to shut the stress response down*. Translated into simpler language, the longer a person experiences chronic stress, the harder it gets for them to stop being stressed, i.e., the stress "becomes progressively harder to reduce." (C) is therefore correct.

(A) is directly contradicted by the passage, which indicates that chronic stress results in chronic exposure to cortisol; and (B) is incorrect because excitement is not mentioned in the passage at all.

Be careful with (D)—the passage does state that stress once *helped our ancestors avoid becoming dinner*; however, that refers to the fight-or-flight response, which is contrasted with the negative of effects of stress that is *severe and sustained*. Again, that leaves (C) as the answer.

Exercise: Matching Phrases

Set #1

1. Investigate an occurrence ________		A. Bolster a hypothesis
2. Become more widely accepted ________		B. Broaden comprehension
3. Strengthen a conjecture ________		C. Study a phenomenon
4. Expand understanding ________		D. Develop immunity
5. Become resistant ________		E. Gain currency
6. Reject a possibility ________		F. Suggest an explanation
7. Posit a theory ________		G. Discard an option

Set #2

1. A reason for hope ________		A. A disputed assertion
2. An esteemed figure ________		B. A cause for optimism
3. An egalitarian system ________		C. A reason for panic
4. A creative approach ________		D. A highly regarded individual
5. A controversial claim ________		E. A persistent enigma
6. A cause for alarm ________		F. A non-hierarchical arrangement
7. A continuing mystery ________		G. An innovative take

Exercise: Literal Comprehension

"My Day," the nationally syndicated newspaper column written by Eleanor Roosevelt, long outlasted her time as first lady. The sheer frequency of the column, which ultimately ran six days a week in 90 newspapers across the United States for more than 20 years, extended Roosevelt's influence immeasurably: it made her a continual presence in the lives of her readers in a manner that anticipated the social-media age.

1 
Mark for Review

Based on the passage, what is true about "My Day"?

Ⓐ It overshadowed Eleanor Roosevelt's accomplishments as first lady.

Ⓑ It exposed a large new audience to Eleanor Roosevelt's work.

Ⓒ It was among the most widely read newspaper columns in the United States.

Ⓓ It was published more frequently than any other column of its time.

Although the Cherokee had a different relationship with the environment than American settlers did, they still altered the landscape around them in distinct ways. Throughout the Tennessee River, for example, Cherokee tribe members constructed stone weirs, rock obstructions designed to catch fish. The weirs did not halt the flow of the river and create large, stagnant pools of water the way dams constructed by settlers did, however. Rather, they depended on the water's continuous motion to sweep fish into traps—a cooperation of sorts between the built and the natural worlds.

2 Mark for Review

According to the text, how did weirs function differently from dams?

Ⓐ They had no effect on their surrounding environments.

Ⓑ They prevented rivers from flowing.

Ⓒ They relied on the water's existing movement.

Ⓓ Their effects on their surrounding environments were unpredictable.

To interrupt people's stereotypes of one another, researchers at Stanford Business School developed an intervention called the daily diary technique, in which randomly assigned people in two countries were given each other's diary to read for a week. They found that over time, this strategy reduced cultural distance compared to when they read diaries written by their compatriots. Participants in the first country began to perceive participants from the second as more ethical, whereas participants from the second country began to view participants from the first as warmer and less rigid.

3 Mark for Review

According to the text, what effect did the intervention developed by Stanford researchers have on participants?

Ⓐ It promoted perceptions of similarity between cultures.

Ⓑ It decreased feelings of antipathy among citizens of the same country.

Ⓒ It caused them to behave in a more ethical manner.

Ⓓ It improved their satisfaction with aspects of their own culture.

The following text is from Georgia Douglas Johnson's 1922 poem "Youth."

The dew is on the grasses, dear,
  The blush is on the rose,
And swift across our dial—youth,
  A shifting shadow goes.
The primrose moments, lush with bliss,
  Exhale and fade away,
Life may renew the Autumn time,
  But nevermore the May!

4 Mark for Review

According to the text, in what way is youth unlike the autumn of life?

Ⓐ It is untouched by shadows.

Ⓑ It cannot be extended.

Ⓒ It remains perpetually fresh.

Ⓓ It is full of bliss.

Geophysicists first began to appreciate the smoldering origins of the land under the sea, known formally as ocean crust, in the early 1960s. Sonar surveys revealed that volcanoes form nearly continuous ridges that wind around the globe like seams on a baseball. Later, the same scientists strove to explain what fuels these erupting mountain ranges, called mid-ocean ridges. Basic theories suggest that because shifting tectonic plates pull the ocean floor apart along the ridges, molten rock deep within the earth's interior must rise to fill the gap. This material is produced in the second layer of the Earth's interior — the mostly solid upper mantle — and makes its way up through the crust. The collision of two plates can also result in a volcano.

5 Mark for Review

Based on the passage, why do undersea volcanoes develop?

Ⓐ Because breaks in the ocean floor allow liquid rock from the mantle to enter.

Ⓑ Because mid-ocean ridges pull apart when the pressure beneath them increases.

Ⓒ Because tectonic plates accumulate along the ocean floor.

Ⓓ Because the Earth's crust collides with the mantle.

The following text is adapted from Edith Wharton's novel *The Custom of the Country*. Mrs. Spragg has recently arrived in New York City with her daughter.

The room showed no traces of human use, and Mrs. Spragg herself wore as complete an air of detachment as if she had been a wax figure in a show-window. Her attire was fashionable enough to justify such a post, and her pale soft-cheeked face, with puffy eye-lids and drooping mouth, suggested a partially-melted wax figure which had run to double-chin.

6 Mark for Review

According to the text, what is true about Mrs. Spragg?

Ⓐ She feels anxious in her environment.

Ⓑ Her clothing is not suited to her position.

Ⓒ Her features are sharp and distinctive.

Ⓓ She appears aloof and disconnected from her surroundings.

The Importance of Being Earnest is an 1895 play by Oscar Wilde.

ALGERNON: Did you hear what I was playing, Lane?

LANE: I didn't think it polite to listen, sir.

ALGERNON: I'm sorry for that, for your sake. I don't play accurately—any one can play accurately—but I play with wonderful expression. As far as the piano is concerned, sentiment is my forte. I keep science for Life.

7 Mark for Review

Based on the text, what is true about Algernon?

Ⓐ	He is embarrassed that Lane has overheard him playing the piano.
Ⓑ	As a musician, he is more concerned with emotion than technical correctness.
Ⓒ	Science appeals to him for the same reasons that music does.
Ⓓ	He wishes that he could play the piano more accurately.

Until the mid-nineteenth century, the outer walls of buildings were load-bearing, so they were generally thick and contained only small windows. By the early 1900s, however, structural advances in engineering had resulted in walls that could be relieved of their weight. As a result, designers were able to increase window sizes so that more light could be admitted into building interiors. Eventually, glass came to be associated with the luxury of being able to pay for the most current building technologies.

8 Mark for Review

According to the passage, how did outer walls constructed in the early 1900s differ from earlier outer walls?

Ⓐ	They did not have to support as much weight.
Ⓑ	They included more windows.
Ⓒ	They were made primarily of glass.
Ⓓ	They became both higher and thicker.

However valuable the information ancient coins provide as individual artefacts, they are even more revealing in larger collections known as hoards. A hoard can be defined as two or more coins deposited together, usually but not always deliberately, and never recovered. In most instances, a hoard's owner intended to claim it, and so the fact of its loss can provide important insight into historical circumstances.

9 Mark for Review

Based on the passage, what is true about hoards?

Ⓐ They were deliberately abandoned by their owners.

Ⓑ They provide more historical information than single coins do.

Ⓒ They were often deposited in combination with other objects.

Ⓓ They do not always consist of multiple coins.

The ice that we encounter in daily life is made up of water molecules arranged in hexagonal patterns stacked on top of one another. Because these crystalline structures are loosely packed, ice is less dense than water. In outer space, however, temperature and pressure conditions may differ dramatically from conditions on Earth, causing water molecules to be arranged in alternate structures. In fact, scientists have identified more than 20 different possible crystalline organizations, as well as two types of amorphous ice: high-density, which is denser than water, and low-density, which is less dense. Though solid in form, these substances are composed of irregularly arranged molecules like those of a liquid. Amorphous ices must be manufactured in a laboratory on Earth, but scientists believe that they could be common in comets, interstellar clouds and icy bodies such as Saturn's oceans.

10 Mark for Review

Based on the passage, what is true about amorphous ice?

Ⓐ It has a well-organized crystalline structure.

Ⓑ It comes in a wide range of molecular organizations.

Ⓒ It does not exist naturally on Earth.

Ⓓ It has been identified in extraterrestrial objects.

Answers: Matching Phrases

Set #1

1. C

2. E

3. A

4. B

5. D

6. G

7. F

Set #2

1. B

2. D

3. F

4. G

5. A

6. C

7. E

Answers: Literal Comprehension

1. B

The key information appears before the colon ("Interesting punctuation") in the third-to-last line. There we learn that Roosevelt's column *extended [her] influence immeasurably*, which is another way of saying that it "exposed a large new audience to [her] work." That makes (B) correct. (A) is incorrect because the passage states that "My Day" *outlasted* Roosevelt's time as first lady, but not that it "overshadowed" her achievement in that role. (C) does not fit because the passage emphasizes the wide reach of "My Day" (*six days a week in 90 newspapers*) but does not explicitly indicate that it was "among the most widely-read columns." (D) does not work either because the passage refers only to the *sheer frequency* of "My Day's" publication but does not make comparisons to any other column.

2. C

In this case, the answer is located in a key location, namely the last sentence. There we learn that weirs relied on *the water's continuous motion*, or how the water naturally moves ("its existing movements"). (C) is thus correct. (A) and (B) are contradicted by the passage, which states that weirs *altered the landscape around them in distinct ways* and that they *did not halt the flow of the river*. Be careful with (D): the passage states only that weirs' effects were *distinct*, not that they were unpredictable.

3. A

The key phrase is in the second sentence, which states that *over time, this strategy* (i.e., reading the diary of a person in another country) *reduced cultural distance*. In other words, it "promoted perceptions of similarity," which is what (A) says. (B) incorrectly concerns citizens of the same country, whereas the findings involved citizens of different countries. Note that you can eliminate this answer for that reason even if you do not know what *antipathy* (dislike) means. (C) is incorrect because reading the diaries only caused participants to perceive people in the other country as more ethical—the passage does not state whether it affected their own behavior. Likewise, (D) is incorrect because the passage makes no mention of how participants' perceptions of their own cultures changed.

4. B

The answer is found in a key place, namely the end of the passage. In context of the poem's title and subject, "Youth," the statement that *Life may renew the Autumn time,/But nevermore the May* means that old age (Autumn) can stretch out for a long time, whereas youth (May) must end—i.e., "it cannot be extended." (A) is contradicted by the passage, which states that *swift across our dial – youth,/A shifting shadow goes*. (C) is incorrect because it states exactly the opposite of the correct answer: by definition, something that "cannot be extended" does not "remain perpetually (forever) fresh." Be careful with (D): the poem only states that youth is *lush with bliss*, but the question asks how youth is "unlike" old age, and the passage does not make that particular comparison.

5. A

The key information appears in the fourth and fifth sentences, which indicate that *erupting mountain ranges* (i.e., volcanoes) are believed to form when the ocean floor is pulled apart and molten (liquid) rock from the upper mantle rises into the resulting space. That corresponds directly to (A). (B) is incorrect because the ridges are pulled apart by shifting tectonic plates, not by pressure. (C) is entirely unsupported by the passage. (D) is incorrect because the passage states that volcanoes can result from *the collision of two plates*, not from the collision between a plate and the mantle.

6. D

All the information you need to answer this question can be found in the first sentence: the phrases *no traces of human use* and *as complete an air of detachment as if she had been a wax figure in a show-window* correspond directly to "aloof and disconnected" in (D). (A) does not work because the passage only states that Mrs. Spragg is completely detached from her environment, not that she is "anxious." (B) is incorrect both because the passage indicates that Mrs. Spragg is dressed fashionably and because it says nothing about her actual position. (C) is directly contradicted by the passage, which indicates that Mrs. Spragg's features recall *a partially-melted wax figure.*

7. B

In his short speech, Algernon reveals that he is uninterested in playing the piano accurately ("technical correctness") and is much more concerned with sentiment ("emotion"), information that eliminates (D) and points directly to (B). (A) is incorrect because rather than being embarrassed by his presumably terrible piano-playing, Algernon seems quite proud of it. (C) is contradicted in the last two sentences, in which Algernon indicates his desire to keep music and science separate.

8. A

This is a second-meaning vocabulary question in disguise. The passage states that *structural advances in engineering resulted in walls that could be relieved of their weight.* In other words, some of the weight could be removed from them, or "they did not have to support as much weight." That makes (A) correct. (B) does not work because the passage only explicitly states that the newer walls could support larger windows—it says nothing about the number of windows. Likewise, (C) is incorrect because the passage indicates only that the windows became larger. It is too much of a stretch to infer that the walls were made "primarily" of glass. (D) does not work either because the passage implies the opposite, indicating at the beginning that outer walls were thick because they were load-bearing. If they had to bear less weight, then logically they could be made thinner.

9. B

Answering this question requires you to integrate information from the beginning and end of the passage. The first sentence indicates that coins are *more revealing* in hoards than as single items, and the last sentence states that hoards *can provide important insight into historical circumstances.* Based on those two statements, it is possible to conclude that hoards "provide more historical information than single coins do." That makes (B) correct. (A) does not work because the passage states that coins were usually *deposited together deliberately*—they were abandoned unintentionally, not deliberately (*in most instances, a hoard's owner intended to claim it*). (C) is incorrect because the passage states only that coins were often deposited together, not that hoards were deposited with other objects. (D) is incorrect as well because the second sentence defines a hoard as consisting of multiple coins.

10. C

If you scan through the text, you'll find that the key term, *amorphous ice*, appears a little more than halfway through. What do we learn about it? That there are two forms of it, not "a wide range of molecular organizations." That eliminates (B). We also learn that it is *composed of irregularly arranged molecules*, which is the opposite of a "well-organized crystalline structure." That eliminates (A). Third, we learn that it *must be manufactured in a laboratory on Earth*—in other words, it "does not exist naturally." That makes (C) correct. (D) does not fit because the passage states only that scientists *believe* amorphous ice exists in comets, interstellar clouds, etc., not that it has actually been found.

6 Reading for Function

If you've already spent some time studying for the SAT, you've most likely had the following experience: you see a question that asks you the primary purpose of a few lines or a passage. You go back, read the lines, and feel pretty confident that you understand what they're saying. When you look at the answers, however, they don't seem to have anything to do with what you've just read.

You go back to the passage, frantically rereading, trying to figure out what you've missed, then look back at the answers. Clear as mud. You get rid of a couple that are obviously wrong but find yourself stuck between (B) and (C), which both seem equally plausible. You remember hearing that (C) is the most common answer, so you decide to just pick it and hope for the best.

This scenario typically stems from the fact that most test-takers don't truly understand that function questions are not asking *what* the lines say but rather *why* they say it. In short, you cannot understand function without understanding content, but understanding content alone is not enough to understand function. Why? Because the SAT not only tests the ability to comprehend *what* is written in a passage but also *why* it's written. Essentially, **function questions ask you to move beyond the literal meaning of a section of a passage, or a passage as a whole, to understanding their larger purpose.**

These questions also generally require you to identify **the point that the information in question supports**. In this sense, function questions are very similar to the "illustrate" questions discussed later on, in Chapter 8: both ask you to work backwards from supporting examples to larger ideas.

However, while answers to function questions are based on the specific wording in the passage, you should keep in mind that **the answers themselves are not stated word-for-word in the text.** In fact, the answers may be phrased in much more general or abstract language than what appears in the passage; you are responsible for drawing the connection between the two. That said, you should **always keep in mind the topic of the passage because the correct answer may refer to it**, either directly or in rephrased form.

Types of Function Questions

Function questions can ask about individual sentences, or even just portions of a sentence, in which case the relevant material will be underlined. They can also ask about passages as a whole. You can expect to encounter both types of question regularly.

They are typically phrased in the following ways:

- The primary purpose of the passage is to…
- Which choice best states the function of the underlined sentence?
- The underlined portion primarily serves to…

And their answers fall into two categories:

1) Those that can **only** be answered by looking at the specific wording in the lines provided in the question. In such cases, the lines will typically contain phrasing, punctuation, or a key transition that points to a particular answer.

2) Those that **cannot** be obtained by looking at the lines provided in the question but that instead depend on contextual information.

For the second type of question especially, a sentence reference simply tells you where the information in question is located—it does <u>not</u> tell you the information's relationship to anything else in the passage. **The section necessary to obtain the answer will often be located either before the portion referenced in the question or, less frequently, after.**

Unfortunately, there is no way to tell upfront which category a particular question will fall into. As a result, **you should generally be prepared to read a sentence or two before and after the sentence referenced**, then focus on the appropriate lines as necessary.

Important: If the underlined section falls relatively close to the beginning of the passage, you should back up and begin reading from there. First sentences will very often give you the main point, making it much easier for you to understand the role of a particular piece of information within the passage. If the underlined portion is located in the middle of the text—especially if the passage is on the longer side—you probably do not need to go all the way back to the beginning but can instead back up a sentence or so as necessary.

Because SAT Reading focuses heavily on relationships between ideas, it follows that questions are frequently based on the places in a passage where ideas come into contact with one another—that is, where new information is introduced or where there is a change in focus.

The relationships between these ideas are sometimes indicated through the use of specific words, phrases, and types of punctuation, which correlate with particular function words. The chart on the next page lists some of the most common examples, along with their functions.

Functions of Key Words and Punctuation

Continuers		Contradictors
Continue Additionally Also And As well as Finally First Furthermore In addition Moreover Next Then **Illustrate, Support** For example For instance One reason/another reason **Explain** Because Explanation That is The answer is The reason is Colon Dash **Define** That is/That is to say Properly speaking Colon Dash Parentheses **Compare** As Just as Like/Likewise Much as Similarly	**Speculate** Could If It is possible May Maybe Might Perhaps **Call attention to Underscore, Highlight Emphasize** Indeed In fact Let me be clear Capital letters Exclamation point Italics Repetition (of a word, phrase) **Indicate Importance** Central Crucial Essential Fundamental Important Key Significant The point/goal is **Draw a conclusion** As a result Consequently Hence So Thereby Therefore Thus **Qualify** Dashes Parentheses	**Contrast** (Al)though But Despite However In contrast In spite of Instead Meanwhile Nevertheless On the contrary On the other hand Otherwise Rather Still Whereas While Yet **Question, Imply skepticism** But is it really true…? Question mark Quotation marks

Now let's look at some examples.

Example #1

To drivers, the color red means stop, but on a map it tells traffic engineers to leap into action. Traffic control centers like the one on the seventh floor of Boston's City Hall—a room cluttered with computer terminals and live video feeds of urban intersections—represent the brain of a traffic system. The city's network of sensors, cables and signals are the nerves connected to the rest of the body. "Most people don't think there are eyes and ears keeping track of all this stuff," says John DeBenedictis, the center's engineering director. But in reality, engineers literally watch our every move, making subtle changes that relieve and redirect traffic.

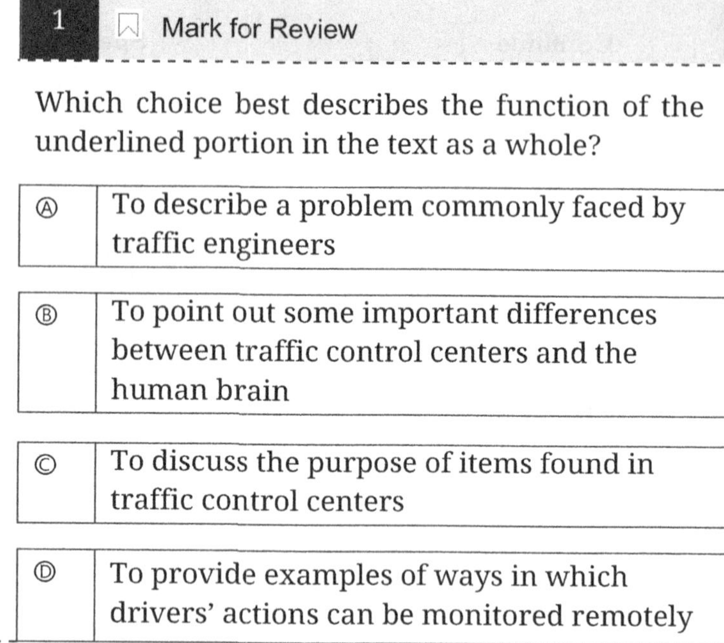

1 Mark for Review

Which choice best describes the function of the underlined portion in the text as a whole?

Ⓐ To describe a problem commonly faced by traffic engineers

Ⓑ To point out some important differences between traffic control centers and the human brain

Ⓒ To discuss the purpose of items found in traffic control centers

Ⓓ To provide examples of ways in which drivers' actions can be monitored remotely

If we wanted to simplify this question, we could say something like, "Why does the passage mention sensors, cables, and signals?" Or, "What point is the reference to sensors, cables, and signals used to support?"

The line reference is smack in the middle of the paragraph, where supporting evidence usually appears. To figure out what point it supports, we must focus on the beginning and the end of the paragraph, where main points are typically stated.

The beginning of the paragraph introduces the comparison between a traffic control center and the brain. Logically, the sentence that includes the key phrase (*The city's network of sensors, cables and signals…*) must serve to further develop that comparison.

The problem here is that no answer is consistent with that idea. As a result, we must read the rest of the paragraph, paying close attention to the last sentence. The presence of the word *but* suggests that it will be very important.

What idea is presented in the last sentence? Traffic engineers are able to watch people's every move. Why? Because of the sensors, cables, and signals that relay information from the streets back to them. So the phrase in question is there to explain how traffic engineers can monitor drivers' behavior from a distance, i.e., remotely. That makes the correct answer (D).

Granted, this question isn't easy; figuring it out without consulting the answers is a challenge. At the same time, however, you cannot assume that you will automatically recognize the correct answer when you see it. Sometimes you will have to do a bit more work upfront than you'd prefer, in order to avoid confusion.

If we wanted to play process of elimination:

(A) To describe a problem commonly faced by traffic engineers

The passage doesn't discuss a problem at all. This is completely off-topic.

(B) To point out some important differences between traffic control centers and the brain

The author draws a comparison between traffic control centers and the brain, but this answer just mentions "differences," which aren't discussed at all. This answer describes exactly the opposite of what's going on in the passage. **One wrong word makes the whole answer wrong.**

(C) To discuss the purpose of items found in traffic control centers

Be careful here. The passage does mention traffic control centers and sensors, cables, and signals in very close proximity to one another; however, it states only that computer terminals and live video feeds are found in traffic control centers. In the next sentence, we learn that sensors, cables, and signals are the *nerves* present throughout the *city*. So (C) is out.

Again, that leaves (D).

If you're stuck between this option and another answer, you can follow the same steps described earlier and read to the end of the paragraph. When you get to the last sentence, you can see that the statement *engineers literally watch our every move* directly corresponds to the idea of monitoring drivers' actions remotely.

Example #2

In August 2009, a consortium of European observatories reported the discovery of COROT-7c, a second planet orbiting COROT-7. Using the data from both planets, they were able to calculate that COROT-7b has an average density about the same as Earth's. This means it is almost certainly a rocky planet made up of silicate rocks like those in Earth's crust. Not that anyone would call it Earth. <u>The planet and its star are separated by only 1.6 million miles, 23 times less than the distance between the parboiled planet Mercury and our Sun.</u> Because the planet is so close to the star, it is gravitationally locked to it in the same way the Moon is locked to Earth.

2 Mark for Review

Which choice best describes the function of the underlined portion in the text as a whole?

Ⓐ It emphasizes an important distinction between COROT-7b and Earth.

Ⓑ It suggests that COROT-7b could eventually come to resemble Earth.

Ⓒ It supports the hypothesis that Earth and COROT-7b may share a common origin.

Ⓓ It explains how Mercury came to occupy its position within the solar system.

Before we look at any of the answer choices, we're going to start by restating the question so that we understand exactly what it is asking:

Rephrased:

What is the purpose of the underlined statement within the passage as a whole?

OR:

What point does the underlined statement serve to support?

Next, we're going to check the lines in question and make sure we understand exactly what they're referring to:

The planet and its star are separated by only 1.6 million miles, 23 times less than the distance between the parboiled planet Mercury and our Sun.

The sentence begins with *the planet,* so we need to back up as far as necessary and determine what "that planet" is. We find the answer in the second sentence: COROT-7b. This is the noun referred to as *it* in the third and fourth sentences. That fact becomes very important because the fourth sentence gives us the purpose of the underlined sentence. So that's the part we're really interested in.

What does the fourth sentence tell us? That no one would mistake COROT-7b for Earth. In other words, it is an extremely different place. Logically, the purpose of the underlined sentence must be to expand on that idea. And that is exactly what (A) says.

One more.

Example #3

Scientists have long known that color plays a role in warning animals about danger. Only recently, however, have they begun to understand how wavelengths of light (and thus color) appear at different depths and how various marine creatures' eyes perceive this light and each other—far differently than humans see them. Where waters are murky, the majority of creatures employ nonvisual forms of communication such as smell, taste, touch, and sound. <u>But in the clear waters of coral reefs, which make up less than 1% of the world's oceans, light abounds, vision predominates, and animals drape themselves in blazing color—not only to menace potential enemies but also to evade predators, hunt for prey, and even hide in plain sight.</u>

3 Mark for Review

Which choice best describes the function of the underlined portion in the text as a whole?

Ⓐ It explains how reef animals use color to hide from predators.

Ⓑ It describes an unusual form of marine communication.

Ⓒ It presents a novel theory about underwater perception.

Ⓓ It emphasizes the controversy surrounding a claim about reefs animals.

In this case, we can get most of the information we need from the underlined sentence itself, although it is also helpful to look at the previous sentence.

The first thing to notice is that the underlined sentence begins with the word *but*, indicating that it includes information opposing the previous sentence or statement, and that it presents a "new idea." So it's not a bad idea to back up and get the context.

The previous sentence tells us that *the majority of [marine] creatures* employ non-visual means of communication, whereas the underlined sentence tells us that reef creatures—which, based on the 1% statistic, we can infer make up only a minuscule percentage of sea life—use vision. Essentially, the underlined sentence is describing a very unusual, or "exceptional" situation.

(B) is thus correct. The relationship is so straightforward that it is unnecessary to seriously consider any of the other answers.

Main Point vs. Primary Purpose

Thus far, we've only looked at questions asking about a specific section of a passage. However, some questions ask about the purpose of a passage as a whole. These questions straddle two categories: they are big-picture questions, but they are function questions as well and must be approached from that standpoint. Otherwise, the answer choices may not fully make sense.

Often, however, when students encounter questions asking about the primary purpose of a passage, they reiterate the main point and then become confused when an option rephrasing it does not appear.

Although the purpose and the point of the passage are related, they are not precisely the same thing, and it important to understand the difference so that you are not surprised by the wording of the answer choices.

> **Main Point** – The primary **argument** the author is making. It is usually stated more or less directly in the passage, usually in the introduction and conclusion.
>
> **Primary Purpose** – The **rhetorical goal** of the passage as a whole (e.g., *explain*, *emphasize*, *describe*). While the primary purpose is based on the overall passage, there is often a key sentence that will point to a particular answer.

In many cases, if you're clear on the main point, making the jump to the primary purpose is relatively straightforward. For instance, if the point of a passage is that Douglas Engelbart's invention of the mouse was inspired by rolling wheels called planimeters (in super-condensed SAT terms, "DE used plnmtrs → mouse"), the answer to a primary purpose question might be something as close and simple as "To describe Engelbart's invention of the mouse."

In other cases, however, the wording may change somewhat between the main point and the purpose. Continuing with the example above, the answer to a primary purpose question could be phrased in more general terms, along the lines of, "To describe the inspiration behind an invention." In that case, you would need to make the connection between the specific noun *mouse* and the more abstract words *inspiration* and *invention*.

Using the First Sentence

If a question asks about the purpose of a passage as a whole, it might seem reasonable to assume that you will need to consider, well, the whole passage. In reality, however, you may sometimes be able to identify the most likely answer based primarily on a single sentence, or even just part of a sentence. And **when it comes to purpose-of-a-passage questions, that sentence is likely to be the first one**. Just make sure you read that sentence—the whole thing—carefully, and that you skim through the rest of the passage to confirm your answer. Trust, but verify.

For example, consider the following passage.

Throughout the dinosaurs' time on Earth, there was an amplification of boniness and spikiness; however, the advantage of skull frills and back plates is hardly self-evident. The solid-domed skull of Pachycephalosaurus seems made for butting—but for butting what? The skull would be all but useless against a predator with the size and power of Tyrannosaurus Rex. The skulls of some Pachycephalosaurs, moreover, were flat and thin—a bad design for contact sports—and the spikes protruding from them were most probably blunt rather than sharp.

1 Mark for Review

Which choice best states the main purpose of the text?

Ⓐ To suggest that a longstanding hypothesis about dinosaurs may be incorrect.

Ⓑ To introduce a study and raise some questions about the validity of its findings.

Ⓒ It describes a dinosaur species in order to illustrate a puzzling trend.

Ⓓ It presents an emerging mystery and discusses an attempt to solve it.

What do we learn from the first sentence? That the *advantage of skull-frills and back plates is hardly self-evident*. In other words, the advantage is unclear. So logically, the purpose of the passage is to discuss that lack of clarity.

Furthermore, the presence of the word *however* in the first sentence suggests that what follows is the "new idea"—no further information will be introduced to contradict it.

The only two answers that contain words consistent with the information we've established should be present are (C) ("puzzling") and (D) ("mystery"). The passage does not provide a possible explanation ("a hypothesis") for the phenomenon in question, nor does it mention a study.

In terms of choosing between (C) and (D), look at how the answer choices are worded. If the mystery were "emerging," the passage would indicate that it was new, but there is nothing here to suggest that is the case. That eliminates (D). In contrast, (C) merely refers to "a puzzling trend." The rest of the answer is consistent with the description of Pachycephalosaurus.

For a fiction example, we're going to revisit the passage below. In Chapter 4, we looked at it in terms of the main point ("Katherine fakes excitement at party"), but now we're going to consider it in terms of its primary purpose.

The following text is adapted from Virginia Woolf's 1919 novel *Night and Day*. Katherine is attending a party hosted by her mother.

Considering that the little party had been seated round the tea-table for less than twenty minutes, the animation observable on their faces, and the amount of sound they were producing collectively, were very creditable to the hostess. It suddenly came into Katherine's mind that if some one opened the door at this moment he would think that they were enjoying themselves; he would think, "What an extremely nice house to come into!" and instinctively she laughed, and said something to increase the noise, for the credit of the house presumably, since she herself had not been feeling exhilarated.

1 Mark for Review

Which choice best states the main purpose of the text?

Ⓐ To describe how the party guests convey their appreciation for the hostess's work

Ⓑ To portray a contrast between Katherine's external animation and internal lack of excitement

Ⓒ To explain why Katherine feels less excited than the other guests do

Ⓓ To depict the enjoyment felt by the people sitting around the tea-table

If you encounter a purpose-of-a-passage question right after you've finished reading, your first thought might be, "Oh no, I was so focused on trying to get what was going on that I wasn't really thinking about the purpose. You mean now I have to go back and reread the passage?"

In this case, if you keep the main point in mind, the primary purpose isn't an enormous leap. In fact, the correct answer, (B), simply rewords it from a slightly different, more abstract angle: Katherine does not feel *exhilarated* (internal) but behaves (external) as if she were enjoying herself. There is no need to complicate things further.

Playing Positive and Negative with Function Questions

One of the simplest ways to approach function questions and eliminate answer choices quickly is to play positive/negative. Positive passages or portions of passages typically have positive answers, while negative passages and portions of passages typically have negative ones.

Although answer choices often contain function verbs that are more neutral than the language of the passage itself, the information in the rest of the answer may be distinctly positive or negative. Even if this strategy alone does not get you all the way to the correct answer, it can allow you to quickly eliminate one or two choices upfront, giving you more time to focus on smaller distinctions between the remaining answers.

The chart on p. 129 provides some examples of common positive, negative, and neutral function words that are likely to appear in answer choices.

Let's look at an example:

On what seems like a monthly basis, scientific teams announce the results of new experiments, adding to a preponderance of evidence that we've been underestimating animal minds, even those of us who have rated them fairly highly. New animal behaviors and capacities are observed in the wild, often involving tool use—or at least object manipulation—the very kinds of activity that led the distinguished zoologist Donald R. Griffin to found the field of cognitive ethology (animal thinking) in 1978: octopuses piling stones in front of their hideyholes, to name one recent example; or dolphins fitting marine sponges to their beaks in order to dig for food on the seabed; or wasps using small stones to smooth the sand around their egg chambers, concealing them from predators.

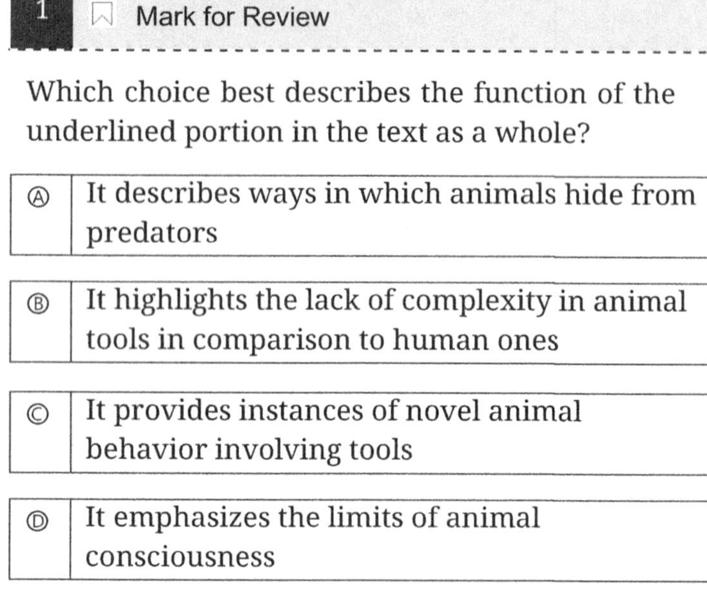

1 Mark for Review

Which choice best describes the function of the underlined portion in the text as a whole?

Ⓐ It describes ways in which animals hide from predators

Ⓑ It highlights the lack of complexity in animal tools in comparison to human ones

Ⓒ It provides instances of novel animal behavior involving tools

Ⓓ It emphasizes the limits of animal consciousness

This is a science passage, so its tone is relatively neutral. If we look closely at the first sentence, however, the phrase *a preponderance* (very large amount) *of new evidence* implies that the author has a positive attitude toward the subject. This suggests that the correct answer will be either positive or neutral and that any negative option can be eliminated.

When we look at the answer choices, we can notice that (B) and (D) contain negative phrasing ("less complex" and "limits"). Both answers can thus be eliminated immediately.

That leaves us with only two possibilities, but we still have to be careful. Remember that answers to function questions are often found **before** the underlined portions, and (A) refers to something mentioned **after**. The answer is constructed this way because many students will begin reading at the beginning of the lines referenced and overlook the information before it. Here, small stones are discussed only in relation to wasps; they are unrelated to the other animals/examples mentioned.

The point of the underlined section is actually found all the way back in the second sentence: *New animal behaviors and capacities are observed in the wild, often involving tool use.* In addition to the word *new*, the dashes in that sentence indicate that it is important. (C) rephrases that sentence, so it is correct.

Shortcut: (C) uses the word "novel" in its second meaning ("new"). Even in the absence of any other information, that usage suggests that (C) has an above-average chance of being correct.

Very important: While most answers contain neutral function words (e.g., "describe," "emphasize"), you may occasionally encounter more extreme ones, either positive ("prove") or negative (e.g., "call out"). Answers with this type of wording are usually **incorrect**. In particular, Science and Social Science passages often discuss theories that are taken seriously but have not yet been definitely (dis)proven, so answers indicating otherwise are inconsistent with how scholarly research works.

Common Function Words and Phrases

Positive	Negative	Neutral
Support Advance (a claim) Affirm Bolster Claim Defend Exemplify Illustrate Prove* Provide (evidence) Offer (an example) Substantiate **Praise** Celebrate **Acknowledge** **Propose** Imply Suggest **Emphasize** Call attention to Focus on Highlight Reinforce Reiterate Underscore **Explain** Account for Articulate Clarify Define Explicate Justify* Qualify Specify **Persuade** Advocate Encourage Promote	**Refute** Call out* Challenge Contradict Criticize Debate Decry Deny Discredit* Dismiss Dispel Disprove* Imply skepticism Question Undermine* **Warn** Raise concern **Concede** Acknowledge Recognize **Exaggerate** **Downplay** Minimize*	**Describe** Characterize Convey Depict Discuss Dramatize Evoke Portray Present Represent Show Trace **Indicate** Identify Point out Reveal **Introduce** **Shift** Change Digress* **Restate** Paraphrase Summarize **Hypothesize** Speculate **Analyze** Consider Describe Develop Explore Reflect on **Attribute** Cite Allude to

***Signals an answer that is likely to be incorrect.**

For a glossary of selected function words, see p. 135.

Exercise: Function

Far below the mid-ocean ridge volcanoes and their countless layers of crust-forming lava is the mantle, a 3,200-kilometer-thick layer of scorching hot rock that forms the earth's midsection and surrounds its metallic core. At the planet's cool surface, upthrusted mantle rocks are dark green, but if you could see them in their rightful home, they would be glowing red- or even white-hot. The top of the mantle is about 1,300 degrees Celsius, and it gets about one degree hotter with each kilometer of depth. The weight of overlying rock means the pressure also increases with depth about 1,000 atmospheres for every three kilometers.

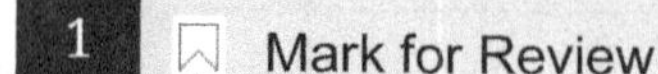

1 Mark for Review

Which choice best states the function of the underlined sentence within the text as a whole?

Ⓐ To convey the intense pressure that pervades the mantle

Ⓑ To suggest that scientific understanding of mantle rocks is limited

Ⓒ To describe a difference between mantle rocks and other types of rock

Ⓓ To emphasize a difference between mantle rocks in different locations

The Awakening is an 1890 novel by Kate Chopin. Edna Pontellier, the protagonist, is on vacation with her husband and children at Grand Isle resort in Louisiana.

Edna Pontellier could not have told why, wishing to go to the beach with Robert, she should in the first place have declined, and in the second place have followed in obedience to one of the two contradictory impulses which impelled her. A certain light was beginning to dawn dimly within her. In short, Mrs. Pontellier was beginning to realize her position in the universe as a human being, and to recognize her relations as an individual to the world within and about her.

2 Mark for Review

Which choice best states the primary purpose of the text?

Ⓐ To highlight Edna's tendency to behave in contradictory ways

Ⓑ To present a situation in which Edna must make a momentous decision

Ⓒ To describe Edna's newfound insight into her interior and exterior existence

Ⓓ To convey Edna's sense of duty toward her family

In order to better understand people's receptiveness to opposing viewpoints, public policy scholars Julia Minson of Harvard University and Frances Chen of the University of British Columbia reviewed dozens of studies spanning 1984 to 2021. Among their findings was the fact that people who feel strongly about an issue can be receptive to others' views without altering their own opinions. <u>As the researchers point out, two thoughtful people might examine each other's ideas seriously and, recognizing that it is possible for reasonable people to hold either perspective, respectfully agree to disagree.</u>

3 Mark for Review

Which choice best states the function of the underlined sentence within the text as a whole?

Ⓐ It highlights a potential outcome of a strong disagreement.

Ⓑ It describes a process by which people's opinions can evolve.

Ⓒ It emphasizes the importance of considering multiple perspectives.

Ⓓ It discusses a strategy that permits opposing parties to reconcile their differences.

In the brain, sleep is manifested through changes in the activity of neuronal cells. The transition from wakefulness into sleep is accompanied by a shift into defined wave-like patterns, with different patterns associated with different stages of sleep. As the body relaxes, the brain moves into relatively rapid alpha waves. And when a person dozes off, it transitions into slower theta waves, before finally settling into the deepest stage of slow-wave sleep. At times, the brain also shifts into rapid eye movement (REM) sleep. This stage of sleep, which is when dreams occur, is characterized by rapid eye movements behind closed eyelids, and brain patterns during REM sleep most closely resemble those of the awake brain.

4 Mark for Review

Which choice best states the primary purpose of the text?

Ⓐ To discuss the stage of sleep during which dreams occur

Ⓑ To compare brain activity during wakefulness to brain activity during sleep

Ⓒ To provide an overview of brain-wave patterns in various stages of sleep

Ⓓ To explain the difference between REM sleep and other stages of sleep

The following text is from Charlotte Grimké's poem "Wordsworth."

Poet of the serene and thoughtful lay!
In youth's fair dawn, when the soul, still untried,
Longs for life's conflict, and seeks restlessly
Food for its cravings in the stirring songs,
The thrilling strains of more impassioned bards;
Or, eager for fresh joys, culls with delight
The flowers that bloom in fancy's fairy realm —
We may not prize the mild and steadfast ray
That streams from thy pure soul in tranquil song

5 Mark for Review

Which choice best describes the function of the underlined portion in the text as a whole?

Ⓐ To criticize the human tendency toward conflict

Ⓑ To describe the power of music to express emotions

Ⓒ To highlight the consequences of uncontrolled restlessness

Ⓓ To convey the soul's youthful desire for excitement

One of the most persistent and problematic biases in science involves motivated reasoning—that is, the tendency to interpret observations to fit preconceived notions. According to Professor Brian Nosek, a specialist in human biases and co-founder of the Center for Open Science at the University of Virginia, psychologists have demonstrated that "most of our reasoning is in fact rationalization." In other words, people begin by making decisions about what to think or do, and their "explanation" later serves as a means to justify what they believed or how they intended to act in the first place.

6 Mark for Review

Which choice best states the primary purpose of the text?

Ⓐ To describe a widespread shortcoming in scientific research

Ⓑ To suggest that true objectivity in science cannot be attained

Ⓒ To emphasize the inaccuracy of many scientific conclusions

Ⓓ To call attention to the dangers of motivated reasoning

In recent years, many companies have shifted from a model in which workers are placed in individual cubicles to one based on open-office plans, with the goal of fostering employee interaction and collaboration. Studies suggest, however, that such strategies may backfire, increasing job dissatisfaction and leaving workers no more likely to work together than before. Researchers theorize that employees' tendency to avoid one another in open offices may be attributable to the "fourth wall"—the imaginary curtain that prevents actors from being distracted by the audience and preserves the imaginary world of a play. To preserve a sense of psychological autonomy, employees in open offices establish their own fourth walls, which their colleagues quickly come to respect.

7 Mark for Review

Which choice best describes the function of the underlined portion in the text as a whole?

Ⓐ To describe a drawback of open offices

Ⓑ To present an explanation for an unintended phenomenon

Ⓒ To emphasize the importance of collaboration in the workplace

Ⓓ To compare office work to theatrical work

Throughout history, though, toys were not designed with children specifically in mind, and it was not customary for children to play alone. Rather, children played with other children, and only rarely with adults. They made up their own narratives while playing with sticks, mud, or household, even religious, objects. It was not until clocks were invented, then, that the miniaturization of the cosmos and the growing desire for control over it led to the profusion of automated toys seen in the nineteenth and twentieth centuries. From toy makers in Germany came mechanized ducks that walked and quacked, while figures in crib scenes hammered and sawed.

8 Mark for Review

Which choice best describes the function of the underlined portion in the text as a whole?

Ⓐ To describe a consequence of the invention of clocks

Ⓑ To provide examples of toys that were popular in the nineteenth and twentieth centuries

Ⓒ To point out that early toymakers were largely indifferent to children's interests

Ⓓ To emphasize a shift in the toys that children preferred

While each person gets dressed at least 29,000 times in the course of their lives, empirical science has paid little attention to why we select the everyday clothes that help mold our image. In a study designed to assess the relationship between style preferences and other aspects of personality, researchers led by Young-Jin Hur used an online questionnaire to survey 506 people in the United Kingdom about their clothing choices. They identified four main categories of preferences: essential, comfortable, feminine, and trendy. Further analysis found that preferences across each of these styles were associated with the color preferences and the self-reported traits of study participants.

9 Mark for Review

Which choice best states the primary purpose of the text?

Ⓐ To analyze the researchers' motivations for conducting the study

Ⓑ To summarize the aims and findings of the study

Ⓒ To criticize the process used to recruit study participants

Ⓓ To explain the significance of the study's results

Antarctica is a tough place to work, for obvious reasons—it's bitterly cold, remote, and wild. However, it's one of the best places in the world to hunt for meteorites. That's partly because Antarctica is a desert, and its dry climate limits the degree of weathering the meteorites experience. On top of the dry conditions, the landscape is ideal for meteorite hunting: the black space rocks stand out clearly against snowy fields. <u>Even when meteorites sink into the ice, the glaciers' churning motion against the rock below helps re-expose the meteorites near the surface of the continent's blue ice fields.</u>

10 Mark for Review

Which choice best describes the function of the underlined portion in the text as a whole?

Ⓐ To describe the difficulties faced by meteorite hunters in the Antarctic

Ⓑ To explain how Antarctica's blue ice fields affect meteorites' composition

Ⓒ To compare the surface conditions of Antarctica to the conditions in outer space

Ⓓ To emphasize a feature of the Antarctic landscape that allows meteorites to become exposed

Glossary of Function Words

Account for – explain

Acknowledge (a point) – recognize the merit or validity of an idea

Advocate – synonym for *promote* and *encourage*

Bolster – support, provide additional evidence for an idea

Call out – draw attention to for the purpose of criticizing

Concede (a point) – recognize the merit or validity of an opposing idea

Discredit – disprove (literally, demonstrate a lack of credibility); this word is likely too extreme to appear in a correct answer

Dismiss – deny the importance or validity of an idea

Downplay – deliberately understate, imply that something is unimportant

Evoke – summon, call up (a memory, impression, etc.), recreate through description

Explicate – explain in great detail

Highlight – emphasize, call attention to

Minimize – deliberately understate the importance of an idea; synonym for *downplay* and *trivialize*

Qualify – provide more information about a statement in order to make it seem less strong or blunt, or to indicate the conditions under which it would be true

Substantiate – give evidence or support for, prove; usually too extreme to be correct

Undermine – weaken or attack the foundation of; usually too strong to be correct

Answers: Reading for Function

1. D

This is a good example of a function question whose answer depends only on the underlined sentence itself rather than on the information before or after it. The key word *but* occurs halfway through the sentence and indicates that its purpose is to describe a contrast: the first half of the sentence describes mantle rocks at the surface (green), whereas the second half describes them deep beneath the earth (very hot). In other words, it "emphasizes a difference between mantle rocks in two locations," making the answer (D). (A) is incorrect because the underlined sentence focuses on heat, not pressure. (B) is entirely off-topic, and (C) does not fit because the underlined sentence describes mantle rocks only.

2. C

The transitional phrase *In short* at the beginning of the last sentence signals that the author is about to summarize an essential idea, and indeed, the key information is located right afterwards. It involves Edna's sudden realization ("newfound insight") about herself and her position relative to the world around her ("her interior and exterior existence"). That corresponds to (C). (A) is incorrect because it takes a word from the passage (*contradictory*) and twists it beyond the scope of the passage: the narrator states only that Edna experiences contradictory impulses when Robert asks her to accompany him to the beach—we cannot infer that she has a general "tendency to behave in contradictory ways." (B) is incorrect because it is Edna's realization that is "momentous," not her decision. (D) is contradicted by the passage: the primary focus is on Edna's discovery about herself, not on her sense of obligation towards her family.

3. A

The underlined sentence begins with the phrase *As the researchers point out*, indicating that the information that follows will focus on an implication or conclusion of the research described in the previous sentences. The previous sentence discusses the finding that *people who feel strongly about an issue can be receptive to others' views without altering their own opinions*, and the underlined sentence expands on that idea. (A) is correct because disagreeing respectfully is something that people with strongly opposing opinions might choose to do at the end of an argument—that is, "a potential outcome." (B) and (D) are both contradicted by the passage. The focus here is on people whose views do <u>not</u> evolve, or who do <u>not</u> reconcile (bring together) their differences. Although the passage does discuss how individuals with different perspectives might interact, (C) is incorrect because the sentence in question does not mention "the <u>importance</u> of multiple perspectives."

4. C

Although the passage is fairly dense and contains a lot of information, the purpose is essentially introduced in the second sentence: *the transition from wakefulness to sleep is accompanied by a shift into defined wave-like patterns, with different patterns associated with different stages of sleep*. The rest of the passage is then devoted to briefly describing those different stages. In other words, the purpose of the passage is to "provide an overview of brain-wave patterns in various stages of sleep." (C) is thus correct. (A) does not work because it is too specific: REM sleep is mentioned at the end of the passage, but this stage is not the primary focus. (D) is incorrect for the same reason. (B) does not fit either because there is no specific discussion of brain activity during wakefulness, and so there is no comparison.

5. D

Although the underlined portion appears close to the start of the poem, in this case the first sentence is simply an exclamation that does not provide any useful information for the question. As a result, it is necessary to focus on the wording of the underlined portion, which describes the soul's search for *life's conflict, food for its cravings...the thrilling strains of more impassioned bards*—in other words, "excitement," which corresponds to (D). (A) is incorrect because the poem is strongly positive, whereas "criticize" is negative. (C) is fairly negative as well, and the underlined section does not mention any "consequences." (B) is off-topic: while the word *songs* appears in the sentence, music is not the focus.

6. A

Although the question asks about the passage a whole, you can get a sense of the answer by using only the first sentence. (In a passage this short, the primary purpose is essentially required to be presented very close to the beginning.) The phrase *One of the most persistent and problematic biases in science* indicates that the passage will present and discuss this problem. The language is moderate and neutral, suggesting that the correct answer will be so as well. (A) is consistent with the stated purpose and does not go outside the bounds of the passage, so it is correct. (B) is too extreme—the passage only states that motivated reasoning is a problem, not that "true objectivity cannot be attained." Be careful with (C): the passage only indicates that scientists have *a tendency to interpret observations to fit preconceived notions*—it does not go so far as to emphasize that "many scientific conclusions" are actually wrong, only that they have been arrived at in a way that is not fully objective. (D) is too extreme and too negative, and the passage never explicitly discusses any dangers.

7. B

The fastest way to answer this question is to focus on the word *theorize* in the underlined portion—it indicates that the sentence in question serves to present an argument or explanation. The only answer consistent with this purpose is (B), which contains the word "explanation." Otherwise, (A) is incorrect because the underlined portion does not "describe a drawback of open offices" but rather offers a theory about why a drawback (increased job dissatisfaction) exists. The beginning of the passage indicates that open offices are intended to promote collaboration but then moves to a discussion of why it does not take place, making (C) incorrect. Although the underlined portion does draw a comparison between open-office workers' behavior and the "fourth wall," which is an element of the theater, the main purpose of the underlined sentence is not to compare office and theatrical work but rather to explain why open offices backfire.

8. A

This is a function question whose answer depends on information presented in the sentence before the underlined one. There, we learn that the invention of clocks led to *the profusion* (large increase) *of automated toys seen in the nineteenth and twentieth centuries.* The underlined sentence then cites mechanized ducks and figures that *hammered and sawed* as examples of that automation. That function corresponds to (A). (B) and (D) are incorrect because the passage does not mention whether the toys were popular or whether children preferred them. (C) is contradicted by the passage. Although the first sentence states that toys were not traditionally designed with children in mind, the rest of the passage describes a shift away from children inventing their own toys and toward professional toymakers designing miniature objects specifically for children.

9. B

The passage as a whole serves to provide a general overview of the study: why it was conducted (it was *designed to assess the relationship between style preferences and other aspects of personality*) and what was discovered (*They identified four main categories of preference... Further analysis found...*). That corresponds to (B). (C) is incorrect because the participant-recruitment process is not discussed in the passage at all, but be careful with (A) and (D). Although the first sentence indicates that fashion preferences are an under-studied topic, the passage does not "analyze" this fact, as (A) states, and it is not mentioned again after the initial reference. (D) is incorrect as well because the end of the passage conveys the basics of the researchers' findings but does not discuss their larger significance.

10. D

To answer this question, you must back up to the previous sentence, whose potential importance is suggested by a colon. That sentence provides the point that the last sentence serves to support, namely that *the [Antarctic] landscape is ideal for meteorite hunting*. The underlined sentence emphasizes that idea by pointing out that meteorites eventually become exposed—and thus easier to find—*even when [meteorites] sink into the ice*. (D) is thus correct. (A) states exactly the opposite of the point: the passage states that Antarctica is *one of the best places in the world to hunt for meteorites*. (B) and (C) are both off-topic—the passage mentions blue ice fields but says nothing about their composition, and there is no comparison between conditions in Antarctica and those in outer space.

7 Text Completions

Every SAT contains a number of text completions: short passages that present a theory or argument and that ask you to identify the statement that logically completes the text. For example, consider the passage below. We'll look at the answer choices on the next page.

> Up close, regal angelfish flash eye-popping bands of yellow, violet, and white. But recent studies show that as regals swim against a coral reef's visually complex background, their contrasting lines merge in a predator's brain, allowing them to evade capture. According to marine biologist Gil Rosenthal, as a reef fish retreats, distance and motion can make it difficult for predators to perceive fine details and distinguish closely spaced outlines of contrasting colors. Therefore, from far away, _____

To answer this question, you must use the information presented before the blank in order to infer how reef fish would be perceived by a predator far away.

Although you must make a leap of logic in order to answer a question such as this, it is only a very small leap. The most important thing to understand about text completions is that they are essentially literal comprehension questions with a twist. All of the necessary information is there; you just have to put the pieces together and make explicit an idea the passage leaves unstated.

Although answers will not normally be stated word-for-word in the passage, **the text will always contain specific wording that clearly corresponds to a particular statement in the correct answer.** And very often, **the key information will appear very close to the blank**, the earlier part of the passage serving primarily to provide background for the argument.

To minimize your chances of confusion, you can follow the sequence below. You don't need to adhere to it rigidly for every question, but it provides a solid general roadmap.

1) Carefully read the claim or theory in question.

Usually this will be presented right before the blank.

2) Restate it in your own words.

If it is particularly dense or confusing, jot down a quick (3-6) word summary on your scratch paper. For the passage on the previous page, we could write something like "RF retreat → blend w/background." (When reef fish retreat, they blend in with their background.)

3) Work out the implications, sticking as close to the passage as possible.

Given the summary above, we can conclude that *from far away*, predators have a hard time seeing brightly colored reef fish because they blend in with their background. If that seems too obvious, well... that's the point.

4) Look for the answer that matches.

Keep in mind that it may use wording very different from that in the passage.

Having gone through steps #1-3, we're going to look at the answers.

Up close, regal angelfish flash eye-popping bands of yellow, violet, and white. But recent studies show that as regals swim against a coral reef's visually complex background, their contrasting lines merge in a predator's brain, allowing them to evade capture. According to marine biologist Gil Rosenthal, as a reef fish retreats, **distance and motion can make it difficult for predators to perceive fine details and distinguish closely spaced outlines of contrasting colors.** From far away, ______

1 Mark for Review

Which choice most logically completes the text?

Ⓐ the bright colors of the fish can easily be perceived, even when the water is clouded by sediment.

Ⓑ marine predators must rely on the visual aspects of their prey.

Ⓒ spots and stripes blur together, allowing even stationary fish to merge into the background.

Ⓓ the fish appear as a single mass rather than a group of individual creatures.

(A) and (B) are both directly contradicted by the passage—the whole point is that predators cannot rely on visual information to identify reef fish that they hunt. Be careful with (D): the issue is not that predators see the fish as a group, but rather that they cannot distinguish the fish from the background of the reef at all. (C), the correct answer, is directly consistent with the correct idea, which we determined beforehand: for a faraway predator, the bright patterns on the fish blend into, i.e., "merge," with the background, allowing them to escape capture.

When Is a Conclusion Valid?

When working through text completions, it can also be helpful to know something about how wrong answers are constructed. Some incorrect options will be directly contradicted by the text or be so far outside its bounds that they obviously do not fit. Identifying and eliminating these answers is a straightforward matter of reading the passage carefully and understanding the necessary vocabulary.

Other answers will be wrong in subtler ways, though. For example, they may involve **speculation**—that is, an answer *could* be true based on the information in the passage, but there isn't enough information to determine whether it is *actually* true. Half-right, half-wrong options may sound so plausible that it seems as if they should be true. (In fact, some of them may even be true in the real world.) Answers in this category can be tempting because they generally refer to claims or people that are directly mentioned in the passage.

Remember, however, that correct answers are likely to include language somewhat different from that used in the passage. It is thus crucial to not eliminate any answer without making sure you really understand what it is saying. **You must be able to distinguish between wording that <u>rephrases</u> important ideas from the text (valid inference) vs. wording that is genuinely off-topic (invalid).**

In addition, keep in mind that **one of the simplest ways to create a logical inference is to rewrite a statement from a different angle**—something that may involve **negative language**, e.g., the word *not* or the prefix *-un* or *-im*. For example, if a researcher claims that a star is **older** than the Earth, a correct answer might state that the star is **not younger** than the Earth.

You should also pay particularly close attention to answers that contain **double negatives**, which create a **positive meaning**. For instance, something that is "not impossible" is possible, and something that is "not unimportant" is important. This language can be very tricky, and you may need to take a few moments to work out exactly what it means.

All that said, we're going to look at a few examples of how valid conclusions can be formed.

Example #1

> Researchers in Japan and Brazil have found that a particular type of muscular contraction, which occurs only when people lower weights, is most effective at increasing muscle strength and size.

There are a couple of key pieces of information here. First, the passage concerns a type of muscular contraction that is *<u>most effective</u> at increasing muscle strength and size.* We can therefore conclude that all other types of muscular contractions are <u>less effective</u> or <u>not as effective</u> at producing this outcome.

Next, this type of contraction occurs *only when people lower weights*, i.e., when they are <u>not raising</u> them.

If we put those statements together, we can logically conclude that people who want to build muscle strength and size should focus on exercises that involve lowering weights; or that raising weights is a <u>less effective</u> way of building muscle strength and size than lowering weights is.

Example #2

> Sea turtle conservation efforts largely focus on protecting vulnerable hatchlings once they emerge. The newly hatched turtles are directed away from the bright lights of towns and encouraged to move towards the sea.

The first sentence states that conservation efforts *largely focus on protecting...hatchlings once they emerge.* We can therefore conclude that conservation efforts are less focused on protecting hatchlings before they emerge, i.e., while they are still in their shells.

Because the first sentence tells us that sea turtle hatchlings are vulnerable and need protection, we can conclude from the second sentence that *the bright lights of towns* represent danger, and that encouraging the hatchlings to move towards the sea is a way of protecting them.

We **cannot**, however, conclude that protecting sea turtles after they hatch is the only way or the best way to conserve the species. The same is true for directing the hatchlings away from towns and toward the sea. The passage only tells us that these methods are used—it tells us nothing about their effectiveness, either in absolute terms or in comparison to other approaches.

Example #3

> About 14% of major earthquakes since 2000 have been supershear events, which occur when a fault ruptures faster than seismic shear waves can travel through rock. Until recently, these earthquakes were believed to occur much less frequently because researchers had mostly looked for them on land.

We can draw several conclusions from these statements.

- If 14% of earthquakes since 2000 have been supershear events, then most earthquakes (76%) since 2000 have been other types.
- Supershear quakes occur much more frequently than researchers used to believe.
- If researchers obtained their inaccurate estimate by looking mostly at supershear quakes on land, then many supershear quakes must not occur on land. Logically, they must occur underwater instead—that is the only other option on Earth.

We **cannot**, however, draw conclusions about earthquakes—supershear or otherwise—before 2000.

Likewise, we **cannot** infer anything about why researchers focused primarily on land and neglected to consider the oceans.

Now we're going to work through a couple of additional test-style examples.

Let's start with something relatively straightforward. You don't get to see the answers just yet.

> Some people naturally exhibit a low response to training—an inability to reap the full physiological benefits of aerobic exercise. A study led by Sarah Lessard at the Joslin Diabetes Center found that participants with a low response had high levels of blood sugar—a condition known as hyperglycemia. While this condition is often associated with diabetes, it is common in non-diabetics as well. Lessard and her colleagues **predicted** that if people with hyperglycemia received a drug designed to lower blood sugar levels, they would therefore
>
> ______

We're going to begin by summarizing the scenario presented in the simplest possible terms. Do not underestimate the importance of writing things down when you are asked to juggle multiple ideas.

- People with hyperglycemia show low response to exercise.
- So: if a drug reduces hyperglycemia, **the response to exercise should get higher**.

Or, in super-condensed SAT language:

- HG ↑, exercise response ↓
- If drug makes HG ↓, exercise response ↑

The correct answer should therefore indicate Lessard + colleagues predicted that taking a drug to reduce hyperglycemia would result in an improved response to exercise.

Notice that there's nothing in there about diabetes – that information is just a distraction from the main argument. Keep that in mind when you look at the answer choices.

Ⓐ	be more likely to incorporate exercise into their daily routine.
Ⓑ	lower their risk of developing diabetes.
Ⓒ	demonstrate an improved physiological response to aerobic training.
Ⓓ	experience less severe spikes in blood sugar after consuming certain foods.

If you held onto the idea that reducing hyperglycemia would logically cause people to develop a higher response—i.e., "an improved physiological response"—to exercise, you could probably jump right to (C). The answer is so strong that it is unnecessary to consult any of the other options.

If you did want to play process of elimination, however, all the other answers are off-topic. The passage suggests nothing about lowered hyperglycemia prompting people to exercise regularly or lower their risk of developing diabetes (although the latter may be true in reality). That eliminates (A) and (B). Likewise, it says nothing about reduced hyperglycemia's influence on blood sugar after eating, eliminating (D). Again, that leaves (C) as the only option.

As a side note, the logical prediction here was actually confirmed by Lessard's study. The persistent inability of certain patients to respond normally to exercise was a mystery in the medical world for many decades, and Lessard along with her colleagues at Joslin finally solved it.

Let's look at another example—it's a bit more challenging language-wise than the previous one. We're going to use the full question from the start this time, but try to practice avoiding the answers until you've done some basic legwork.

Fully one-third of the human brain is devoted to processing visual information; in contrast, only five percent involves smell. As a result, modern neuroscience has focused most intensely on deciphering sight, with olfaction often treated as a bonus sense. That is reflected in the paucity of language to describe it, a situation that poses a problem for scientific investigation. There are countless adjectives to describe what things look—and sound—like, but humans' vocabulary for olfactory perception is fragmentary and highly inconsistent. Therefore, ______

1 Mark for Review

Which choice most logically completes the text?

Ⓐ olfactory researchers are seeking higher levels of funding to study how people process odors.

Ⓑ people often cannot explain how things smell to them in a way that is comprehensible to researchers.

Ⓒ people must be able to process visual and olfactory information simultaneously in their daily lives.

Ⓓ people should focus on sensations rather than words when they encounter new scents.

To begin, reiterate the key information from the passage and the question. Try to focus on the fundamentals and not get too distracted by challenging language. Even if you don't know what "olfaction" is, you can figure out that it refers to smelling ability: the first sentence states that only 5% of the brain involves smell, which corresponds to the idea that olfaction is treated as a *bonus sense.*

Basically, the human brain largely focuses on processing visual information and neglects scents (olfactory information). As a result, people don't have a lot of words to talk about smells. This creates a problem for studying smells scientifically.

When we summarize things this way, the question more or less answers itself. Logically, studying smells scientifically would be hard **because** people don't have a consistent vocabulary to discuss them.

If we then consider the answer choices with that information in mind, we can see that (B) is an excellent match for that idea: if people can't accurately or consistently describe what they're smelling, it becomes very difficult for researchers to gather information about how people use that sense.

Playing process of elimination, (A) is completely off-topic—the passage only states that researchers have a "problem" studying scent perception. Assuming that they are asking for more money to study it goes *way* beyond the bounds of the text.

(C) is incorrect because while people obviously do need to process both visual and olfactory (smell) information at the same time in daily life, that fact has nothing to do with the passage. It merely indicates that a much larger portion of the brain is devoted to vision and that people do not think about smell as much. This answer takes two pieces of factual information and puts them together in a way that sounds vaguely intimidating but is actually insignificant.

(D) does not fit because the passage implies no recommendations regarding what people *should* do when they encounter new scents. It only indicates that they have trouble describing smells in general.

Again, that leaves (B) as the answer.

To sum up:

Because text completions are an important part of SAT Reading, the ability to break down challenging questions of this type in a logical, step-by-step manner can have a real impact on your score.

Now, can working this carefully be a pain? Absolutely. It's much easier to just crash through questions and hope for the best. However, the bottom line is that this approach *works* (and I say this from personal experience). The SAT is a reasoning test, and these questions are explicitly constructed so that if you think carefully and reason your way through them, you can eventually find your way to the right answer.

Remember that no matter how strong your reading and/or reasoning skills are, the usefulness of taking a pencil and working out each step of the argument **by hand** on your scratch paper should not be underestimated. Again: this is not just about getting questions right but also a matter of ensuring that you do not get them wrong. After all, if you can get the points, why would you pass them up?

Exercise: Text Completions

Physicists have yet to figure out what exactly happens at the singularity of a black hole: matter is crushed, but what becomes of it then? The event horizon, by hiding the singularity, isolates this gap in our knowledge. All kinds of processes unknown to science may occur at the singularity, yet they have no effect on the outside world. Astronomers plotting the orbits of planets and stars can safely ignore the uncertainties introduced by singularities and _____

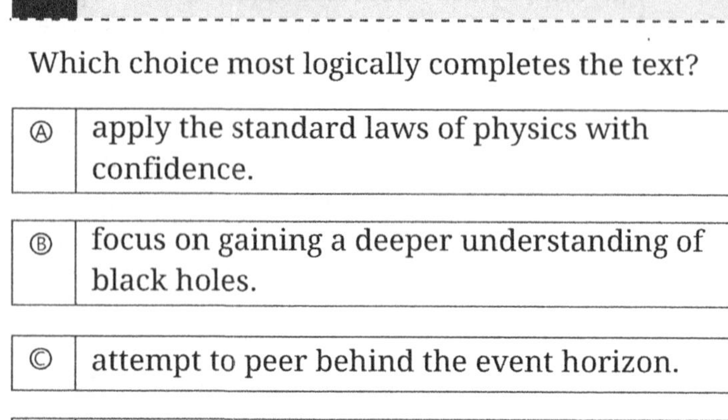

1 Mark for Review

Which choice most logically completes the text?

Ⓐ apply the standard laws of physics with confidence.

Ⓑ focus on gaining a deeper understanding of black holes.

Ⓒ attempt to peer behind the event horizon.

Ⓓ uncover phenomena not currently known to science.

Most grocery stores spray produce with water on a regular basis in order to ensure that they maintain a wholesome, fresh-picked appearance. However, according to Martin Lindstrom, author of *Brandwashed: Tricks Companies Use to Manipulate Our Minds and Persuade Us to Buy*, not only does this liquid lack any practical purpose, but it actually has a deleterious effect: _____

2 Mark for Review

Which choice most logically completes the text?

Ⓐ shoppers are unlikely to purchase fruits and vegetables that appear dry and withered.

Ⓑ moisture causes picked vegetables to spoil more quickly than they otherwise would.

Ⓒ certain vegetables lose some of their nutrients when they are boiled.

Ⓓ produce must be watered at predictable intervals in order to appeal to consumers.

Although it is widely assumed that cognitive bias clouds our assessment of the people around us, a group of researchers at the Santa Fe Institute has found that people's estimations of what their friends and family believe are often largely correct. That's because as highly social creatures, we have become very good at sizing up those around us—what researchers call "social sensing." It is therefore possible ______

3 Mark for Review

Which choice most logically completes the text?

Ⓐ to gather highly accurate information about trends by asking about individuals about their social circles rather than their own beliefs.

Ⓑ to determine people's views on a variety of topics by analyzing the ways in which they interact with others.

Ⓒ to discover what people truly believe about an issue by asking them to reflect on their personal biases.

Ⓓ to develop an algorithm that reliably predicts people's preferences about a wide range of items.

One of the most startling discoveries of the early 21st century was that Indo-European languages seem not to have been spread by Anatolian farmers living in what is now Turkey, as was commonly thought, but rather by a people called the Yamnaya, horse-herding nomads who lived on the Eurasian steppes more than 5,000 years ago. A host of linguistic evidence suggesting this possibility was first compiled persuasively by archaeologist David Anthony in 2007; DNA evidence later proved he was on target, showing that ______

4 Mark for Review

Which choice most logically completes the text?

Ⓐ members of tribes from the steppes arrived in Germany sometime between 2500 and 2000 BCE.

Ⓑ the Yamnaya were a genetic blend of three separate Eurasian populations.

Ⓒ around 5,000 years ago, the Yamnaya's genes began to appear throughout Europe and Asia.

Ⓓ the Yamnayans were linguistically unique in comparison to other groups from the same period.

When Isaac Newton published the *Principia* in 1687, his laws of motion solved numerous problems in physics; however, they also introduced a new conundrum, which was not fully grasped until centuries after Newton and which still poses a problem for cosmologists today. Essentially, Newton's laws work about twice as well as they are intended: they describe the everyday world that people move through, but they also account perfectly well for a world in which people walk backwards, clocks tick from evening to morning, and ______

5 Mark for Review

Which choice most logically completes the text?

Ⓐ objects interact unpredictably with one another.

Ⓑ planets that are in motion remain in motion.

Ⓒ particles of different weights move at varying speeds.

Ⓓ apples rise from the ground to the branches of a tree.

Exactly how Mars was formed approximately 4.5 billion years ago is a mystery, although there are several theories. One idea is that the planet was created via a titanic collision of rocks in space, spawning an all-encompassing magma ocean. When it cooled, a crust with high levels of basalt was formed. Another possibility is that parts of the first crust on Mars had a different origin, one that would primarily show large concentrations of silica. Planetary geochemist Valerie Payré and her partners analyzed data for the planet's southern hemisphere, the planet's oldest region. They discovered nine locations rich in feldspar, a mineral associated with lava flows that are higher in silica than basalt. This finding led them to conclude that ______

6 Mark for Review

Which choice most logically completes the text?

Ⓐ portions of Mars' surface were never covered by a crust.

Ⓑ the magma ocean formed from rocks colliding in space was not all-encompassing.

Ⓒ the southern hemisphere of Mars contained more silica than was previously believed.

Ⓓ the first crust on Mars did not develop until long after the planet was formed.

Liquid interfaces—the boundaries where two groups of liquid meet—are only a few atoms thick and until recently were almost impossible to study: the large bulk of molecules that clump on either side of the interface drowned out signals from the interface itself and created a lot of noise in experimental data. Researchers at the SLAC National Energy Laboratory may have found a solution, however: by shooting fine jets of water and oil at each other, they created liquid layers only a few hundreds of atoms thick. As a result, ______

7 Mark for Review

Which choice most logically completes the text?

Ⓐ the two substances emerged in purified form.

Ⓑ the groups of molecules surrounding the interface became even thicker.

Ⓒ tiny crests of waves caused the water to behave as if it were a gas.

Ⓓ the interfaces where the liquids interacted could be more easily observed.

To find out how the brain processes multiple languages, a team of cognitive scientists led by Ev Fedorenko and Saima Malik-Moraleda scanned the brains of 25 polyglots. Using imaging technology, they mapped neural language networks while study participants listened to brief recordings in familiar and unfamiliar languages. The researchers found that when participants heard any of the foreign languages they had studied, the same brain regions were always activated, although responses were strongest when languages were close to a person's native tongue. When subjects heard the language to which they had been exposed since birth, however, their neural networks were much less active. This trend held even when they were fluent in their other familiar languages, suggesting that ______

8 Mark for Review

Which choice most logically completes the text?

Ⓐ people can achieve fluency in a foreign language until relatively late in life.

Ⓑ learning a new language increases the efficiency of neural processing.

Ⓒ the brain processes languages acquired early in life with greater efficiency.

Ⓓ native-level fluency cannot be achieved in a language learned after early childhood.

Lightning is typically associated with storm clouds, which consist of turbulent masses of water droplets. In these clouds, water droplets drawn to the top of the cloud by updrafts freeze. When they are eventually pushed downward, the frozen droplets collide with uprising liquid droplets. The impact strips electrons from the molecules, resulting in the electrification of the cloud. However, scientists have found that coarse marine aerosols, such as salt from sea spray, can reduce the frequency of lightning. The particles weaken updrafts within the cloud, causing droplets to fall as rain instead of rising upward to form ice and thus ______

9 Mark for Review

Which choice most logically completes the text?

Ⓐ minimizing the chance that clouds will become electrified.

Ⓑ increasing thunderstorms' power.

Ⓒ creating unpredictable weather patterns.

Ⓓ making lightning more likely to strike over water than on land.

It was once thought that acquiring perfect pitch depended on a "critical period" early in life during which children could acquire this skill with training, or that only some children with a specific genetic endowment could acquire perfect pitch during this period. Adults, it was believed, could not acquire perfect pitch once that developmental window closed. However, research has shown that with only a short period of training, some adults can learn to remember notes, and can correctly identify them even months later with higher accuracy than they had been able to beforehand. The researchers therefore concluded that ______

10 Mark for Review

Which choice most logically completes the text?

Ⓐ to develop perfect pitch, children should begin musical training at a young age.

Ⓑ the influence of genetics on musical ability is extremely limited.

Ⓒ the development of perfect pitch may depend on general auditory capabilities.

Ⓓ the process of acquiring perfect pitch is more flexible than previously believed.

Answers: Text Completions

1. A

The second-to-last sentence includes the transition *yet*, which indicates key information: although singularities may involve all sorts of mysterious processes, they have no real-world effect. Thus, scientists can ignore them. The correct answer must restate or be consistent with this idea. (A) is correct because if singularities don't have an effect, then scientists can treat everything as normal and apply the usual laws of physics. (B) is unrelated to the required idea, and (C) and (D) both contradict the idea of ignoring puzzling aspects of black holes and maintaining the existing scientific framework.

2. B

The key phrase occurs right before the blank: *not only does the liquid [used to water fresh produce] lack any practical purpose, but it has a deleterious* (damaging) *effect*. The information that follows must logically explain that effect. (A) does not explain the negative impact of watering on already-picked fruits and vegetables—the fact that shoppers are unlikely to select produce in poor condition is irrelevant to this section of the passage. (C) is incorrect because the passage focuses only on the effects of water on uncooked vegetables. (D) incorrectly states a positive effect of watering produce. (B) is correct because faster spoilage is a negative effect of spraying fresh fruits and vegetables with water.

3. A

This is a good example of a question in which the answer is very nearly stated in the passage. The text makes clear that people are generally pretty accurate in identifying the beliefs of their friends and family members, so logically it must be possible to gather accurate information about trends by asking individuals what the people close to them think rather than what they themselves think—which is exactly what (A) says. (B) is incorrect because the passage focuses on beliefs, not interactions. (C) says exactly the opposite of what is indicated by the passage—reliable information can be obtained by asking people about others, not themselves. (D) goes way beyond the scope of the passage, which does not discuss the role of technology in determining people's preferences at all.

4. C

The statement immediately before the blank indicates that David Anthony was *on target*, so the blank must refer to evidence supporting his theory. What was Anthony's theory? That Indo-European languages were spread by the Yamnaya, *horse-herding nomads who lived on the Eurasian steppes more than 5,000 years ago*. Note that to identify this information, you must essentially back up to the beginning of the passage—the phrase *this possibility* in the last (second) sentence refers to an idea described in the previous (first) sentence, and there is no way to make sense out of the passage without knowing what that idea is. The correct answer must support it with information indicating that the Yamnaya moved throughout the regions, plural, where Indo-European languages became established. (A) focuses on Germany, which is only one area, so it can be eliminated. (B) is off-topic—the Yamnaya's genetic roots are irrelevant to the argument. (D) does not fit because the correct answer must involve the Yamnaya's migration and its eventual effects. Even though this option mentions the Yamnaya's language, it does not mention how its influence was spread. Only (C) contains that information: if "the Yamnaya's genes appeared throughout Europe and Asia," these people must have been present in many regions, hence the spread of their language.

5. D

The first two examples in the list describe situations in which things run backwards, so logically, the final item in the list must describe a normal occurrence that is reversed. Objects interacting unpredictably; planets remaining in motion; and particles of different weights moving at varying speeds are not examples of a phenomenon running backwards. Only apples rising back to a tree, rather than falling from one, illustrates the required idea. (D) is thus correct.

6. B

This is a complicated question, so we're going to break it down into parts. Notice that the process outlined here requires you to work backwards through the passage. First, what is the finding? That nine regions of Mars were rich in feldspar, which is *associated with lava flows that are higher in silica than basalt.* What is the significance of this finding? It supports the theory that *parts of the first crust on Mars had a different origin.* A different origin from what? From the *all-encompassing magma ocean* that was created from rocks colliding in space. Logically, if parts of the crust were formed from something other than the magma ocean, then the ocean could not have been *all-encompassing* (covering everything). And that is what (B) says. (A) is incorrect because the passage only discusses the origins of the first crust that did exist on Mars—there is nothing to suggest that there were places without a crust. (C) is incorrect because the passage indicates only that feldspar, which is found in Mars's southern hemisphere, is *higher in silica than basalt.* The passage does not indicate how much silica researchers previously believed was present. (D) does not work either because the passage only mentions that Mars was formed around 4.5 billion years ago and the southern hemisphere is Mars's oldest region—there is no mention of when the crust formed, and the amount of feldspar and silica in that area is not discussed in relation to any particular timeline.

7. D

To answer this question, you must identify the problem that the experiment was designed to solve—otherwise, you will have no way of determining the answer. The passage explains that liquid interfaces are *almost impossible to study* because the molecules of liquid "clump" on either side of the interface—that is, the boundary between the two substances—preventing researchers from understanding what happens there. The experiment used fine (very thin) jets to prevent that clumping so that they could better observe how the molecules behaved at the boundaries, i.e., the interfaces "could be more easily observed." That corresponds directly to (D). (A) and (C) are completely off-topic, and (B) indicates exactly the opposite of what would be expected—the fine jets were used to prevent clumping.

8. C

Start by breaking the argument down: the study found that listening to a known foreign language activated language networks in the brain (i.e., neural language networks). However, listening to one's native language—which the subjects obviously knew best of all—did not result in the same level of activation. In other words, the brain didn't have to work very hard. Why would this be the case? Logically, because understanding one's first language—a language acquired from birth—is an automatic process, one that requires very little effort and is therefore "very efficient." The only answer consistent with that idea is (C). In contrast, (A) is unsupported by the passage. The text only indicates that some of the participants were fluent in at least one other language—it says nothing about when those languages were learned. (B) contradicts the text: study participants' brains worked harder (i.e., were less efficient) when they listened to a foreign language they knew. Be careful with (D): the text states only that participants' neural networks were activated when they heard a foreign language that they spoke fluently (the implication being that they had to work harder to understand it than their first language). The passage does not, however, indicate what level of fluency those people had achieved, nor does it go so far as to imply that native-level fluency in a second language cannot be achieved at all.

9. A

The key piece of information occurs in the second-to-last sentence, which contains the key word *found.* What did scientists find? That *coarse marine aerosols...can reduce the frequency of lightning*. The last sentence explains how this is accomplished. As a result, the text must be completed with a statement indicating that lightning occurs less often or, in other words, that the "chance that clouds will become electrified" is "minimized." (A) is thus correct. (B) says exactly the opposite of what the passage implies, and (C) and (D) are both unsupported by the relevant section of the passage.

10. D

(A) is contradicted by the passage, which states that some adults can acquire the ability to remember notes. That means that it is not necessary to begin developing that skill in early childhood in order to obtain it. (B) is outside the scope of the passage, which focuses specifically on perfect pitch rather than musical ability as a whole. (C) is neither supported nor contradicted by the passage—there is no mention of the relationship between the development of perfect pitch and other "auditory capabilities." (D) correctly states the logical conclusion of the study: if some people are able to develop perfect pitch in adulthood, that contradicts the old assumption that the skill is either completely natural or that it must be acquired very early in life. In other words, the "process of acquiring [it] is more flexible than previously believed."

8 Supporting & Undermining

"Support" and "undermine" questions belong to the same inference family as text completions but require you to go a step further. Rather than just ask you to identify a logical conclusion, they ask you to move beyond a stated hypothesis or conclusion and identify a statement that would either support or undermine (weaken) it.

While some simpler questions asking test-takers to support or illustrate an argument may appear at the beginning of a Reading/Writing section, the most challenging of these items are likely to appear among the later Reading questions—that is, just before the first Writing questions.

As is true for text completions, if you approach these questions methodically, they have the potential to become quite straightforward. **But you can't get impatient, and you can't skip steps.** If you're not really certain what a question is asking, OR you don't feel that you can focus properly, you are better off skipping it and returning to it after you have answered the Writing questions.

The process for answering support/undermine questions can be broken into three main steps:

1) Identify the claim and rephrase it if necessary.

If the claim or theory is stated simply in the question, take a second and process it so that you're clear on what it is. If it is worded more complexly, rephrase it in simpler language and jot it down on your scratch paper. You can't determine whether a set of lines would support or weaken an idea unless you know what that idea is.

2) Determine what sort of information would support or weaken the claim.

You should at least attempt to get a basic sense of this on your own. Do not assume you'll be able to recognize the information from the answer choices, which by definition are written to confuse you.

3) Check the answers.

If you've done steps one and two carefully, the option closest to what you've said should be correct.

Illustrating a Claim

We're going to start with the most straightforward type of "support" question, which asks you to identify the statement that best illustrates a main idea.

In comparison to the question types we'll look at later in this chapter, "illustrate" questions are more likely to accompany **prose fiction** or **poetry** passages. As always, you are not expected to have any pre-existing knowledge of the work in question—all the necessary background information will be explicitly provided.

That said, you may still need to navigate challenging, old-fashioned, and possibly metaphorical language in order to understand what an author or poet is literally saying. For example, consider the following question.

"Slow Through the Dark" is an early 1900s poem by Paul Laurence Dunbar. In the poem, the speaker urges the listener not to lose hope, even in difficult circumstances.

1 Mark for Review

Which quotation from "Slow Through the Dark" most effectively illustrates the claim?

Ⓐ "Slow moves the pageant of a climbing race; / Their footsteps drag far, far below the height,"

Ⓑ "No strange, swift–sprung exception we; we trace / A devious way thro' dim, uncertain light,— ."

Ⓒ "Heed not the darkness round you, dull and deep; / The clouds grow thickest when the summit's nigh."

Ⓓ "Who stoppeth here to spend a while in sleep / Or curseth that the storm obscures the sky?"

Let's start by reiterating the basics: the question is asking us to identify the lines in which the speaker urges the listener to remain hopeful in a tough situation. As a result, the correct answer must convey the idea of hope.

We can assume upfront that (D) is incorrect because it cites a question, which goes against the idea of urging (encouraging) someone. (A) does not fit either because its focus is on [dragging] footsteps, which has nothing to do with encouraging someone to be hopeful. (B) can likewise be eliminated: the word *we* includes the speaker, and we want an answer in which the speaker addresses someone else.

(C) is the best fit. The phrase *Heed not the darkness round you*—in other words, do not give into despair— is essentially an order not to lose hope when circumstances are difficult.

Supporting a Claim

"Support" questions are similar to "illustrate" ones, but they are more likely to accompany science or social science passages and involve logical arguments rather than works of literature.

For example, take a look at the question below.

Marketers assume that the more choices they offer, the more likely customers will be able to find just the right thing. They assume, for instance, that offering 50 styles of jeans instead of two increases the chances that shoppers will come across a pair they really like. Nevertheless, research now shows that there can be too much choice; when there is, consumers are less likely to buy anything at all, and if they do buy, they are less satisfied with their selection.

1 Mark for Review

Which finding, if true, would most strongly support the conclusions of the research described in the underlined section?

Ⓐ People faced with choosing among a large number of options experience physical symptoms associated with feeling overwhelmed.

Ⓑ Consumers given a choice of 10 jams in a taste test were more likely to make a purchase than consumers who were offered only five.

Ⓒ Shoppers who purchased food from multiple stores spent more on groceries than shoppers who purchased all their food from a single store.

Ⓓ Some companies have increased the number of products they offer in order to appeal to a wider range of consumer preferences.

As always, we're going to start by summarizing the relevant section of the passage, in this case the research described in the underlined section.

What does that research show? That when faced with too many choices, consumers are less likely to make a purchase, and if they do make one, they are less likely to be happy with it. The correct answer must include a finding consistent with that idea.

(B) can easily be eliminated since it directly contradicts the passage—people given more choices would be less likely to buy jam, not more. (C) and (D) go in the wrong direction as well since they imply that more choice leads to a positive outcome.

Only (A) fits. Feeling overwhelmed when confronted with too many options would make people less likely to make a choice or be happy with a choice they've made. (A) is thus correct.

Let's look at another, more challenging question.

As a person sleeps, the motor cortex—the part of the brain that controls movements—replays skills that it learned during the day. In a recent experiment run by the BrainGate consortium, researchers observed that the pattern of firing neurons sped up during sleep, echoing findings from previous animal studies. The scientists were also interested to note that replay took place not during REM sleep, which is when people normally dream, but during deep, slow-wave sleep, which occurs in the first three or four hours of the night. They theorize that replay during this period helps the brain consolidate new information, moving it from short-term to long-term memory.

1 Mark for Review

Which finding, if true, would most strongly support the scientists' theory?

Ⓐ Athletes who slept for at least seven hours before a game competed at a higher level than ones who slept for less time.

Ⓑ People whose neuron firings increased in speed during REM sleep retained new information over a longer period of time than people whose neurons fired more quickly early in their sleep cycle.

Ⓒ Students who slept for only a few hours before an exam showed no difference in performance when compared to students who slept for a full night.

Ⓓ Dancers who slept for several hours shortly after learning a new routine knew it better two weeks later than a group that stayed awake.

The question indicates that we will need to identify a statement that supports the scientists' theory, so it is necessary to read the passage with that key word in mind. It appears in a different form in the last sentence, telling us scientists ***theorize*** *that replay during the period* (i.e., during slow-wave sleep, early in the night) *helps the brain consolidate new information, moving it from short-term to long-term memory.*

Next, we need to think about what type of scenario would support the claim that replaying new skills during slow-wave sleep helps people retain what they have learned in the long term.

(A) No. This answer only involves an amount of sleep; it says nothing about consolidating new skills.

(B) No, but be careful. This choice refers to "retaining new information" but incorrectly ties it to REM sleep. The passage, in contrast, discusses a phenomenon that does NOT occur during REM sleep.

(C) No. The passage discusses an effect that improves learning—if two groups performed identically, that would not be the case.

(D) Yes, this fits. The passage discusses a phenomenon that happens early in the sleep cycle, which means that it would occur in people who only slept for several hours. If dancers who slept that amount after learning a new routine knew it better after two weeks (i.e., longer-term) than dancers who did not sleep at all, that supports the idea that replay early in sleep consolidates learning.

Undermining a Claim

"Undermine" or "weaken" questions are based on the same logic and involve the same process as "support" questions—they just go in the opposite direction, asking you to identify the statement most <u>in</u>consistent with a given theory or conclusion.

For example, consider the passage below.

Dinosaurs, with the exception of the ancestors of birds, disappeared during a mass extinction 65 million years ago when an asteroid struck the Earth. Because a high metabolic rate has generally been suggested as one of the key advantages when it comes to surviving mass extinctions, some genetic paleontologists have proposed that birds survived while non-avian dinosaurs did not because of the birds' increased metabolic capacity.

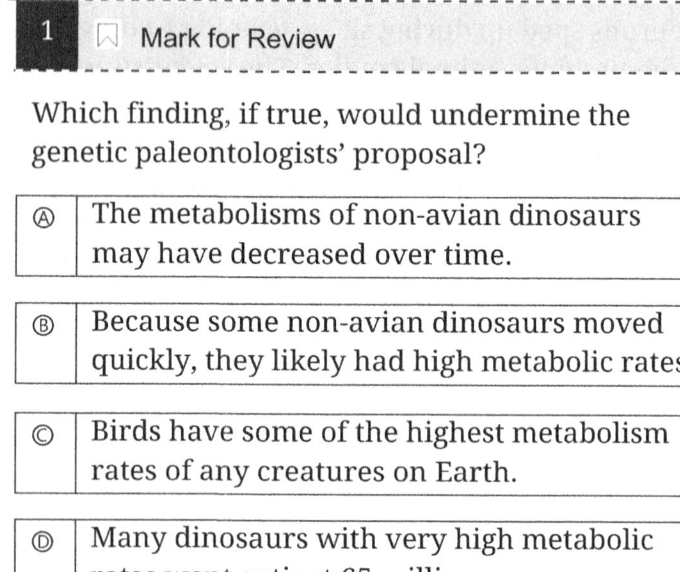

1 Mark for Review

Which finding, if true, would undermine the genetic paleontologists' proposal?

Ⓐ The metabolisms of non-avian dinosaurs may have decreased over time.

Ⓑ Because some non-avian dinosaurs moved quickly, they likely had high metabolic rates.

Ⓒ Birds have some of the highest metabolism rates of any creatures on Earth.

Ⓓ Many dinosaurs with very high metabolic rates went extinct 65 million years ago.

The first step is to identify the genetic paleontologists' proposal—without that information, we cannot know what sort of statement would weaken it. The information appears in the last sentence: *birds survived [the mass extinction 65 million years ago] while non-avian dinosaurs did not because of the birds' increased metabolic capacity.*

In other words, metabolic capacity ↑, chances of surviving a mass extinction ↑.

To weaken that claim, we need to find an answer supporting the opposite:

- Metabolic capacity ↑, chances of surviving a mass extinction ↓.

OR:

- Metabolic capacity ↑, no effect on chances of surviving a mass extinction.

If we hold very tight to that idea and don't allow ourselves to become confused by any of the other options, we can identify (D) as the sole choice consistent with that idea. By definition, the extinction of creatures with high metabolic rates contradicts the claim that having a high metabolic rate prevents animals from going extinct.

Note that not trying too hard to wrap your head around the wrong answers is really key here. If you got caught up in trying to work out the logic behind them, you could really waste a lot of time—which is itself a sign that those options are incorrect.

Exercise: Supporting and Undermining

"Gerarda" is an 1895 poem by Eloise Bibb. In the poem, Bibb emphasizes the contrast between the way in which objects are depicted in Gerarda's paintings and their true appearance, writing ______

1 Mark for Review

Which quotation from "Gerarda" effectively illustrates the claim?

Ⓐ But in her spiritual world she leaves
Her mind, her thoughts, her soul, her brain,

Ⓑ Her paintings hang upon the wall,
The power of genius stamps them all;

Ⓒ Now to-day o'er canvas bent,
She strives to place these visions sent

Ⓓ And thus her pictures plainly show,
Not nature's self but ideal glow.

"Frederick Douglass" is an 1895 poem by Paul Laurence Dunbar. In the poem, Dunbar praises Douglass for his honesty and refusal to be intimidated, writing ______

2 Mark for Review

Which quotation from "Frederick Douglass" effectively illustrates the claim?

Ⓐ No miser in the good he held was he,--
His kindness followed his horizon's rim

Ⓑ A hush is over all the teeming lists,
And there is pause, a breath-space in the strife;

Ⓒ And he was no soft-tongued apologist;
He spoke straightforward, fearlessly uncowed;

Ⓓ He was her champion thro' direful years,
And held her weal all other ends above.

"Left-digit" bias, in which people focus on the first digit of a number and ignore the last, is a well-documented phenomenon that explains why prices tend to end in "9". According to a recent study by researchers in California and Sweden, it also influences journalists' coverage of unemployment rates. When jobless levels and the amount of change in unemployment rates are similar in two regions, crossing a round number informs reporters' assessment of the story's newsworthiness—even when both figures fall within the same margin of error.

3 Mark for Review

Which finding, if true, would most directly support the researchers' finding?

Ⓐ The Bureau of Labor Statistics publishes a report of unemployment rates by state, rounding its statistics to the nearest decimal place.

Ⓑ The mention of high unemployment figures in a newspaper caused consumer spending to drop by almost 2.5% in one city.

Ⓒ A city newspaper ran several stories about joblessness when the unemployment rate reached 5% but quickly stopped coverage of the issue.

Ⓓ A newspaper published significantly fewer stories about local unemployment when the jobless rate was 3.9% than when it rose to 4.1%.

One argument that is commonly cited to support the idea that birds lack a sense of smell is that some birds' olfactory bulbs are relatively small. As a result, many scientists concluded that these creatures gave up smell in favor of improved eyesight. This notion became so pervasive that it once was repeated to avian expert Danielle Whittaker as fact by a prominent neurobiologist.

4 Mark for Review

Which finding, if true, would most undermine the neurobiologist's statement?

Ⓐ An analysis of avian genomes revealed the presence of proteins that bind to odors and relay a signal to the brain.

Ⓑ The number of olfactory neurons is much smaller in birds than in most other animals.

Ⓒ The odors that birds depend on for food and social relationships are quickly dispersed in the wind.

Ⓓ Birds sometimes overlook strongly scented prey in favor of animals that are more visually striking.

New research suggests that coffee could have a positive effect on cardiovascular health. Although caffeine is coffee's most well-known constituent, the beverage contains more than 100 biologically active components. In a study led by Jiyoung Kim, researchers at Seoul National University concluded that non-caffeinated compounds likely play a role in the positive relationship between coffee consumption and health.

5 Mark for Review

Which finding, if true, would most directly support the researchers' conclusion?

Ⓐ Whereas regular coffee contains from 70-140 mg of caffeine per cup, decaf contains approximately 0-7mg.

Ⓑ Decaffeinated coffee causes cells to produce NQO1, an enzyme that has neuroprotective benefits.

Ⓒ Extracts from caffeinated coffee have been shown to aid weight loss more than a placebo.

Ⓓ People who drink several cups of coffee every day are less vulnerable to certain diseases.

Scientists have long known that self-pollination can inhibit plants' ability to adapt to environmental changes, but until recently they did not know exactly how or how quickly the changes occurred. A group of researchers at Washington State University set up a controlled greenhouse experiment in which a group of monkeyflower plants were isolated from the bumblebees that normally pollinate them. Initially, the plants produced few seeds, but as they adapted to the self-pollination process, their seed production increased dramatically. In addition, their flowers changed shape to facilitate the transfer of pollen. However, scientists expected that the plants would eventually become more vulnerable to shifts in their environment.

6 Mark for Review

Which finding, if true, would most directly support the scientists' expectation?

Ⓐ Some flowers also received pollen from nearby flowering plants, a process that is known as geitonogamy.

Ⓑ The plants' genetic variation decreased by 25% over nine generations, making them more susceptible to a variety of pathogens.

Ⓒ None of the plants contained the types of genetic defects that are typically found in the wild.

Ⓓ By eliminating the transfer of pollen grains, the plants were able to reduce the amount of pollen wasted by 60%.

It was only when Alma Thomas turned away from figurative art and toward abstraction that she rose to acclaim as an artist. When the solidity of her line gave way to broken, vibrant colors, the beauty she had long seen emerged.

7 Mark for Review

Which choice, if true, would most effectively support the writer's claim?

Ⓐ Her painting *Starry Night and the Astronauts* (1972) includes a small kaleidoscope of red, orange, and yellow that suggests the spaceship Apollo 10.

Ⓑ Thomas was fascinated by the natural world, incorporating everything from the flowers in her garden to the stars in the night sky into her paintings.

Ⓒ Her *Still Life with Vases and Flowers* (1964), which contains realistic images, feels labored, whereas *Lunar Surface* (1970) glows with rich splashes of purple and blue.

Ⓓ Although Thomas's own works focused on nature, she believed that art could also evoke the energy of airplanes, cars, skyscrapers, and electric signals.

Middlemarch is an 1871 novel by George Eliot. In the story, a young woman named Dorothea Brooke becomes engaged to a scholar named Mr. Casaubon. In describing Dorothea's motives for marriage, Eliot emphasizes her belief that she and Mr. Causabon have a great deal in common.

8 Mark for Review

Which quotation from *Middlemarch* effectively illustrates the claim?

Ⓐ Dorothea by this time had looked deep into the ungauged reservoir of Mr. Casaubon's mind, seeing reflected there in vague labyrinthine extension every quality she herself brought;

Ⓑ If it had really occurred to Mr. Casaubon to think of Miss Brooke as a suitable wife for him, the reasons that might induce her to accept him were already planted in her mind.

Ⓒ His notes already made a formidable range of volumes, but the crowning task would be to condense these voluminous still-accumulating results and bring them to fit a little shelf.

Ⓓ But in this case Mr. Casaubon's confidence was not likely to be falsified, for Dorothea heard and retained what he said with the eager interest of a fresh young nature to which every variety in experience is an epoch.

To find out whether people are more likely to follow recommendations in auditory or visual form, researchers Shwetha Mariadassou, Christopher Bechler, and Jonathan Levav ran a series of experiments in which participants were exposed to recommendations either spoken aloud or printed on a screen. They found that people were consistently more likely to adhere to the spoken recommendations, even ones from an electronically generated voice. Further investigation revealed that the auditory messages were more effective because they disappeared immediately after being spoken and were thus perceived as more urgent. The researchers therefore concluded that the length of exposure rather than specific visual or auditory properties was responsible for the differing responses.

9 Mark for Review

Which finding, if true, would most directly support the researchers' conclusion?

Ⓐ People are more likely to listen to recommendations conveyed in both auditory and print form than to recommendations conveyed in a single form.

Ⓑ When printed recommendations are flashed on a screen for no more than a few seconds, they are as likely to be followed as spoken recommendations.

Ⓒ Auditory recommendations that are spoken slowly are more likely to be followed than ones that are spoken quickly.

Ⓓ Although recommendations spoken by an electronically generated voice are less effective than those spoken by a human voice, they are more likely to be followed than printed recommendations.

The Romans began making concrete more than 2,000 years ago, but the formula used to mix it resulted in a substance that was not as strong as the modern product. However, structures such as the Pantheon and the Colosseum have survived for centuries, often with little to no maintenance. The properties of Roman concrete were traditionally attributed to its use of volcanic ash, which can react with water to produce a strong concrete. Small, white chunks of lime known as clasts were also present, but researchers believed that these were the result of poor mixing and did not affect the concrete's durability.

10 Mark for Review

Which finding, if true, would most directly contradict the researchers' belief?

Ⓐ When limestone is heated to high temperatures, it produces a highly reactive powder known as quicklime.

Ⓑ Lime clasts are made of calcium carbonate and formed at very high temperatures.

Ⓒ Clasts are associated with a type of concrete that sets more quickly than other types.

Ⓓ Lime reacts with water to form a calcium-rich solution capable of gluing cracks in concrete together.

Answers: Supporting and Undermining

1. D

The question indicates that the correct answer must support the idea that Bibb "emphasizes the contrast between appearance and reality." As you read through the answer choices, look for a word such as *but* or *yet* that will indicate a contrast: (A) and (D) both contain *but,* whereas (B) and (C) do not include this type of language and can be assumed to be incorrect. (A) does not fit because it does not mention Gerarda's paintings, whereas (D) both mentions her "pictures" and refers to "not nature's self (= reality) but ideal glow (= appearance)." (D) is thus correct.

2. C

Start by defining the claim: *Dunbar praises Douglass for his honesty and refusal to be intimidated.* The correct answer must be positive and illustrate these qualities. (A) refers to "kindness," but that is not quite a match, so this option can be eliminated. (B) is a relatively neutral description that does not involve the necessary criteria. Although (D) is positive, this answer is off-topic as well. (C) is correct because it indicates that Douglass felt no need to apologize, spoke in a "straightforward" manner, and was "fearlessly uncowed" (not intimidated).

3. D

If you scan the passage, you'll find the word *researchers* in the second sentence. The rest of the passage is essentially dedicated to describing what they found: "left-digit" bias affects whether journalists cover unemployment rates, and employment figures that cross a round number (a number ending in zero) attract more attention than ones that do not. The correct answer must therefore provide an example of a situation in which coverage of a jobless rate increased when it crossed a round number. The only answer that meets this requirement is (D): the change from 3.9% to 4.1% unemployment was very small, but the jump over a round number correlated with greater coverage of the issue. (A) is completely off-topic, and (B) does not fit because the passage does not even mention consumer spending. (C) describes an increase in unemployment coverage when the jobless rate reached a round number (5%), but the last part of the answer ("quickly stopped coverage") does not fit. There is also no comparison to the amount of coverage unemployment received when the rate was below 5%, making this a weaker answer than (D).

4. A

What did the neurobiologist say? That *these creatures* (i.e., birds) *gave up smell in favor of improved eyesight.* This is an "undermine" question, so the correct answer must contradict that idea. Most logically, it will indicate that birds have both good eyesight and a sense of smell. The relationship between (A) and the claim in question may not be immediately obvious, but consider it carefully: if avian (bird) genomes suggest that birds are physiologically capable of perceiving odors, that would suggest they do in fact have a sense of smell. So keep (A). The presence of an unusually small number of olfactory neurons in birds would support rather than undermine the claim in question, so (B) can be eliminated. (C) and (D) have the same problem. In (C), if birds cannot rely on odors to find food, that would support the idea that they did not evolve a sense of smell. And in (D), ignoring strong scents in favor of visual information suggests a poor sense of smell.

5. B

What is the researchers' conclusion? That *non-caffeinated compounds likely play a role in the positive relationship between coffee consumption and health*. The correct answer must therefore be consistent with the idea that something other than caffeine is responsible for coffee's health benefits. (A) has no relationship to this argument; the fact that decaf contains trace amounts of caffeine is irrelevant. (C) is incorrect because it focuses on the health benefits of caffeinated rather than decaffeinated coffee, and (D) does not quite work because it does not indicate what type of coffee is involved. It supports the idea that coffee has health benefits, but not the idea that something other than caffeine is responsible for them. Only (B) works: if decaf causes the production of an enzyme with "neuroprotective benefits" (i.e., that protects the brain), then caffeine is presumably not the cause.

6. B

What is the scientists' expectation? If you're not sure where to look for this information, focus on the end of the passage, where key information in support/undermine questions (and text completions) is most likely to be located. Indeed, the word *expected* appears in the last sentence. Basically, the scientists expected that although the self-pollinating plants appeared to be doing well, they would eventually develop a weakness that would make them *more vulnerable to shifts in their environment*. The correct answer must be consistent with that idea. (A) and (D) are off-topic and can be eliminated. (C) would weaken rather than support the expectation: plants without genetic defects would be <u>less</u> likely to become vulnerable to disease. (B) is correct because an almost 25% decrease in genetic diversity that left plants more "susceptible" (i.e., *vulnerable*) to diseases would be directly consistent with the researchers' expectations.

7. C

What is the writer's claim? That the beauty of Alma Thomas's work emerged when she moved away from figurative art and began to work abstractly. The correct answer must support or illustrate that idea. (A) mentions Thomas's use of color but does not indicate whether this painting was figurative or abstract. (B) is off-topic, focusing on the subject matter of Thomas's work rather than its style. (D) is incorrect for the same reason. Only (C) offers an explicit contrast between Thomas's "labored" early figurative work and "glow[ing]" abstract later work.

8. A

What is the claim? That Dorothea believes she and Mr. Casaubon have many things in common. The correct answer must therefore emphasize Dorothea's belief in their similarity. The main challenge in this question is sorting through the dense, old-fashioned language and understanding what each quotation is literally saying. (A) is correct because it indicates that Dorothea sees "every quality" of her own reflected in Mr. Casaubon. In other words, she perceives him as very similar, if not downright identical, to her. (B) indicates only that Dorothea ("Miss Brooke") is already interested in marrying Mr. Casaubon—this answer says nothing about their similarities. (C) is off-topic, focusing on Mr. Casaubon and not mentioning Dorothea at all. (D) is incorrect as well because it only conveys the idea that Dorothea is extremely interested in what Mr. Casaubon has to say because of her youth; it does not explicitly mention that she views him as being similar to her.

9. B

To identify what sort of information would logically support the researchers' conclusion, you must identify the key phrase—*length of exposure*—because it tells you that the correct answer must focus on time. The phrases "no more than a few seconds" in (B) and "very slowly" in (C) suggest right away that one of these answers is correct and that the others are off-topic. (C) does not work, however, because it implies the opposite of the researchers' findings, namely that recommendations become more effective when they are presented quickly. (B) is correct because it supports this idea: if people are more likely to follow spoken recommendations because the words disappear immediately after being said, then logically they are also likely to follow written recommendations if the words disappear quickly ("are flashed on a screen").

10. D

The question asks about the researchers' "belief," so the key information is located in the last sentence, which states that *researchers believed that [the lime clasts] were the result of poor mixing and did not affect the concrete's durability* (i.e., its ability to last a long time). The correct answer must therefore convey the opposite idea, namely that lime clasts make concrete stronger and more able to last a long time. The only answer that contains information with this implication is (D): if lime helps "[glue] cracks in concrete together," then logically it makes concrete stronger and more durable. The other answers neither support nor contradict the idea that lime clasts make concrete stronger.

9 Graphs & Charts

Graph- and chart-based questions come in a variety of shapes, sizes, and layouts, and range from simple and straightforward to seemingly very complex. While they tend to involve scientific topics, you are likely to encounter some social science ones as well. They may also overlap with other question types, for example doubling as text completions or support/undermine questions. If you do well in Reading/Writing Module 1, you should expect to encounter one or two more challenging items in Module 2.

In general, the information most directly relevant to the question will be presented at the **end** of the passage. As is true for text completions, the first sentence or two will often serve primarily to provide context. In many if not most cases, you can therefore skim through the introductory material and then slow down towards the end, paying very close attention to the last sentence. If you find it helpful to do so, you may even want to highlight the key words so that you know exactly what type of information you are looking for.

In principle, graph questions are designed to make you synthesize multiple sources—a passage, a question plus answer choices, and a graphic. In reality, however, these items are rarely as complicated as they appear.

The first thing to keep in mind is that you are not expected to have any prior knowledge of the topics. No matter how complex the terminology may seem—and you are likely to encounter some very technical and unfamiliar terms—all of the information you need to answer the questions will be right there in front of you. Provided that you get the gist of the key facts, you do not need to understand every word to get questions right.

The second thing to understand is that **while some questions may genuinely require you to use the passage along with information from the graph or chart, many answers can be identified based strictly on the wording of the question and the answer choices—it is unnecessary to look at the graphic at all**. This is particularly true for very complex-looking questions, which are essentially constructed to make you think that they are much harder than they actually are.

Even if information from the graph or chart is required to answer the question, you should **always begin by carefully reading the passage—usually the last sentence—and the question because these places tell you what claim or conclusion to focus on. In addition, you should pay close attention to key words such as *majority, half,* and *most common*.** Only a portion of the graph will be relevant to the question, and if you don't know where to focus your attention, you will waste time and energy.

In some instances, multiple answer choices will cite accurate information from the graphic; however, only one option will correspond to the specific focus in the question. Thus, **it is entirely possible to interpret a graph or chart perfectly and still end up with the wrong answer**. In such cases, ignoring the chart and focusing on the phrasing in the text portion of the question may, paradoxically, give you a much better chance of getting the question right.

While it is not a bad idea to double-check your answer against the graph, just to make sure you haven't overlooked anything, be careful not to start second-guessing yourself. If only one option matches the specific criteria indicated in the question, then it must be the correct answer by default.

Starting below, we're going to look at some examples of how to work through graphic-based questions, both when the graph is necessary and when it isn't.

Example #1

Let's start with something reasonably straightforward.

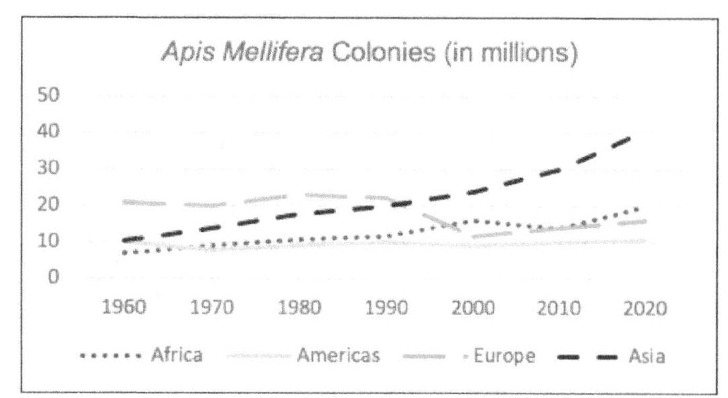

As part of a unit on pollination, a biology student is researching Colony Collapse Disorder, the mysterious disappearance of millions of honeybee (*Apis mellifera*) colonies in the early 2000s. Although many wild bee populations have continued to decline, the number of honeybees has actually increased on every continent. The student wants to **<u>emphasize</u> that in some regions, honeybee populations had not only <u>rebounded</u> by 2020 but also reached their <u>highest level</u> in 60 years.**

1 Mark for Review

Which region included in the graph should the student cite to support this claim?

Ⓐ Africa

Ⓑ Americas

Ⓒ Europe

Ⓓ Asia

As discussed earlier, we're going to start by focusing on the passage, particularly the last sentence. The word *emphasize* tells us that the key information will follow.

What does the "student" want to emphasize about honeybee populations in some regions in 2020? The sentence tells us that there are two conditions that must be met:

1) They had rebounded (i.e., increased after a decline).

2) They had reached their highest level since 1960 (the beginning of the graph).

For an answer to be correct, **both** of these things must be true.

In this case, the question is constructed so that we have no choice but to look at the graphic—the answer choices themselves provide no clue as to which option might be correct.

The graph itself does not contain any tricks: the four lines correspond to rises and falls in honeybee (*Apis mellifera*) populations on four continents during a 60-year period (1960-2020).

- To meet the "rebound" requirement, the correct line must go down and then up.

- To meet the "highest point" requirement, the line must be higher for the 2020 point than for any other year since 1960.

The only line that fits both those criteria is the line for Africa: there is a dip between 2000 and 2010, and the highest point (20 million) corresponds to 2020. (A) is thus correct.

Although the changes in the correct line are subtle in comparison to the changes for Europe and Asia, notice that the line's attachment to the "20 million" mark at the last data point clearly puts it higher in 2020 than at any other point.

Example #2

Next, we're going to look at a non-science example. Notice that the answer choices here contain much more information than the ones in the previous question.

The length of the answer choices suggests that the graph may not be important, so we're going to start by just looking at the passage and the questions. We'll consider the graph later, if we need it.

Despite steady gains in readership and overall popularity, e-books are hardly positioned to replace print books. Rather, the two types of media complement each other, providing the same content in different forms. Print books and e-books each have unique attributes and serve distinct purposes, which vary by demographic and situational factors. Researchers Yin Zhang and Sunali Kudva used data from the National Reading Habits Survey to examine book-format preferences in a variety of situations. Although the pair found that e-books are firmly established as an option due to ease of accessibility, they also **concluded that print books offer greater appeal to most readers in certain situations.**

1 Mark for Review

Which choice best describes data from the chart that supports Zhang and Kudva's finding?

Ⓐ A large majority of readers seeking immediate access to a book preferred the electronic option, with less than 25% of readers opting for print.

Ⓑ The percentage of readers who choose a format based on the variety of titles available was about 50% for both print books and e-books.

Ⓒ More than 75% of readers preferred print books for reading to a child, and more than 60% preferred print books for sharing with other readers.

Ⓓ When concerned about quick access or reading during travel, most readers preferred books in the same format.

The wording of the last sentence is key because it tells us what the researchers **concluded**: most readers—that is, **more than 50%**—prefer print books (dark gray bar) sometimes. Any answer that contradicts this idea or that has a different focus can be eliminated.

- (A) can be eliminated because the focus is on a situation in which readers prefer e-books.
- (B) doesn't fit because the focus is on a situation in which the numbers are roughly equal.
- (D) doesn't provide enough information to judge, although it is reasonable to assume that most readers who were traveling or seeking quick access to a book would want the electronic version.

(C) is a match, citing situations in which a clear majority of readers (75% and 60%, respectively) prefer print books. It's almost certainly the right answer, but we're going to look at the graph to be safe.

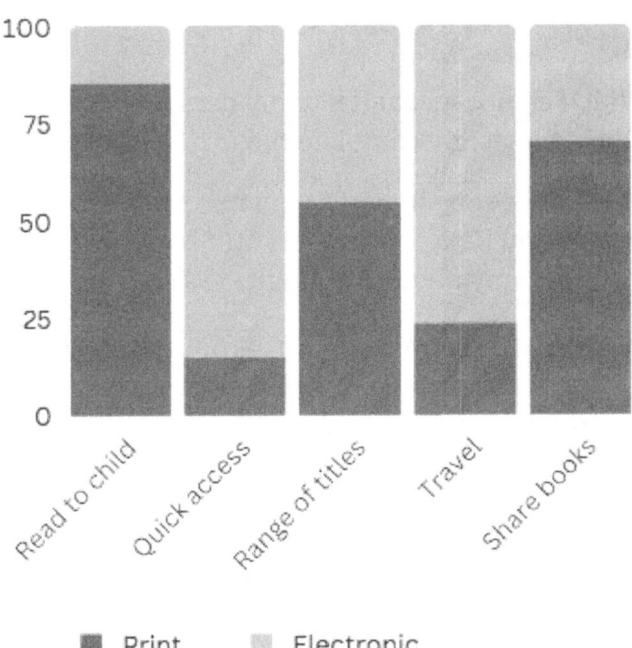

Despite steady gains in readership and overall popularity, e-books are hardly positioned to take over print books. Rather, the two types of media complement each other, providing the same content in different forms. Print books and e-books each have unique attributes and serve distinct purposes, which vary by demographic and situational factors. Rearchers Yin Zhang and Sunali Kudva used data from the National Reading Habits Survey to examine book-format preferences in a variety of situations. Although the pair found that e-books are firmly established as an option due to ease of accessibility, they also **concluded that print books offer greater appeal to most readers in certain situations.**

1 Mark for Review

Which choice best describes data from the chart that supports Zhang and Kudva's finding?

Ⓐ A large majority of readers seeking immediate access to a book preferred the electronic option, with less than 25% of readers opting for print.

Ⓑ The percentage of readers who choose a format based on the variety of titles available was about 50% for both print books and e-books.

Ⓒ More than 75% of readers preferred print books for reading to a child, and more than 60% preferred print books for sharing with other readers.

Ⓓ When concerned about quick access or reading during travel, most readers preferred books in the same format.

Yes, the print-book bars (dark gray) for "Quick access" and "Travel" are both much smaller than the e-book bars (light gray) on top. That indicates that a much smaller percentage of readers prefer print books in these situations. (D) can thus be conclusively eliminated, making (C) correct.

Example #3

Now back to a science passage. Once again, we're going to start by ignoring the graph entirely.

MRSA—*Methicillen-resistant Staphylococcus aureus*— is a type of bacteria that is frequently responsible for hospital-acquired infections and is known for being resistant to common antibiotics. When a group of these medications were compared in terms of their ability to cure MRSA infections versus a variety of other infections, researchers **found that an antibiotic could demonstrate a high level of general effectiveness but that the same medication could be significantly less effective in combatting MRSA**. For example, ______

1 Mark for Review

Which choice most effectively uses data from the table to logically complete the text?

Ⓐ Erythromycin had a general effectiveness of nearly 32%, whereas its MRSA effectiveness was only about five points lower.

Ⓑ whereas Mupirocin was around 17% less effective against MRSA than against general infections, the gap for Clindamicin was only about 14%.

Ⓒ only Vancomycin was fully effective in combatting both general and MRSA bacteria.

Ⓓ Rifampicin showed a general effectiveness rate of more than 85%, whereas it was just over 60% effective against MRSA.

The key piece of information occurs in the sentence before the blank, which tells us that the **same** antibiotic can show **very different** effectiveness rates in general vs. against MRSA.

As a result, the correct answer must fulfill two conditions:

1) It must mention just **one** antibiotic.

2) It must include a statistic indicating a **significant difference** between general effectiveness and effectiveness against MRSA.

On that basis:

- We can eliminate (A) because 5% indicates a small gap.
- We can eliminate (B) because it compares two different medications.
- We can eliminate (C) because the effectiveness rates of Vancomycin were the same.

That leaves (D), which correctly cites an example of a single drug with a large difference (>25%) in effectiveness.

For the record, this is what the entire question looks like:

Antibiotic	General Effectiveness %	MRSA Effectiveness %
Erythryomycin	31.94	26.92
Vancomycin	100	100
Mupirocin	90.28	73.08
Penicillin	5	0
Clindamicin	83.33	69.23
Rifampicin	86.11	61.54

MRSA—*Methicillen-resistant Staphylococcus aureus*— is a type of bacteria that is frequently responsible for hospital-acquired infections and is known for being resistant to common antibiotics. When a group of these medications were compared in terms of their ability to cure MRSA infections versus a variety of other infections, researchers found that an antibiotic could demonstrate a high level of general effectiveness but that the same medication could be significantly less effective in combatting MRSA. For example, ______

Which choice most effectively uses data from the table to logically complete the text?

Ⓐ Erythromycin had a general effectiveness of nearly 32%, whereas its MRSA effectiveness was only about five points lower.

Ⓑ whereas Mupirocin was around 17% less effectiveness against MRSA than against general infections, the gap for Clindamicin was only about 14%.

Ⓒ only Vancomycin was fully effective in combatting both general and MRSA bacteria.

Ⓓ Rifampicin showed a general effectiveness rate of more than 85%, whereas it was just over 60% effective against MRSA.

We could, of course, double-check (D) against the table, in which case we would see that the information is indeed cited accurately. But given that this answer is the only option that fulfills the requirements specified in the question, it must be correct regardless.

Note that all of the answer choices provide accurate descriptions of information in the graph, so if you looked only at the answers and the graph, you would have no way of determining the correct option.

Alternately, you might start by checking (A), notice that it was consistent with the graph, and choose that answer without bothering to check the others. **But to reiterate: an answer can accurately summarize information from the chart and still be wrong.**

If, on the other hand, you started with the passage and the question, you would avoid that trap completely and focus only on the relevant information from the start.

"Backwards" Graphs (Higher Is Not Always Better)

In general, higher bars on a graph are associated with positive effects, whereas lower bars are associated with negative (or less positive) ones. In some cases, however, the situation may be reversed: higher bars may signal an increase in something **negative**.

"Backwards" graphs of this sort are not a major focus of the exam—and if they do appear, you may not even need to consult them—but given that most questions involve a step of interpretation beyond what the graphic most obviously shows, they are not outside the scope of what you could encounter. For example, consider the graph below:

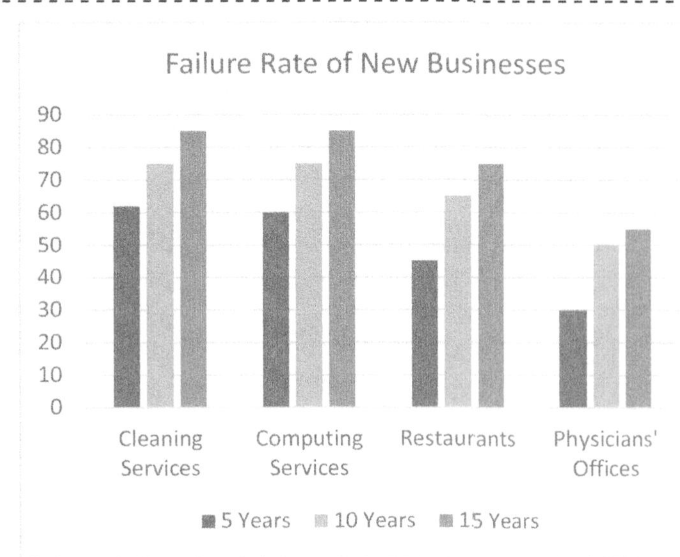

Among new businesses, restaurants have long had a reputation for experiencing rapid failure at an unusually high rate. For many years, this belief was supported with anecdotal accounts or small datasets. In 2014, however, two economists examined the question using a data set covering 98% of businesses in the United States. Tracking non-chain restaurants from 1992 to 2011, they found that in the short term, **these establishments achieve success at levels comparable to or even better than businesses in other sectors**. For example, _____

1 Mark for Review

Which choice most effectively describes data from the graph that supports the economists' findings?

Ⓐ about 45% of restaurants failed within five years, in comparison to 60% of computing services.

Ⓑ 30% of physicians' offices were open after five years, in comparison to about 45% of restaurants.

Ⓒ in comparison to restaurants, a higher percentage of cleaning services remained open after five years.

Ⓓ a similar percentage of cleaning and computing businesses closed after five years.

The title indicates that the graph shows the **failure** rate of various types of new businesses. **High bars = more failure = less successful**, whereas **lower bars = less failure = more successful**. The correct answer must therefore support the idea that a smaller percentage of restaurants failed than did businesses in another sector—the "restaurant" bar will be **equal to or lower than** the comparison bar. Only (A) is consistent with that requirement, making that answer correct.

Exercise: Graphs and Charts

	Heating Energy (kilowatts/m^2)	Cooling Energy (kilowatts/m^2)
Office	65	35
Medical	220	75
Retail	180	90
Education	275	180
Hotels	215	125
Residential	150	65

A student in an environmental science class is doing a project on the amount of energy used by different types of buildings in a large city. He wants to focus on structures where people do not live and that use at least twice as much energy for heating as for cooling. Based on the information provided, the student should choose ______

1 Mark for Review

Which choice most effectively uses data from the chart to complete the text?

Ⓐ residential buildings.

Ⓑ office buildings.

Ⓒ retail buildings.

Ⓓ hotels.

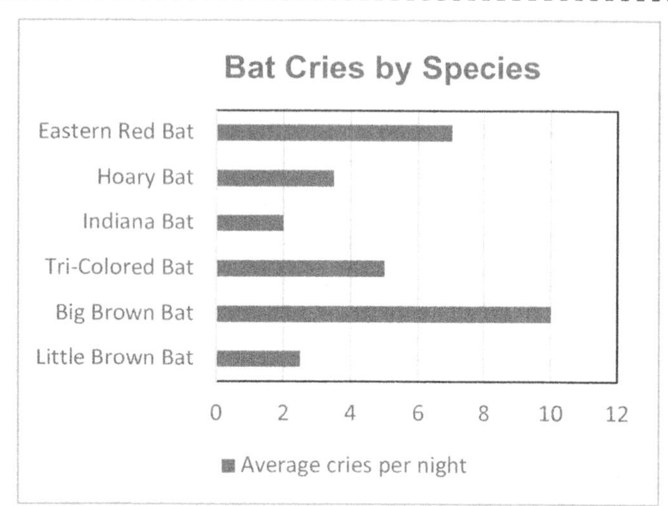

A student studying the presence of white-nose syndrome, a disease that has decimated bat populations across North America since 2007, examined data about the number of bats in a protected area. Because bats live in the dark and their cries are inaudible to people, biologists must use acoustic detectors to record their sounds and then analyze them to identify the species present in a given location. Observing that the highest number of cries came from big brown bats (*Eptesicus fuscus*), the student concluded that brown bat species were not affected by the disease.

2 Mark for Review

Which statement best describes data from the graph that would undermine the student's conclusion?

Ⓐ No bat species emitted more than 10 cries on average per night.

Ⓑ The number of cries from little brown bats was among the lowest of any species.

Ⓒ More cries were recorded for tri-colored bats than for hoary bats.

Ⓓ Eastern red bats were more vocally active than big brown bats.

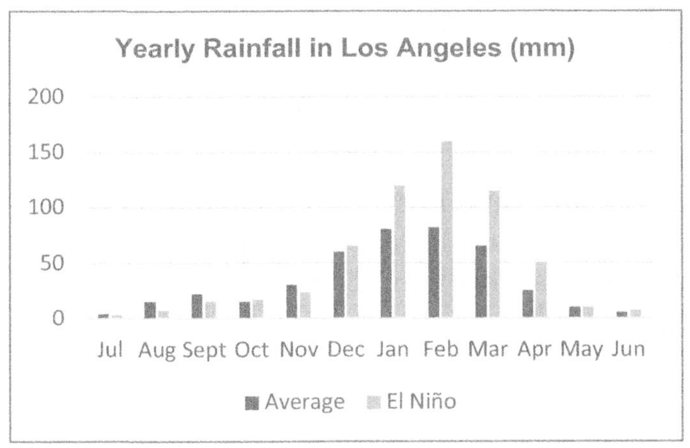

El Niño is a climate pattern in which water in the Pacific Ocean near the equator becomes hotter than usual, affecting the atmosphere and weather around the world. Although El Niño climate conditions are unpredictable, they typically occur every few years and can change the weather in the United States, particularly in the southern states and in California. Climatologists have found that although El Niño years do not bring heavy rains every month, the difference in rainfall during the winter in El Niño years can be much greater than the difference during other seasons. Los Angeles, for example, receives around 15mm of rain in May on average and during El Niño years, whereas ______

3 Mark for Review

Which choice uses data from the graph to logically complete the text?

Ⓐ 5mm more rain than average falls in October when El Niño is present.

Ⓑ more than 100 mm of rain falls in January during El Niño years.

Ⓒ the amount of rainfall in August and September is lower than average during El Niño years.

Ⓓ the amount of rainfall in February during El Niño years is 100 mm higher than average.

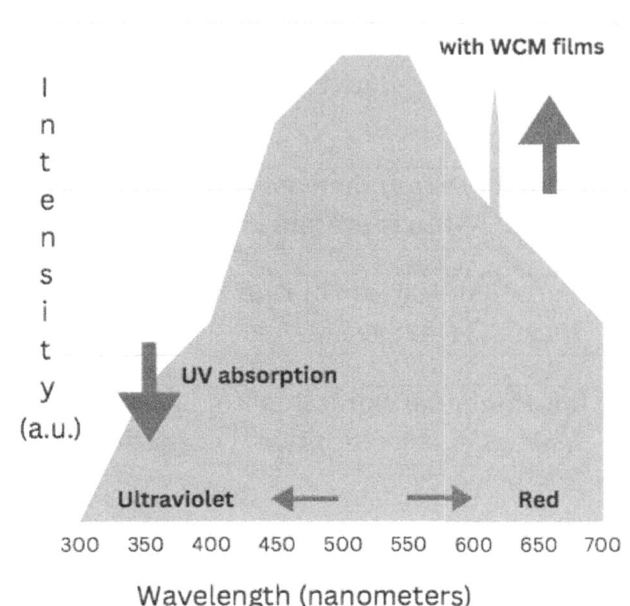

Plants use photosynthesis to create energy from visible light from the sun. In addition to visible light, however, sunlight contains ultraviolet (UV) light. Researchers at the University of Hokkaido wondered whether it would be possible to provide plants with additional visible light by employing a wavelength converting material (WCM) capable of transforming UV light into red light. They created a thin-film WCM coating and applied it to clear plastic sheets, which were placed next to Swiss chard plants. A control group used sheets without the coating. In the summer, when sun irradiation was strong, no significant difference was observed between the two groups. In winter, however, the plants with the WCM films were significantly taller and contained more biomass after 63 days as compared to the control group. The researchers concluded that this accelerated growth was caused by the increased supply of red light provided by the WCM films.

4 Mark for Review

Which choice uses data from the graph to support the researchers' conclusion?

Ⓐ Light that is less than 400 nanometers long had a much lower level of intensity than light that is more than 450 nanometers long.

Ⓑ Light ranging from 500 to 550 nanometers had the highest level of intensity.

Ⓒ The intensity of light waves more than 600 nanometers long that passed through the films increased to nearly peak levels.

Ⓓ UV absorption declined steeply in light waves that are less than 450 nanometers.

Study	No. of Participants	Sample
Erickson, 2010	39	Young adults, 18-28
Basek, 2011	20	Older adults, avg. 70.1
Vo, 2011	34	Young adults, 18-22
McGarry, 2013	7	Older adults, avg. 85
Kühn and Gallinat, 2014	62	Young adults, avg. 28.4
Szabo, 2015	56	Adults, avg. 36.8
Zhang, 2015	45	Adolescents, avg. 16.9
Takeushi, 2016	189	Children, 5-16
Takeushi, 2016	240	Children, avg. 11.1

Despite the sensationalist claims about the effects of video games on children's development that regularly appear in the media, a growing body of research purports to demonstrate that game players outperform non-gamers on a range of cognitive measures, and some studies suggest that the skills acquired through gaming can be transferred to real-world situations. However, these studies employ a variety of methodologies, criteria, and types of participants. Marc Palaus and colleagues at Oberta University in Spain conducted a review of 116 studies, aiming to better understand the relationship between gaming and cognitive development. While they concluded that it is possible to establish links between video games and skills involving attention, cognitive control, and visuospatial processing, they also observed that the lack of standardization could contribute to inconsistencies in the findings of similar studies.

5 Mark for Review

Which choice most effectively uses data from the graph to support the researchers' observation?

Ⓐ The studies run by Takeushi relied on larger sample sizes and involved younger participants than any of the other studies.

Ⓑ Few of the studies included participants under the age of 18.

Ⓒ Each study focused on participants in a particular age range and did not include members that were much older or younger.

Ⓓ The participants in the studies conducted by Erickson, Vo, and Kühn and Gallinat were all under the age of 30.

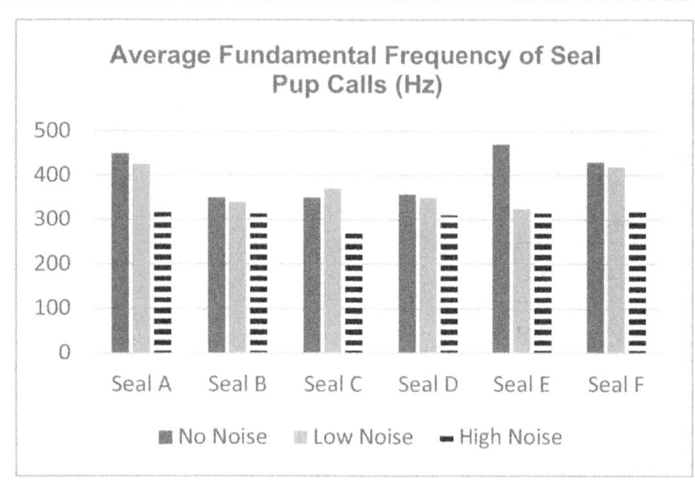

Seals are among the few mammals other than humans that are capable of learning new types of vocalizations. Whereas it is well established that adult harbor seals can acquire new vocal patterns, until recently this phenomenon had never been studied in pups. In 2021, researchers at the Max Planck Institute for Psycholinguistics and a group of colleagues conducted a study in which they played a series of pre-recorded sounds for a group of harbor seal pups ranging from one to three weeks old. They found that the baby seals were able to modify their vocalization patterns: overall, the pups lowered the fundamental frequency (FO) of their calls in response to increased noise. In some cases, the response was highly pronounced, with the same animal emitting vocalizations at much lower frequencies in high noise than in low noise.

6 Mark for Review

Which choice most effectively uses data from the table to support the researchers' finding?

Ⓐ Seal B emitted vocalizations of 330 Hz in low noise and 300 Hz in high noise.

Ⓑ The fundamental frequency of Seal A's vocalizations in high noise was 100 Hz lower than in low noise.

Ⓒ Whereas the fundamental frequency of Seal A's call was 125 Hz lower in high noise than in no noise, the frequency of Seal B's call dropped by less than 50 Hz.

Ⓓ In both low and high noise, the fundamental frequency of Seal E's call was around 150 Hz than it was without noise.

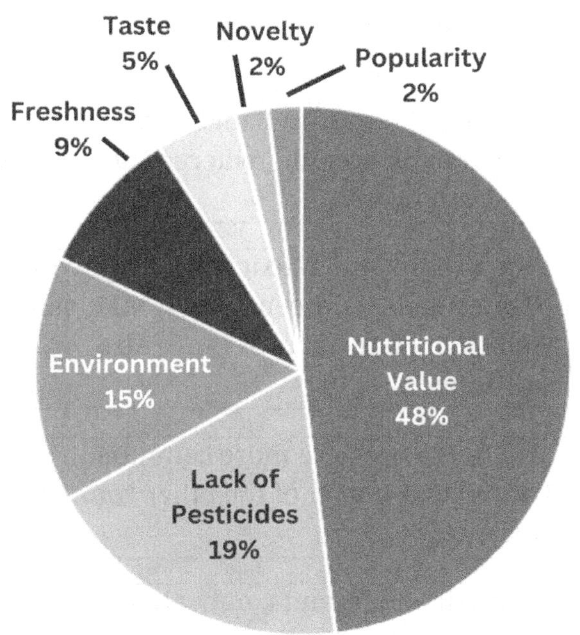

Many consumers perceive organic foods as more nutritious, natural, and environmentally friendly than conventional items. Since 1990, when the "organic" label was first applied to foods, studies on purchasing behavior have contributed significantly to its rise. Researchers Raghava Gundala and Anupam Singh collected data from 770 consumers in the Midwestern United States. They found that consumers were most commonly driven to buy organic products for their ______

7 Mark for Review

Which choice most effectively describes data from the graph that supports the researchers' findings?

Ⓐ freshness and lack of pesticides, although they also considered nutritional value.

Ⓑ lack of pesticides, although they were similarly driven by environmental concerns.

Ⓒ nutritional value, although concerns about the environment played nearly as large a role.

Ⓓ nutritional value, with desire to try new items playing a much smaller role.

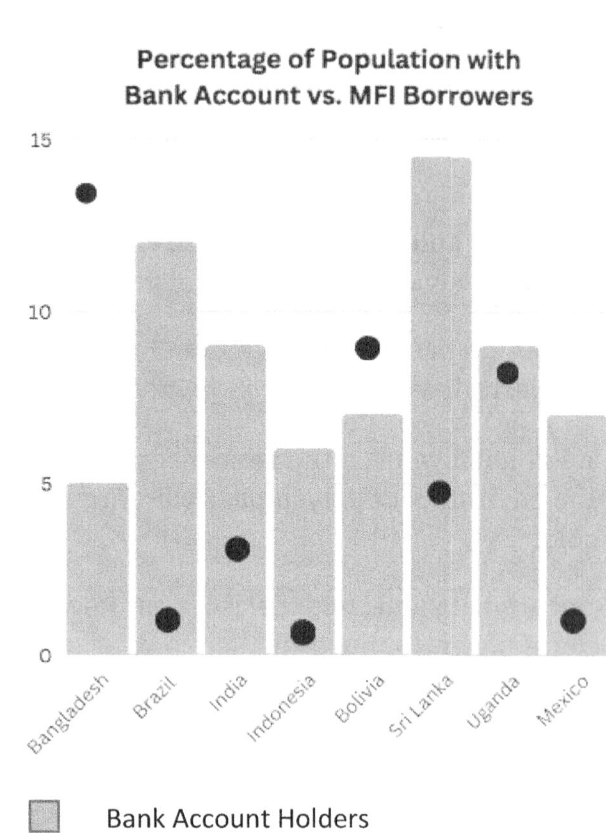

Adapted from IZA World of Labor

Pioneered in Bangladesh in the early 1980s, microfinance (MFI) is a system in which small-scale loans are made available to groups without requiring any collateral. Over the past several decades, micro-loans have allowed thousands of individuals, particularly women, to start their own businesses in developing countries. Some researchers have therefore concluded that microfinance serves as an effective substitute for traditional banking in countries where only a small portion of the population participates in traditional banking.

8 Mark for Review

Which statement best describes data from the graph that would undermine the researchers' conclusion?

Ⓐ Only 5% of adults in Bangladesh have a formal bank account, whereas about 13% are MFI borrowers.

Ⓑ In Indonesia and Mexico, which have some of the smallest percentages of MFI loans, traditional bank accounts are also uncommon.

Ⓒ MFI borrowers are more common in Sri Lanka than in any of the other countries surveyed.

Ⓓ In Brazil and Uganda, only about 1% of the population has received an MFI loan, but a much larger percentage of Brazilians have a bank account.

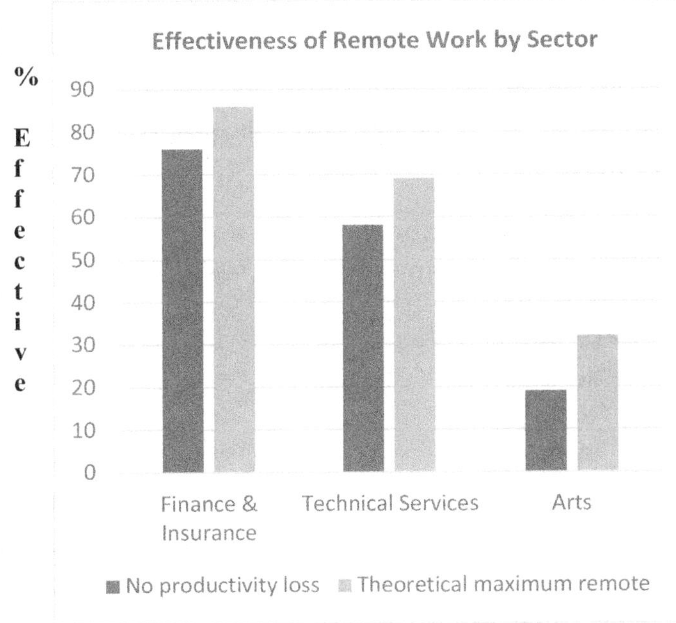

While workers in many industries now do their jobs remotely, the effectiveness of this arrangement depends on the specific activities undertaken and on their physical and social requirements. For example, activities such as operating machines and running laboratory experiments cannot be carried out remotely. On the other hand, jobs involving information and instruction can be done from almost anywhere. A group of economics experts compared the amount of time a job could clearly be performed remotely without any decline in productivity to the total amount of time it could reasonably be done off-site. Based on their findings, they concluded that employees in the finance and insurance industries were most likely to be able to perform their jobs remotely without compromising their output.

9 Mark for Review

Which choice most effectively describes data from the graph that supports the researchers' conclusion?

Ⓐ The difference between remote work with and without any productivity loss is larger for finance and insurance workers than for technical workers.

Ⓑ Finance and insurance workers can theoretically spend more than 80% of their time working remotely, which is significantly higher than the amount of time for technical and arts workers.

Ⓒ Finance and insurance employees can work remotely more than 70% of the time without any loss of productivity, in comparison to less than 60% of technical workers and 20% of art workers.

Ⓓ Unlike arts workers, finance and insurance as well as technical workers can spend the majority of their time working remotely without any loss of productivity.

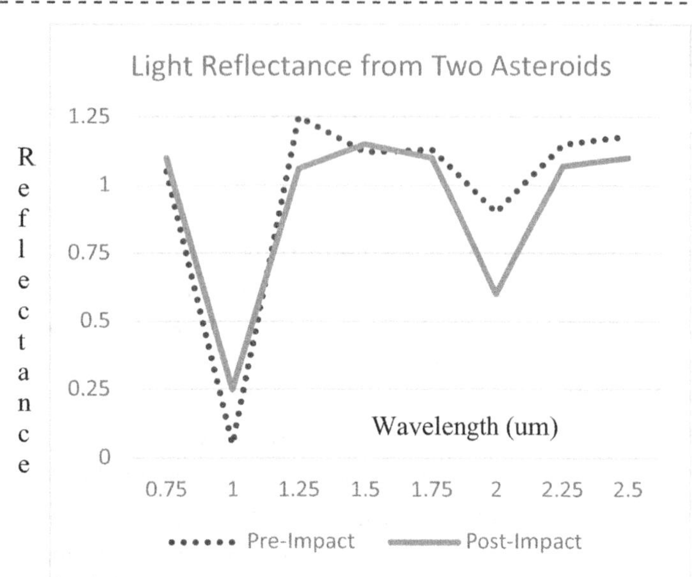

Adapted from Johns Hopkins Applied Physics Laboratory

Launched in November 2021, the Double Asteroid Redirection Test (DART) was a NASA space mission designed to assess the extent to which a half-ton spacecraft could shift a Near-Earth Object's path away from the Earth through a direct collision with a binary asteroid system. The mission also enabled scientists to investigate whether the system, which consisted of asteroids referred to as Didymos and Dimorphos, had the same composition. To accomplish this, they observed the spectra of the sunlight reflected off the asteroids, both pre-impact (when Didymos reflected the vast majority of the light) and post-impact (when around 70% of the reflected light came from debris shed by Dimorphos). Based on the presence of characteristic dips at the same point in the spectra created by Didymos and Dimorphos, they concluded that the two asteroids were likely composed of the same materials.

10 Mark for Review

Which choice most effectively describes data from the graph that supports the researchers' findings?

Ⓐ At 1um and 2um, there was a decline in both pre- and post-impact reflectance.

Ⓑ Pre-impact reflectance fell to its lowest points at 1um and 2um.

Ⓒ The pre-impact decrease in reflectance at 2um was larger than the pre-impact decrease at 1um.

Ⓓ At 1um, pre- and post-impact reflectance were identical, whereas they differed by around 1 point at 2um.

Answers: Graphs and Charts

1. C

The passage lays out two conditions that the correct answer must meet. First, it must involve buildings where people do <u>not</u> live. That eliminates (A) because residential buildings are by definition designed to be lived in. Second, the amount of heating energy must be at least twice as high as cooling energy—that means, exactly twice as or higher. (B) can be eliminated because 65 is not higher than 35 x 2, and (D) does not work because 215 is not higher than 125 x 2 either. Only (C) fits: 180 = 90 x 2.

2. B

Although it may look complicated, this question is actually quite straightforward. What is the student's conclusion? That *brown bat species were not affected by [white-nose syndrome]* because the highest average number of cries recorded came from big brown bats. If you look at the graph, you can see that there are actually two brown bat species listed, and the number of cries for the other species (little brown bat) is at the very low end—a finding that would imply some brown bats are in fact affected. That is what (B) says, so it is correct. All of the other answers are off-topic.

3. D

Although the passage is fairly long, the key information—as usual—appears at the end. You cannot just read the last sentence, however: it includes the transition *for example*, which means that you need to back up and find the idea that the sentence is illustrating. You'll find it in the previous sentence, which states that although El Niño does not result in consistently heavy rains throughout the year, *the <u>difference</u> in rainfall during the winter in El Niño years can be much greater than the <u>difference</u> during other seasons*. Los Angeles is then cited as an example of a city where this is the case. The last sentence indicates that average and El Niño rainfall are the same in May (in a season other than winter), and the word *whereas* before the blank indicates that the remainder of the sentence must describe the opposite—a winter month in which the difference between average and El Niño rainfall is large. The correct answer must therefore include a comparison between El Niño rainfall and average rainfall.

(B) does not include a comparison, so this answer can be eliminated immediately. Be careful with (A): this answer does mention a month in which El Niño is associated with more rain than average, but 5mm is a very small amount, and the correct answer must involve an amount that is *much greater*. (C) does not fit because the correct answer must involve months in which El Niño rainfall is higher, and there is also no information about the size of the differences. (D) correctly cites an example of a winter month (February) in which El Niño is associated with rainfall that is much higher than the average (100 mm).

4. C

Don't be intimidated by the seeming complexity of the graph—this question is much easier than it looks. What is the researchers' conclusion? You'll find it in the last sentence: the accelerated growth of the plants with WCM films *was caused by the increased supply of red light.* The correct answer must support the idea that the films increased the red-light supply.

Shortcut: (C) is the only answer that mentions the films, so start by checking it. Indeed, the fact that the light that passed through the films increased to "peak levels" of intensity in the "red" area of the graph directly illustrates the idea that the films caused the plants to receive more red light. (C) is thus correct. The other answers include information about light wavelength, intensity, and absorption but do not explicitly mention the effect of the films.

5. A

What is the researchers' observation? That *the lack of standardization [among studies] could contribute to inconsistencies in the findings of similar studies.* The correct answer must therefore mention a factor that varies from study to study and include a comparison of some type. The words "Each study" in (C) and "all" in (D) indicate that these answers are discussing factors that remain the same across studies, so both choices can be eliminated. (B) is off-topic: even though the studies involve video games, the relative lack of children among the participants is not the issue indicated by the passage. Only (A) mentions an inconsistency that illustrates the researchers' observation: the studies run by one of the participants differed noticeably from the other studies in that they involved far more participants. In other words, it shows that the studies were not standardized.

6. B

What is the researchers' finding? It appears in the last sentence: the seal pups changed their vocalizations in response to the sounds, and in some cases, the same animal might produce vocalizations with much lower fundamental frequencies in high noise than in low noise. The correct answer must therefore focus on one animal only and indicate a large gap in fundamental frequency between low and high noise. (C) makes a comparison between two seals, so it can be eliminated automatically. Be careful with (A): it does compare the frequencies in low and high noise, but the gap is fairly small (30 Hz). (D) is likewise incorrect because the correct answer must cite a large difference in the responses to the two noise levels, and here it is very similar. Only (B) offers an example of a seal whose vocalizations showed a large gap (100 Hz) between low and high noise.

7. D

The key phrase in the passage is *most commonly*, so your first job is simply to identify the largest sector of the graph. That is "Nutritional Value," which at 48% is significantly larger than any of the other sectors. That eliminates (A) and (B). To decide between (C) and (D), focus on the second part of these answers. (C) does not work because it is not true that environmental concerns played "nearly as large a role"—15% is much lower than 48%. (D) is correct because "Novelty" (i.e., "the desire to try new items") is only 2%, so this factor played "a much smaller role."

8. B

What is the researchers' conclusion? That microfinance loans can effectively replace traditional banking as a means to connect potential business owners to startup funds. If that were true, then low levels of participation in traditional banking (gray bars) would correspond to high levels of MFI participation (black dots). The question, however, asks you to identify the option that "undermines" the claim, so the correct answer must show that a low percentage of bank account holders does not correspond to a high percentage of MFI borrowers. Only (B) is consistent with that idea: the fact that countries with a small percentage of bank-account holders have very low MFI participation directly contradicts the idea that MFI can replace traditional banking. Note that you do not need to look at the graph to identify this as the probable correct answer.

(A) is incorrect because it supports the claim rather than undermines it: a low percentage of bank account holders (5%) is paired with a significantly higher level of MFI participation (13%). (C) misinterprets the graph—the gray bar, which represents bank account holders is the highest—and does not make the required comparison between the percentage of bank accounts vs. MFI borrowers. The comparison in (D) fails to undermine the conclusion as well: the issue is not whether countries that are similar in one metric are different in another, but rather the proportion of bank-account holders to MFI borrowers.

9. C

What is the researchers' conclusion? That insurance and finance workers were most likely to be able to do their jobs remotely without a drop in performance (*without compromising their output*). The correct answer must therefore cite statistics consistent with the idea that a higher proportion of these workers can do their jobs at full capacity remotely than workers in one or more of the other sectors included in the graph. (C) correctly focuses on that key factor, citing the 70% of finance and insurance workers who can do their jobs at full capacity vs. the lower 60% and 20% for technical and arts workers, respectively. Note that you do not need to look at the graph to identify this as the probable correct answer.

(A) is incorrect because it compares remote work with and without productivity loss when the key factor is remote work without productivity loss between finance and insurance works and other workers. (B) is incorrect because it refers to the maximum percentage of finance and insurance jobs that can "theoretically" be done remotely—that is, the amount that does involve some loss of productivity. (D) does not work either because the issue is the total amount of time that can be worked without productivity loss, not whether that time is the majority (>50%).

10. A

Why did the researchers conclude that the two asteroids had the same composition? Because of *the presence of characteristic dips at the same point in the spectra*. The correct answer must therefore convey the fact that both pre- and post-impact reflectance dropped at the same points (wavelengths). (A) is correct because it states that both types reflectance declined at 1 and 2 um. Note that you do not need to look at the graph to identify this as the probable correct answer. (B) does not work because this answer mentions pre-impact reflectance only, whereas the correct answer must describe both pre- and post-impact reflectance. (C) can be eliminated for the same reason. (D) incorrectly states that pre- and post-impact reflectance were the same at 1um. This answer also focuses on the wrong factor—the issue is whether the two types of reflectance dropped at the same time, not on the difference between them.

10 Paired Passages

While the digital SAT will consist primarily of single short passages accompanied by one question, it will also contain a set of short paired passages ("Text 1" and "Text 2") that present alternate viewpoints or information about the same topic. These passages will be accompanied by a question asking about the relationship between them.

In previous versions of the exam, and mostly likely in this version as well, the most common relationship between the passages was **disagreement**. However, the two authors—or figures mentioned in one or both of the passages—may **also agree** on certain points. As a result, you must be able to distinguish between aspects of the topic on which the two opinions overlap and those where they differ. **Correct answers can involve areas of both agreement and disagreement.**

In addition, answers to paired-passage questions may depend on an easily overlooked detail in one or both passages. Sometimes that detail will be located in a key place (first sentence, last sentence, close to a major transition), but sometimes it will not. Because you may not remember the key information, you should always return to the passages as needed. You should also make sure not to eliminate any answer you're uncertain about until you have confirmed that it is incorrect.

If you are a strong reader who handles this type of writing well, you can probably approach paired passages much as you approach the other type of passages. However, **if you are not aiming for a very high score and struggle disproportionately with this question type, you should plan to skip it initially and only return after you have answered everything that you can answer easily.**

Even though both passages will be very short, they may still be dense and discuss unfamiliar subjects. In order to avoid confusion, **you should aim to deal with the smallest amount of information possible at any given time**. The more work you do in terms of determining arguments upfront, the less work you'll need to do later. You can move very quickly through the steps outlined on the following page, but for maximum effectiveness, you should not skip any of them.

How to answer paired-passage questions:

1) Read Text 1: Identify main point.
2) Read Text 2: Identify main point.
3) Write the relationship.
4) Answer the question in your own words.
5) Look at the choices, and pick the one closest to your answer.

It is important to **determine the relationship** between the passages upfront because the question will always test your understanding of that connection, typically asking you what the author of one passage would "say about" or "respond to" an idea in the other.

Once you have this information, you've essentially answered the question before you've even looked at it. If the authors of the two passages disagree only, the correct answer will be negative. You can thus eliminate positive and neutral options, which can often be identified from the first few words of the answer. Furthermore, when answers include more detailed information about the passages, you may sometimes be able to use the main points themselves.

You can also use your knowledge of the test's structure to help you make educated guesses. For example, take a look at the question below. We don't even need a set of passages here—our only concern is how to use the framework of the test to predict the most probable answer.

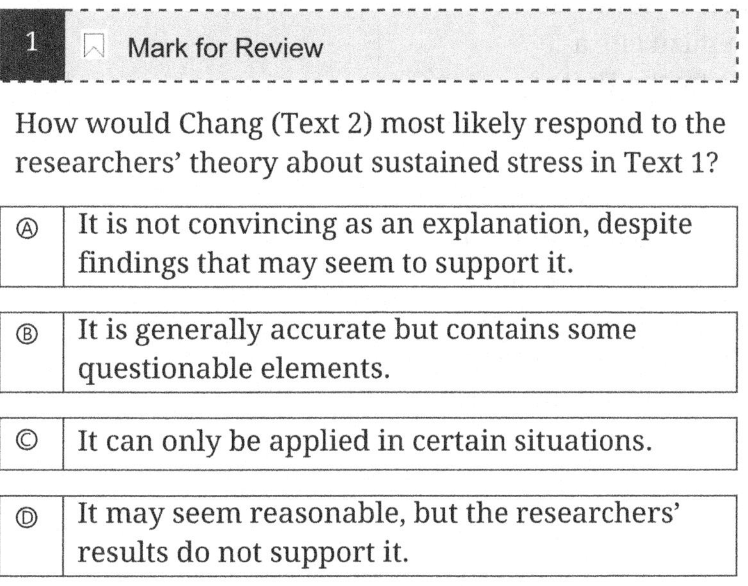

1 Mark for Review

How would Chang (Text 2) most likely respond to the researchers' theory about sustained stress in Text 1?

Ⓐ	It is not convincing as an explanation, despite findings that may seem to support it.
Ⓑ	It is generally accurate but contains some questionable elements.
Ⓒ	It can only be applied in certain situations.
Ⓓ	It may seem reasonable, but the researchers' results do not support it.

Since passages generally disagree, we can assume that the correct answer will be negative. (B) is positive ("generally accurate"), so it's probably wrong. (C) is negative, but it contains the extreme word "only," so we'll eliminate it as well. Between (A) and (D), (D) is more negative, so we're going to give a slight edge to that option. Besides, when there's a mismatch between theory and practice, it's usually because the theory sounds good but doesn't work in practice—not the other way around, as (A) indicates. At this point, we could go back to Text 2 and check for a mention of findings that would support (D). If that didn't work, we would go to (A), then (C).

Now let's look at a full-length example.

Text 1

Our food now travels an average of 1,500 miles before ending up on our plates. This globalization of the food supply has serious consequences for the environment, our health, our communities and our tastebuds. Much of the food grown in the breadbasket surrounding us must be shipped across the country to distribution centers before it makes its way back to our supermarket shelves. Because uncounted costs of this long-distance journey (air pollution and global warming, the ecological costs of large-scale monoculture, the loss of family farms and local community dollars) are not paid for at the checkout counter, many of us do not think about them at all.

Text 2

Just how much carbon dioxide is emitted by transporting food from farm to fork? Pierre Desrochers and Hiroko Shimizu cite a comprehensive study done by the United Kingdom's Department of Environment, Food and Rural Affairs (DEFRA), which reported that 82 percent of food miles were generated within the U.K. Consumer shopping trips accounted for 48 percent and trucking for 31 percent of British food miles. Air freight amounted to less than 1 percent of food miles. In total, food transportation accounted for only 1.8 percent of Britain's carbon dioxide emissions.

1 Mark for Review

Based on the texts, how would Desrochers and Shimizu (Text 2) most likely describe the view presented in Text 1?

Ⓐ It is strongly supported by data compiled by DEFRA.

Ⓑ It overstates the effects of transporting food on the environment.

Ⓒ It appears justified by preliminary findings but has not yet definitively proven.

Ⓓ It is highly implausible because most consumers do not consider the source of their food.

Let's start by breaking things down.

Topic:

Transporting food long distances to sell.

1) Main Point, Text 1:

Transporting food long distances harms environment.

2) Main Point, Text 2:

Transporting food long distances doesn't really harm environment.

3) Relationship:

Disagree.

4) Answers:

(A) Positive - eliminate it.

(B) Negative - keep it.

(C) Positive - eliminate it.

(D) Negative - keep it.

Now, be careful with (D). You might remember something about people not thinking about where their food comes from, but that's in Text 1. If you go back to Text 2, you'll find it says nothing about that idea.

Text 2 does, however, state that *food transportation accounted for only 1.8 percent of Britain's carbon dioxide emissions*, which stands in contrast to the doom-and-gloom environmental scenario presented in the first passage. Based on that statement, you can assume that Desrochers and Shimizu would consider the claim in Text 1 to be somewhat exaggerated, i.e., "overstated." That makes (B) correct.

Exercise: Paired Passages

Text 1

By investigating interactions between tree species, scientists have found that trees leverage similarities and differences in their microbial "makeup" to recognize other trees of their own species, and that they preferentially share nutrients with them through their mycorrhizal network—the systems of roots and fungi that connect them. For example, Douglas Fir trees growing in the same plot have been shown to share more carbon among them than with trees of other species.

Text 2

The notion that trees send out resources to strengthen a community composed of members of their species is unlikely because groups that cooperate would need to win out over groups made up of competing individuals. According to plant ecologist Kathryn Flinn, while trees can sometimes facilitate each other's growth, a forest does not function like a single organism: it includes a vast array of species with a constantly shifting variety of interactions, both cooperative and competitive.

1 Mark for Review

Based on the texts, what would Kathryn Flinn most likely say about the "Douglas Fir trees" in Text 1?

Ⓐ Their mycorrhizal network is not fully understood.

Ⓑ They function as if they were a single organism.

Ⓒ They are also likely to compete among themselves for some resources.

Ⓓ The amount of carbon they share will vary according to environmental conditions.

Text 1

In recent years, there has been an explosion of scientific research revealing precisely how positive feelings are beneficial. We know that they motivate people to pursue important goals and overcome obstacles, offer protective benefits against the effects of stress, improve our social connectedness, and even ward off illness. The science of happiness has spawned a small industry of motivational speakers and research enterprises. Clearly, happiness is popular.

Text 2

Happiness, it turns out, has a cost when experienced too intensely. For instance, we often are told that happiness can open up our minds to foster more creative thinking and help us tackle problems or puzzles. This is the case when we experience moderate levels of happiness. But according to Mark Alan Davis's 2008 analysis of the relationship between mood and creativity, when people experience intense and perhaps overwhelming amounts of happiness, they no longer experience the same creativity boost. What's more, psychologist Barbara Fredrickson has found that too much positive emotion—and too little negative emotion—makes people inflexible in the face of new challenges.

2 Mark for Review

Based on the texts, how would Mark Alan Davis most likely respond to what "we know" in Text 1?

Ⓐ By emphasizing the connection between creativity and negative emotions

Ⓑ By acknowledging the benefits of positivity in moderation but cautioning against it in excess

Ⓒ By questioning the motives of the participants in the happiness industry

Ⓓ By challenging the connection between positive feelings and personal fulfillment

Text 1

Until recently, the concrete psychological effects of fiction on individuals and society were largely a matter of speculation. However, research in psychology is beginning to provide answers about how fiction can expand our moral imaginations. For example, a series of studies conducted by Keith Oatley, Maja Djikic, and Raymond Mar found that fiction measurably improves people's ability to guess others' mental states by looking at only their eyes. They interpreted this finding as evidence for the idea that fiction allows people to connect with something larger than themselves.

Text 2

An empirical approach to the question of whether fiction improves empathy was taken by David Kidd and Emanuele Castano, who conducted five experiments in which participants read fictional excerpts and then responded to images of facial expressions. The results showed that the participants had improved their theory of mind (ToM), or their ability to infer the thoughts and emotions of others. As Kidd points out, however, highly developed ToM does not always translate into more ethical behavior: the ability to manipulate someone, for instance, also requires a heightened understanding of other people's emotions.

3 Mark for Review

Based on the texts, how would Kidd and Castano most likely respond to Oatley, Djikic, and Mar in Text 1?

Ⓐ By acknowledging the importance of connecting with others

Ⓑ By conceding that fiction can allow people to transcend their everyday lives

Ⓒ By pointing out that empathy can have negative as well as positive effects

Ⓓ By emphasizing that individuals with high ToM may sometimes prefer nonfiction

Text 1

On May 21, 2019, midsize black holes were detected for the first time when the U.S.-based Laser Interferometer Gravitational-Wave Observatory (LIGO) and its European counterpart Virgo captured a tremor from a pair of black holes merging deep in space. Priyamvada Natarajan, an astrophysicist who has long worked on black-hole growth models, believes that black holes this size are born in nuclear star clusters, dense collections of stars found near galactic centers. These holes sweep through the cluster, adding gas and dust, until they settle at a single location and cease to expand.

Text 2

Imre Bartos and other researchers working on "hierarchical merger" models, in which black holes grow by eating one another, focus on one major data point in the LIGO/Virgo findings. The angular momentum, or "spin," of a black hole ranges from 0 to 1. When two black holes of similar size combine, the resulting black hole usually has a spin of around 0.7. Significantly, the two black holes involved in the merger recorded by LIGO and Virgo had 0.69 and 0.73 respectively, suggesting that they both might have formed in previous mergers.

4 Mark for Review

Based on the texts, what would Imre Bartos most likely say about Priyamvada Natarajan's belief in Text 1?

Ⓐ It underestimates midsize black holes' spin.

Ⓑ It misstates the time when the merger occurred.

Ⓒ It relies too heavily on data from LIGO/Virgo.

Ⓓ It overlooks the significance of a crucial statistic.

Text 1

To be a female artist in the nineteenth century was challenging enough, but to be a female sculptor was nearly unthinkable. Not only were sculptors expected to have a familiarity with the human form that no respectable woman in that age could acquire, but they had to work with heavy materials, such as blocks of marble weighing many hundreds of pounds. Consequently, most aspiring female artists of the period had no choice but to content themselves with the more ladylike pursuits of drawing and painting.

Text 2

In 1860, American sculptor Emma Stebbins, who was working in Italy, completed two marble figures representing contemporary subjects in the style of classical sculpture. As scholar Melissa L. Gustin has recently demonstrated, Stebbins modeled her work on two ancient marble sculptures that she viewed in Rome: the Spear-Bearer and the Resting Satyr in the Vatican Museum's Braccio Nuovo. The educated and well-traveled viewers of Stebbins's work would have taken pleasure in recognizing her references to specific classical works.

5 Mark for Review

Based on the texts, how would Melissa L. Gustin most likely respond to the discussion of female artists in Text 1?

Ⓐ By emphasizing that some female artists succeeded in overcoming societal restrictions

Ⓑ By acknowledging the difficulties that aspiring female sculptors faced

Ⓒ By challenging the idea that female sculptors faced physical challenges

Ⓓ By pointing out that nineteenth-century women were probably familiar with certain classical sculptures

Answers: Paired Passages

1. C

What does Text 1 say about Douglas Fir trees? When they grow in the same plot, they share more carbon among them than with trees of other species.

Next, what is Kathryn Flinn's position (Text 2)? She asserts that while trees *can sometimes help facilitate each other's growth*, relationships among organisms in forest are *constantly shifting* and include both cooperation and competition.

Logically, how would Flinn respond to the observation that Douglas Firs seem to "prefer" sharing carbon with members of their own species? Given her perspective that species both cooperate and compete, she would probably respond to an example of cooperation by suggesting that the Douglas Firs also compete at times. And that is exactly what (C) says.

(A) and (D) are irrelevant to Flinn's discussion, and (B) is directly contradicted by her assertion that *a forest does not function like a single organism.*

2. B

What does Text 1 state that "we know"? If you scan the passage for these words, you'll find them at the beginning of the second sentence, which tells us that positive feelings are associated with a host of happy outcomes (motivation to achieve goals, overcome obstacles, protect against stress, etc.).

Next, what position does Mark Alan Davis (Text 2) hold? That *when people experience intense and perhaps overwhelming amounts of happiness, they no longer experience the same creativity boost.* In other words, too much positivity is not a good thing.

Logically, how would Davis respond to the example from Text 1? Presumably by reiterating his position that while moderate amounts of happiness are helpful, too much of it is not, i.e., "by acknowledging [the] benefits of positivity in moderation but cautioning against it in excess." (B) is thus correct.

(A) is incorrect because Davis's position on negative emotions is never mentioned. (C) is beyond the scope of what can be inferred from Davis's position.

Be careful with (D): Davis is only mentioned in relation to creativity, not "personal fulfillment," and he does not deny the benefits of happiness—he only indicates that too much of it can be negative.

3. C

What is the position of Oatley, Djikic, and Mar in Text 1? Fiction *improves people's ability to guess others' mental states* and improves their ability to empathize.

What is the position of Kidd and Castano in Text 2? They agree that fiction improves people's understanding of others' mindsets but point out that these skills can be used in negative ways.

Logically, how would Kidd and Castano respond to the position in Text 1? That position only emphasizes the positive aspect of reading fiction, so they would presumably point out the negative one. And that is what (C) says.

(A) is outside the scope of the passages, which focus on the effects of fiction rather than relationships in general. (B) is incorrect because Kidd and Castano only discuss the effects of fiction on theory of mind, not on "transcend[ing] their everyday lives." (D) is entirely off-topic; neither passage discusses or implies anything about the effects of reading nonfiction.

4. D

What is Priyamvada Natarajan's belief in Text 1? That *black holes this size* (i.e., of medium size) come from nuclear star clusters and sweep through them gathering gas and dust.

What is Imre Bartos's position (Text 2)? *Black holes grow by eating one another,* a view that is based on an analysis of black holes' spin— a specific statistic that falls within a narrow range.

Logically, how would Bartos respond to Natarajan? Because it is not mentioned that Natarajan takes "spin" into account, Bartos would presumably focus on the absence of that figure, i.e., "a crucial statistic." That makes (D) correct.

(A) is incorrect because Natarajan's model does not include spin at all. (B) is incorrect because Bartos does mention when the merger occurred. (C) is incorrect because Bartos's model, not Natarajan's, is mentioned as relying on specific data from LIGO/Virgo.

5. A

Don't overthink this question—if you stick to the big picture of each passage, the answer is relatively straightforward.

What does Text 1 tell us about nineteenth-century female artists? That it was almost impossible for them to become sculptors (first sentence) and that they had no choice but to be happy with painting and drawing (last sentence).

What did Melissa L. Gustin demonstrate? That Emma Stebbins—a nineteenth-century female sculptor (as indicated by the date *1860*)—modeled two of her sculptures on ancient Roman works. The fact that viewers of those works were *educated and well-traveled* suggests that Stebbins achieved a significant level of success as a sculptor—the opposite of what Text 1 indicates should have been possible.

Logically, then, Gustin would presumably respond to Text 1 by pointing out that there were exceptions to the situation described there, and that some aspiring female sculptors did manage to break through "societal restrictions" and become very accomplished. That corresponds directly to (A).

(B) states the opposite of Gustin's research: although it is possible (and perhaps likely) that Gustin would in reality acknowledge the obstacles female sculptors historically faced, the passage only cites her work in relation to a successful female sculptor, and the correct answer must be based on that fact. (C) is neither supported nor contradicted by the passage; Gustin's view of the physical challenges faced by female sculptors are not mentioned. (D) is entirely irrelevant to the argument and beyond the scope of the passages. The focus is on whether nineteenth century women could become sculptors, not on whether they were familiar with particular works.

Reprints and Permissions

Adee, Sally. From "Roughnecks in Space: Moon Mining in Science Fiction," *New Scientist*, 27 April 2012. http://www.newscientist.com/gallery/moon-mining

Anft, Michael. "Solving the Mystery of Death Valley's Walking Rocks," *Johns Hopkins Magazine*, 6/1/11. Reprinted by permission of *Johns Hopkins Magazine*. http://archive.magazine.jhu.edu/2011/06/solving-the-mystery-of-death-valley's-walking-rocks/

Austen, Jane. *Northanger Abbey*. Originally published 1803. Excerpted from Chapter 1 through Project Gutenberg, http://www.gutenberg.org/files/121/121-h/121-h.htm

Ball, Philip. From "The Trouble with Scientists," *Nautilus*, 5/14/15. http://nautil.us/issue/24/error/the-trouble-with-scientists

Bibb, Eloise. "Gerarda," 1895. https://www.poetrynook.com/poem/gerarda

Bordal, Laura Torres; Jadoul, Yannick; Rasilo, Heikki; Salazar Casals, Anna; Ravignani, Andrea. "Vocal Plasticity in Harbour Seal Pups,"Comparative Bioacoustics Group, Max Planck Institute for Psycholinguistics, Nijmegen, The Netherlands. https://doi.org/10.1101/2021.02.10.430617

Brauer, Wiebke. Adapted from "The Miracle of Space," *Smart Magazine*, 10/31/14. Reprinted by permission of *Smart Magazine. http://smart-magazine.com/space/the-miracle-of-space/*

Brontë, Emily. *Wuthering Heights*. Originally published 1847. Excerpted from Chapter 20, http://www.online-literature.com/bronte/wuthering/20/

Chopin, Kate. *The Awakening*, originally published 1899, Chapter 6. Accessed through Project Gutenberg, https://www.gutenberg.org/files/160/160-h/160-h.htm

Dickinson, Emily. "Beclouded." Originally published 1896. https://etc.usf.edu/lit2go/114/the-poems-of-emily-dickinson-series-one/2632/nature-poem-29-beclouded/

Dunbar, Paul Laurence. "Frederick Douglass," 1895. https://poets.org/poem/frederick-douglass

Freedman, David. Adapted from "The Truth About Genetically Modified Food," Scientificamerican.com (Nature, Inc.), September 1, 2013. https://www.scientificamerican.com/article/the-truth-about-genetically-modified-food/

Gholipour, Bahar. Adapted from "Sleep Shrinks the Brain's Synapses to Make Room for New Learning," Scientificamerican.com (Nature, Inc.), May 1, 2017. https://www.scientificamerican.com/article/sleep-shrinks-the-brain-rsquo-s-synapses-to-make-room-for-new-learning/

Grimké, Charlotte Forten. "Wordsworth," https://www.beltwaypoetry.com/grimke-charlotte-forten/

Gross, Daniel. From "Will We Ever Be Able to Make Traffic Disappear?" Smithsonian.com, 5/7/2015. http://www.smithsonianmag.com/innovation/will-we-ever-be-able-to-make-traffic-disappear-180955164/

Hamlin, Kimberly. "Monumental Women," *Humanities*, 8/10/2020. https://www.neh.gov/article/monumental-women

Heard, Josephine. "On receiving Tennyson's Poems from Mrs. M. H. Dunton, of Brattleboro, Vt," 1890. https://scalar.lehigh.edu/african-american-poetry-a-digital-anthology/josephine-heard-morning-glories-full-text-1

Hokkaido University, graphic: plants and red light. https://www.global.hokudai.ac.jp/blog/uv-to-red-light-converting-films-accelerate-plant-growth/

Johnson, Georgia Douglas. "Youth," 1922. https://poets.org/poem/youth-2

Johnson, James Weldon. "Beclouded." Originally published 1922 in *The Book of American Negro Poetry.* https://poets.org/poem/mother-night

Kaufman, Les. Adapted from "One Fish, Two Fish, Red Fish, Blue Fish," *National Geographic,* 2005.

Kelemen, Peter B. From "The Origin of the Ocean Floor," *Scientific American,* February 2009. **Reproduced with permission, © 2009, Scientific American, Inc. All rights reserved.** http://www.scientificamerican.com/article/the-origin-of-the-ocean-floor/

Koerth-Baker, Maggie: From "The Power of Positive Thinking, Truth or Myth?" *Live Science,* 8/29/08. http://www.livescience.com/2814-power-positive-thinking-truth-myth.html

Killam, Daniel. El Niño graph, adapted from **"**California Getting Wetter to the North, Drier to the South: Natural Variability or Climate Change?" 10.3390/cli2030168

Lehrer, Jonah. Adapted from "Under Pressure: The Search for Stress Vaccine," *Wired,* 7/28/10, 2:00 p.m. http://www.wired.com/2010/07/ff_stress_cure/

Mills, Mark. From "Every Breath You Take," *City Journal,* 7/2/13. http://www.cityjournals.org/2013/bc0702mm.html

Nuwer, Rachel. "What is a Species?" Smithsonian.com, 11/6/13. http://www.smithsonianmag.com/science-nature/what-is-a-species-insight-from-dolphins-and-humans-180947580/?no-ist

Ostrander, Isabel. "Anything Once," Ch. 6, originally published 1920. https://www.literature.org/authors/ostrander-isabel/anything-once/chapter-06.html

Orwell, George. Adapted from "Keep the Aspidistra Flying," originally published 1936. Accessed from Project Gutenberg, http://gutenberg.net.au/ebooks02/0200021.txt

Palaus, Marc. Chart data adapted from "Neural Basis of Video Gaming: A Systematic Review." *Frontiers of Human Neuroscience,* vol. 11, 2017. https://doi.org/10.3389/fnhum.2017.00248

Panko, Ben. "What Does it Mean to Be a Species? Genetics is Changing the Answer," Smithsonian.com, May 19, 2017. http://www.smithsonianmag.com/science-nature/what-does-it-mean-be-species-genetics-changing-answer-180963380/

"Raining Pebbles: Rocky Exoplanet Has Bizarre Atmosphere, Simulation Suggests," Washington University in St. Louis, 10/1/09. https://www.sciencedaily.com/releases/2009/09/090930165038.htm

Rupp, Rebecca. From "Surviving the Sneaky Psychology of Supermarkets," *National Geographic,* 6/15/15. http://theplate.nationalgeographic.com/2015/06/15/surviving-the-sneaky-psychology-of-supermarkets/

Sainani, Kristin. Adapted from "What, Me Worry?" *Stanford Magazine,* May/June 2014. https://alumni.stanford.edu/get/page/magazine/article/?article_id=70134. Reprinted by permission of the author.

Schwartz, Barry. "More Isn't Always Better," *Harvard Business Review,* June 2006. Reprinted by permission of Harvard Business Publishing. https://hbr.org/2006/06/more-isnt-always-better

"Scientists Discover Salty Aquifer, Previously Unknown Microbial Habitat Under Antarctica," © 2015, Dartmouth College. http://www.sciencenewsline.com/articles/2015042815560014.html

Sullivan, John Jeremiah. "One of Us," *Lapham's Quarterly*, Spring 2013. http://www.laphamsquarterly.org/animals/one-us

Taylor, Astra. "A Small World After All," *Bookforum*, June/July/August 2013. http://www.bookforum.com/inprint/020_02/11685

Thompson, Helen. "Yawning Spreads Like a Plague in Wolves," Smithsonian.com, 8/27/14, http://www.smithsonianmag.com/science-nature/yawning-spread-plague-wolves-180952484/

Tregaskis, Sharon. "The Buzz: What Bees Tell Us About Global Climate Change, *Johns Hopkins Magazine*. 6/2/2010. Reprinted by permission by *Johns Hopkins Magazine*. http://archive.magazine.jhu.edu/2010/06/the-buzz-what-bees-tell-us-about-global-climate-change/

Updike, John. Adapted from "Big Bad Bizarre Dinosaurs {Extreme Dinosaurs}, *National Geographic*, December 2007.

Waters, Mary Yukari. "Rationing," *The Missouri Review*, 3/1/02. https://missourireview.com/article/rationing/

Wayman, Erin. "The First Americans," Smithsonian.com, 11/28/11. http://www.smithsonianmag.com/science-nature/the-first-americans-889302/

Wharton, Edith. *Summer*, originally published 1917. Excerpted from Chapter 1 through Project Gutenberg, http://www.gutenberg.org/files/166/166-h/166-h.htm

Wilde, Oscar. *The Importance of Being Earnest*, originally published 1895. Excerpted from Act I, Scene I through Project Gutenberg, https://www.gutenberg.org/files/844/844-h/844-h.htm

"Why Eat Locally?" *The Regal Vegan*, http://www.regalvegan.com/site/local-yokels/

Woolf, Virginia. *Night and Day*, Ch. 1, originally published 1919. https://www.literature.org/authors/woolf-virginia/night-and-day/chapter-01.html

Zhang, Y. and Kudva, S. "E-books versus print books: Readers' choices and preferences across contexts," Journal of the Association for Information Science & Technology, Association for Information Science & Technology, vol. 65(8), pages 1695-1706, August. Graphic information based on Pew Research Statistics.

ABOUT THE AUTHOR

Erica Meltzer earned her B.A., magna cum laude, from Wellesley College and spent more than a decade tutoring privately in Boston and New York City, as well as nationally and internationally via Skype. Her experience working with students from a wide range of educational backgrounds and virtually every score level, from the third percentile to the 99th, gave her unique insight into the types of stumbling blocks students often encounter when preparing for standardized reading and writing tests.

She was inspired to begin writing her own test-prep materials in 2007, after visiting a local bookstore in search of additional practice questions for an SAT Writing student. Unable to find material that replicated the contents of the exam with sufficient accuracy, she decided to write her own. What started as a handful of exercises jotted down on a piece of paper became the basis for her first book, the original Ultimate Guide to SAT Grammar, published in 2011. Since that time, she has authored guides for SAT reading and vocabulary, as well as verbal guides for the ACT®, GRE®, and GMAT®. Her books have sold more than 300,000 copies and are used around the world. She lives in New York City, and you can visit her online at www.thecriticalreader.com.

Made in the USA
Coppell, TX
04 January 2026

68138589R10116